Students' Right to Speak

Students' Right to Speak

The First Amendment in Public Schools

Erica R. Salkin

McFarland & Company, Inc., Publishers
Jefferson, North Carolina

LIBRARY OF CONGRESS CATALOGUING-IN-PUBLICATION DATA

Names: Salkin, Erica R., 1974– author.
Title: Students' right to speak : the First Amendment in public schools / Erica R. Salkin.
Description: Jefferson, N.C. : McFarland & Company, Inc., Publishers, 2016. | Includes bibliographical references and index.
Identifiers: LCCN 2016015921 | ISBN 9781476662923 (softcover : acid free paper) ∞
Subjects: LCSH: Freedom of speech—United States. | Students—Civil rights—United States.
Classification: LCC KF4772 .S25 2016 | DDC 344.73/0793—dc23
LC record available at https://lccn.loc.gov/2016015921

BRITISH LIBRARY CATALOGUING DATA ARE AVAILABLE

ISBN (print) 978-1-4766-6292-3
ISBN (ebook) 978-1-4766-2374-0

© 2016 Erica R. Salkin. All rights reserved

No part of this book may be reproduced or transmitted in any form or by any means, electronic or mechanical, including photocopying or recording, or by any information storage and retrieval system, without permission in writing from the publisher.

Front cover photograph © 2016 XiXinXin/iStock

Printed in the United States of America

McFarland & Company, Inc., Publishers
Box 611, Jefferson, North Carolina 28640
www.mcfarlandpub.com

To my loving family: Lee, Marian and Nic.
You make life utterly fascinating
and I can't wait for our next adventure.

Acknowledgments

This work was a labor of love, and I could not have completed it without the support of some very special people.

Many thanks to my mentors throughout the years, especially David Wallner, Dr. Robert Drechsel and Dr. Katy Culver. You put me on the path and gave me the push I needed to walk it.

Many thanks to my amazing friends and colleagues at Whitworth University, especially Dr. James McPherson, Dr. Gordon Jackson, Dr. Mike Ingram, Dr. Alan Mikkelson, Dr. Ron Pyle and Joy York. Special thanks to Anne Wilcox for her feedback and her general amazing attitude toward life.

I am forever grateful to the friends who have listened to me talk about this work with good humor and patience, especially Dr. Robert E. Gutsche, Jr., Kristen Krause and Kelli Willard West.

Table of Contents

Acknowledgments vi

Preface 1

Introduction: Welcome to the Conversation! 3

1. What Does the Law Say About Children? 11
2. The Constitution Goes to Public School 25
3. You Can't Say That in a Public School— or Can You? 38
4. What Is a Student? 77
5. Why Free Speech for Students at All? 98
6. A Foot in Both Worlds: The Special Case of Student Newspapers 127
7. Facebook and Twitter and Texting, Oh My! Cyberspeech 142
8. Starting Your Own Conversation About Student Speech 156

Chapter Notes 169

Works Cited 191

Cases Cited 198

Index 203

Preface

I have been intrigued by the subject of student speech rights in public schools since my own experience as a high school newspaper editor in southcentral Wisconsin. We were the lucky ones, with an adviser ready to go to bat for us should the administration attempt to restrict our speech, and willing to allow us to make our own mistakes (and pay the consequences for them) as well. It wasn't until my university years that I learned not all students had such a great experience. As I followed the subject through my graduate studies, I realized that free speech in public schools was a challenging topic for all involved parties.

This book explores student free speech in public K–12 schools with a slightly different perspective than others in the field. While most work in public school student speech rights focuses primarily (or exclusively) on the law, I was interested in what other disciplines had to contribute. What we could learn from a more multidisciplinary examination could potentially help teachers, administrators and school boards create stronger, proactive student speech policy that flexes with new innovations in communication while remaining true to the dual interests of the First Amendment and the need for an effective educational environment.

In the following pages, you'll see plenty of legal discussion—we can't ignore what the courts and the states have said about student speech. But you'll also see interwoven throughout that discussion background on children and the law, the constitution in the schools, the history and sociology of American public K–12 education and a little bit of teenage neuroscience in an effort to look at the question of student speech rights from as broad a perspective as possible.

One thing this book does not do, however, is provide you with *the*

Preface

answer. There is no one right answer to the question of public student speech rights—as you'll see in the following pages, there are many crucial factors that will be highly specific to your community and your school district. What this book will do, however, is delve into a background that may initiate some conversations and give you a foundation on which to build an approach to student speech that is right for you.

Make no mistake, the ability to engage in rational discussion with people who hold a range of opinions is a valuable skill in a modern democracy. A glance at the current Common Core learning goals for English and Social Sciences shows they include the ability to make and sustain an argument—to achieve this goal, one must be able to disagree or dissent civilly. If students are not given some breathing room to practice this vital skill, it won't develop. If they are given an unfettered marketplace of ideas in which to play, the educational environment may suffer. A balance must be found. That is the discussion that this book begins.

Introduction
Welcome to the Conversation!

One balmy[1] afternoon in 1858, a young man was driving his father's cow home when he happened to pass his schoolteacher's residence. In a brazen act of cheek (at least, by mid–19th century standards) and in the presence of both the teacher and several other classmates, the young man called out "Old Jack Seaver!" The next day, the teacher reprimanded the saucy youth: first with a lecture on respect for one's elders, and then with a rawhide whipping.

The young man's father sued the teacher, claiming the teacher had acted beyond the authority granted by the school, and that the boy's act of disrespect was, in fact, a parent's right and responsibility to punish. The Supreme Court of Vermont sided with the teacher, deeming the discipline appropriate to the infraction.[2] Further:

> [W]here the offense has a direct and immediate tendency to injure the school and bring the master's authority into contempt, as in this case, when done in the presence of other scholars and of the master, and with a design to insult him, we think he has the right to punish the scholar for such acts if he comes again to school.[3]

For more than 150 years, then, courts have been taking up questions of student speech and its potential to impact the academic day, the ability of teachers or schools to punish disruptive speech, and the extent of the school's authority to discipline speech that occurs off school grounds or outside the school day. While modern student speech cases are complicated by constitutional mandates, legislative policies, and global communication platforms, the core questions we face today are not all that different from those of *Lander's* Vermont courtroom. How do we assess the impact of student speech? How does

Introduction

a school balance discipline and responsibility? And how do we draw the lines of the school's authority geographically, temporally and socially?

Ever since the Supreme Court noted in *Tinker et al. v. Des Moines Independent Community School District* that "it can hardly be argued that either students or teachers shed their constitutional rights to freedom of speech or expression at the schoolhouse gate,"[4] the First Amendment has been a part of the student speech discussion in courtrooms and school board meetings. *Tinker* was not the final word on student speech, however, and judicial attitudes toward freedom of speech for our nation's public school students have shifted. For example, in 2007 Justice Clarence Thomas argued, "In my view, the history of public education suggests that the First Amendment, as originally understood, does not protect student speech in public schools" as he concurred with the student speech restriction in *Morse v. Frederick*.[5]

Tinker and *Morse*, two United States Supreme Court cases separated by 38 years, highlight the challenge faced by public schools and educators trying to create sound student speech policy for their students. If the nation's highest court is conflicted about if or how students have free speech rights within public schools, how are administrators and teachers supposed to make confident decisions about student speech policy or regulation?

Most First Amendment analysis involves balancing of some kind,[6] but the balance in school speech cases is tough because the scales are inconsistent. Two public school principals in Pennsylvania learned this the hard way: both learned students at their schools had created mock profiles of them on MySpace suggesting professional and sexual improprieties. Both principals discovered the student creators of these false profiles and punished those students. Both principals faced First Amendment challenges to their disciplinary actions and eventually came before separate three-judge panels from the Third Circuit, who came to *opposite* conclusions (one disciplinary action was upheld, the other struck down as unconstitutional) using the same case precedents to justify their decisions.[7]

Part of the challenge of finding a clear path regarding student speech freedom stems from what Redish and Finnerty called "a seemingly intractable paradox: the very process that is essential for the success of democracy threatens the fundamental preconditions of

Welcome to the Conversation!

democracy."[8] Schools[9] are charged with teaching the next generation about the fundamentals of citizenship, including the rights and responsibilities inherent in the U.S. Constitution. Schools are also required to maintain an effective learning environment so education can happen.[10] Thus the clash: encouraging students to better understand how to handle free expression may lead them to exercising that skill in such a way as to create a disturbance in the ability to educate.

Free speech and education commentators argue both sides of this clash. Dupre wrote that the state rightly "takes away some liberty from the individual student in order to preserve the liberty of a nation,"[11] while Roe observed the unclear suppression of student speech "creates a dissonance between the school's declared doctrine and its actual educational process."[12] The conflict between teaching a constitutional right and allowing its exercise unveils a trickier question: are schools places in which students may practice citizenship, or places in which they merely read about the rights and responsibilities of democracy?

Those who advocate for greater student speech rights argue (often passionately) that schools are the wellsprings of democracy, places for growth and exploration, and environments in which restrictions or regulations of thought and expression should be made only in the face of the most overwhelming need. In a 1974 study of student press, then-editor of the *St. Petersburg Times* Eugene Patterson noted:

> Freedom is a difficult art. To teach it, one must practice it. Students are quick to identify lip service. And if a school administration forces timidity, conformity, insincerity and hypocrisy on its student editors, they are going to grow up thinking that is the way America works, or else they are going to take a cynical view of American freedoms as being empty words.[13]

There is equal passion in the argument for the need to regulate student speech within schools. Teachers and administrators know that words can hurt, especially in the modern era; studies suggest nine percent to 35 percent of children between the ages of 12 and 17 have experienced some form of electronic aggression.[14] High-profile cases of cyberbullying leading to injury or death have led parents and advocacy groups to call for legislators to get tough on online speech and for schools to get tough with offenders, regardless of any potential First Amendment implications.

Compounding the safety concern is the perception that schools have become more dangerous places. Massive acts of violence such as

Introduction

the shootings at Columbine High School in 1999 and Sandy Hook Elementary School in 2012 have shaken the image of the safe, protected school environment. Schools began to adopt strict zero-tolerance policies in an effort to regain their lost sense of the security, and courts emphasized student welfare as a compelling interest that could potentially overcome the First Amendment right to free speech.

Standing back and attempting to look at the big picture, the pro-student speech argument stresses education for a rising generation of citizens, while the pro–school regulation argument focuses on today's educational environment. Each side has its advocates, and each has had its day in the courts. But more court decisions aren't going to resolve this conflict of ideas and ideals. It's time for schools to go on the offensive, to create clear student speech policy that respects both the First Amendment and the responsibility of public education to teach effectively. It's time to combine what we know about the law with what we know about theories of free speech, the educational environment, the development of young minds and the impact of technology. It's time to go beyond the courts, which have yet to incorporate any significant educational theory[15] or existing First Amendment theory into their student speech deliberations.[16] In fact, the Second Circuit Court of Appeals has gone so far as to say such theoretical underpinning was unnecessary.[17]

Exploring the "why" behind student free speech, however, gives us a chance to look at this issue with new eyes. Theory provides some of that "why," giving us a foundation of purpose beneath our policies that can remain firm even as policies adapt to changing needs. The idea that law should be guided by theory isn't new: Bork's chief argument against the "right of privacy" established in *Griswold v. Connecticut*[18] was that it lacked any theoretical foundation to justify its creation.[19] Without a strong theory base under student speech law, students can't predict if their speech will be protected, administrators can't predict if their regulations are constitutional and courts can't be predicted at all.

Looking at student speech though the lens of a range of disciplines forces us to take a step back and ask some very important questions before analyzing specific situations. Before we ask if speech disrupted school activities, before we engage in complicated forum analyses, let's first explore if schools are "First Amendment institutions"[20] where free

Welcome to the Conversation!

speech has benefit and value, and examine where the line between "student" and "citizen" lies. Theory refocuses our attention from the specifics of what one student said to these larger questions, and while it doesn't always make questions easier to resolve, it gives us a common starting point.

Currently, the common starting point in student speech discussion is *Tinker's* "schoolhouse gate" and "material disruption" standards. But the First Amendment protects speakers and speech, not places,[21] which means instead of looking at the gate, we're better served by exploring what makes a "student" a "student" and what differentiates student speech from citizen speech. Law alone can't tell us this, but a combination of law, history, philosophy and sociology can offer more tantalizing answers and help schools create or revise policies that better protect student speech *and* uphold the school's ability to carry out its educational mission. Good policy is the rising tide that lifts all boats, as students will know their outlets for free expression, teachers and schools will be more confident in their exercise of authority and perhaps most importantly, there will be less reliance on courts to sort out school issues.

To stay consistent with the First Amendment's approach to free speech ("Congress shall make no law…"), a discussion of student free speech begins with the idea that "the First Amendment does apply in schools, not that it doesn't."[22] We see this concept emerge in the *Tinker* decision of 1969, the first Supreme Court case to look at pure student speech (as opposed to speech related to another constitutional right, such as religious expression).[23] This is an important starting point, because it sets the level of expectation for the entire discussion. By presuming that student speech has First Amendment protection, our challenge becomes determining when there is a compelling enough reason to seek to override that protection.[24]

But *Tinker* is the start of the discussion, not the end of it. To create strong, confident student speech policy, we combine *Tinker* and its descendants with First Amendment theory, the history and culture of American education, and the societal and individual impact of public schools. Public schools are complex environments with significant historical, political, and cultural functions. Thomas Jefferson called education the "best safeguard against tyranny,"[25] and though the federal government toyed with the idea of a national school system,[26] that

Introduction

responsibility was ultimately shifted to the states with the expectation that education would prepare young people to participate in all levels of their democratic government.

Education has been seen as both a civic and a moral enterprise, one that helps a person develop a "democratic self" as well as the self-understanding necessary to develop individual opinions on political and social issues.[27] Modern public education still focuses on training for citizenship—in 2010, more than two-thirds of fourth-grade students explored key civics topics like politics, democracy or the Constitution, along with 85 percent of eighth-grade students and 97 percent of high school seniors.[28]

The rise of the common school movement of the mid–1800s revealed another goal of public education—socialization into American culture. Schools seemed to be the best way to quickly inculcate American values into the influx of immigrants and their children.[29] Today, schools still strive to provide support for their students' moral and social growth,[30] walking the thin line between generally agreed-upon values and those that may be derived from particular philosophical or religious viewpoints.

These two goals of education—teaching democracy and inculcating values—bring us back to the paradox suggested by Redish and Finnerty. Ideally, teaching the rights and responsibilities of a citizen in a democracy, including free speech, would involve not only study and preparation, but also practice. Yet, allowing such speech may contradict the values espoused by the school, undermining both its mission and authority.[31] In other words, if we let the students speak freely, they may say something that contradicts a value the school is trying to inculcate, like honesty, fairness or tolerance. Strong student speech policy has to address and account for the dual goals of education and respect the needs of the institution that makes a student a student in the first place.

We can fairly say a school makes a student, as we don't start calling children "students" until they formally enroll in some kind of learning experience. Enrollment is where "student" begins, but where does it end? This question needs to be answered to understand when a young person is a "student" and when he or she is a "citizen" under the law. When a teenage boy is sitting in a classroom, responding to a teacher's question, it's easy to place the label of "student" on him. Does that label

Welcome to the Conversation!

remain when that boy goes home for the day, for the weekend, or for the summer? Is his speech still "student speech" and under the authority of the school? Separating different personas under the law isn't unique—Supreme Court decisions have helped us determine when public employees, like schoolteachers, speak as "employees" as opposed to "citizens."[32] For schools to create strong student speech policy, a similar split is needed for "student" and "citizen" (or to be more accurate, "minor citizen" as most K–12 students are under the age of legal adulthood and thus have reduced First Amendment rights[33]).

The separation of student from citizen may be difficult, but we do so in recognition that the person speaking is in a different role than that of citizen, and the government figure seeking to regulate is in a different role than that of sovereign. This isn't an attempt to ignore age—minors are still minors and children are treated differently under the law. Great student speech policy doesn't ignore age, but acknowledges that student status can be shed, much like public employee status.[34]

By bringing together several disciplines—law, history, sociology, education and communication—we can create a more comprehensive "why" behind student speech rights that may guide administrators and districts toward creating proactive policy that protects speech rights and academic environments, and is fluid enough to adapt to changing communication. We don't need the perfect case to come before the Supreme Court to answer our questions about student social media speech or regulating off-campus expression—the answers can be found by expanding our search beyond four core Supreme Court precedents and looking at the wide world of theory and scholarship that underpin them.

In an age when we see levels of civic engagement dropping[35] and rising generations feeling a disconnect from their government, we must ask what we risk if student speech policies in public schools discourage young people from engaging in expression. Hundreds of "what-if" scenarios could be raised here, ranging from the utter chaos of allowing students to run their schools to *1984* analogies of a population subdued into mindless complacency. The realistic scenario is far less extreme but still a concern—a rising generation of citizens unaware of the power of speech to spur positive change, less capable of engaging in productive debate with people of differing opinions, and uncertain of the value

Introduction

of their own contributions to the marketplace of ideas. There is no argument that a stable educational environment is necessary for effective teaching to occur. With a strong student speech policy, we can honor both the immediate value of order and discipline with the long-term goal of producing democratically involved citizens.

1

What Does the Law Say About Children?

"Protect the children!" has been a rallying cry for a range of legal, economic, moral and social issues, and speech and expression are not exempt. Most of the nation's 49.8 million public K–12 students are under the age of 18 and therefore considered children under the law.[1] When courts look at the K–12 students before them, they often see kids—so to understand the legal concerns in play when we talk about students, it's useful to understand current approaches to children's constitutional rights and responsibilities.

Using chronological age to determine the boundary between childhood and adulthood is beautifully clear and simple. Birth is generally a well-documented event, firmly establishing a date by which one's age can be verified.[2] However, the black-and-white distinction of under/over age 18 creates the pragmatic question of the difference of a day. Can 24 hours really separate a child of 17 years, 364 days and an adult of 18? Justice Oliver Wendell Holmes wrote that such debate was unproductive:

> When he has discovered that a difference is a difference of degree, that distinguished extremes have between them a penumbra in which one gradually shades into the other, a tyro thinks to puzzle you by asking where you are going to draw the line, and an advocate of more experience will show the arbitrariness of the line proposed by putting cases very near to it on one side or the other. But the theory of the law is that such lines exist, because the theory of the law as to any possible conduct is that it is either lawful or unlawful.[3]

Rather than argue the age of majority, it's far more useful to understand it. The "age of majority," or the age at which courts and governments consider a person to be an adult, had long been 21 in the United

States. Some historians suggest the age of 21 was selected in the Middle Ages because that was the age at which a man presumably could wear full armor.[4] In the modern era, a more likely rationale is that psychological and social research support 21 as the age at which most people are able to make mature, responsible life decisions.[5]

The age of adulthood adjusted in the 1970s, largely in response to the Voting Rights Act Amendments of 1970 lowering the federal voting age from 21 to 18. Because 18-year-olds could participate in two significant aspects of adult civic life—military service and voting in federal elections—states ratified the 26th Amendment changing the voting age for all elections to 18 and creating a new definition for adulthood.[6]

The age line of majority was redrawn, but the core rationale for it remained. People younger than 18 did not have the rationality or autonomy needed to engage with the full rights and responsibilities of adulthood, echoing the views of John Stuart Mill's *On Liberty*:

> It is perhaps hardly necessary to say that this [liberty] doctrine is meant to apply only to human beings in the maturity of the faculties. We are not speaking of children, or of young persons below the age which the law may fix as that of manhood or womanhood. Those who are still in a state to require being taken care of by others, must be protected against their own actions as well as against external injury.[7]

Withholding greater liberties from children, who are not able to understand the full consequences of their actions, protected them as well as the public from foolhardy decisions made as a result of that immaturity.

Examining the Immaturity Argument

There's a reason many video games reward players with "experience points"—the immature, the inexperienced, the novice tend to make mistakes. The inexperience of children requires that others care for them to protect "against their own actions as well as against external injury."[8] We see the immaturity rationale appear strongly in three areas of age-based legal restrictions: rights over one's own body, the ability to engage in activities within adult society, and rights/duties of citizenship.

1. What Does the Law Say About Children?

Rationality (or the lack thereof) plays a large role in supporting age-based restrictions on what people may put in or do to their own bodies, such as alcohol use (age 21), smoking (age 18) and tattoos or body piercings (age 18).[9] The chief reason for placing age restrictions at or beyond the age of majority is the belief that minors are not rational enough to understand the harm they are doing to their bodies. Research has established the impact of alcohol on developing brains, the impact of tobacco smoke on lung tissue and the short-term hazards of tattoos (such as infection due to poor aftercare) as well as the long-term ones (social stigma, cost and discomfort of removal).[10] While this information is readily available, those who advocate restriction believe minors, especially adolescents, lack the life experience to understand the long-range impact of these actions. In essence, children need to be protected from themselves.[11]

One interesting twist to the above is the ability of minor females to obtain contraception or an abortion without their parents' permission or notification. Twenty-six states and the District of Columbia allow minors 12 and older to independently consent to contraceptive services, and two states and the District of Columbia explicitly allow all minors to consent to abortion services.[12] In these very specific areas, courts and legislatures see significant privacy concerns of the young women involved and work to balance them against the rights of the young women's parents or guardians. The 1976 *Planned Parenthood of Central Missouri v. Danforth*[13] case and subsequent *Bellotti v. Baird*[14] decision affirmed a parent's right to be a part of his or her child's medical choices but allowed an exception for a minor who could convince a judge both that she was mature and rational enough to understand the decision she was making and that making the decision without the input or knowledge of her parents was necessary.

Danforth and *Bellotti* affirmed an age-based restriction but suggested that the immature assumption about age could be overridden should the minor prove herself competent to make the decision. While a "proof of rationality" test is impractical for every aged-based situation, these two Supreme Court cases open the door to the idea that some minors may possess the rationality or autonomy generally considered only present over the age of 18.

The second grouping of age-based restrictions involves privileges[15] restricted to adult society, including driving (age 16),[16] marriage, signing legal contracts, gambling, and purchasing pornography (all age 18). The reasoning behind these restrictions links to the ripple effect of bad decisions. Driving is the most obvious example, as a lack of experience behind the wheel combined with poor decision-making can lead to injury or death not only of the driver, but also of others.

Not all harm has to be as obvious as car accidents. For example, in *Ginsberg v. New York*,[17] the Supreme Court upheld the constitutionality of variable obscenity, or the idea that speech can be considered obscene for minors but not for adults. In that case, "safeguarding such minors from harm"[18] to their moral and ethical development was a compelling enough interest to overcome the First Amendment challenge to a New York state statute restricting the sale of otherwise legal sexual publications to minors. No harm had to have occurred, nor did the likelihood of harm have to be supported through scientific research. Rather, the Court upheld the law by applying an intuitive approach to support the belief that sexual material was likely to be harmful for the development of young people.[19]

The third group of age-based regulations is similarly rooted in concern for the community and focuses on civic rights and duties such as voting or running for elected office. The concern in these age-based regulations is not protecting the minor from harm, but protecting the public from an immature or unprepared elected official, or an election outcome determined by immature voters who may be uninformed and irrational. An age line works to keep the voting privilege among those who will wield it responsibly.[20]

Such a concern is best seen in the debates in the early 1970s preceding the passage of the 26th Amendment, which lowered the voting age from 21 to 18.[21] Though West Virginia Senator Jennings Randolph had introduced the measure in Congress for nearly 30 years straight, it had not been seriously considered until the height of the Vietnam War, when the slogan "Old Enough to Fight, Old Enough to Vote" brought home the injustice of disenfranchising 18- to 20-year-old soldiers and veterans.[22] Congressional representatives jumped on board; Senator Birch Bayh of Indiana stated, "The surest and most just way to harness the energies and moral conscience of youth is to open the door to full citizenship by lowering the voting age. Youth cannot be expected to work within the system when they are denied that very opportunity."[23]

1. What Does the Law Say About Children?

The ability to run for elected office is guarded by age restrictions on local, state and federal levels. Minimum age requirements for local and state elected offices vary between 18 and 25, while the U.S. Constitution sets age minimums of 25 for members of the House of Representatives,[24] 30 for members of the U.S. Senate[25] and 35 for the president of the United States.[26] Legislative records indicate that these age restrictions were created to ensure public officeholders are mature enough to deal with their duties effectively.[27] As with voting, the concern is less for the younger person attempting to secure political office, but rather for the needs of his or her possible constituents.

Age restrictions for voting and holding office are prohibitive for minors, but the protective nature of age lines can also hold great benefit for children. Consider the approach to juvenile crime and punishment—the juvenile court system, created at the turn of the 20th century, was made to protect minors and focuses more on rehabilitation than punishment. Juvenile records are generally closed and juvenile offenders' names often protected from the public record. *In re Gault*[28] assured that juvenile proceedings still afforded minors the benefits of due process, including the right to formal charges, to counsel, to confront accusers and to cross-examine them. The Supreme Court declared the Eighth Amendment not only prohibits the death penalty for minors who commit their crimes before the age of 18,[29] but also sentencing a minor to life without parole for non-homicide crimes.[30] Criminal activity committed by minors raises serious questions as to whether the child knew the full consequences of not only the crime, but the penalties should he or she be caught. Immaturity is still a significant motivator in creating law and policy around juvenile crime, but that motivator creates opportunities for children that adults would not normally have.

Protecting individuals -- Protecting the public

Rights over one's body	Adult society privileges	Rights/duties of citizenship
Purchase and use alcohol	*Driving*	*Vote*
Purchase and use tobacco	*Marriage*	*Run for political office*
Tattoos and body piercings	*Ability to sign contracts*	
	Gambling	

Rationality and maturity take time, and the law of age-based regulations recognizes that need. Certain types of rights—control of one's body, one's ability to engage in societal privileges as well as activities related to citizenship—are reduced or restricted because minors are seen as semi-autonomous at best, and communities as a whole need protection from decisions based in immaturity. A small exception to this broad argument is seen in the *Planned Parenthood* and *Bellotti* cases, which allowed for the possibility of a minor to prove to a judge or court that she is rational and autonomous.

Of the three groups of age-based regulations, those related to civic rights and responsibilities hold a special relevance to a discussion of student speech rights, as that group also deals with rights and responsibilities conferred by the Constitution. It's intriguing to note that of the three groups, the civic-oriented restrictions are the only ones to see an age line reduced. In the first group, the age for purchasing and consuming alcohol was increased from 18 to 21, largely in response to the federal government's threat to withhold highway funds from states that did not increase the age.[31] From the second group, many states have changed their drivers' license regulations to introduce a graduated process, withholding full driving rights from minors until they are 18. Yet the age for voting was lowered, suggesting a desire on the part of legislatures to further involve young people in government and civic life—the same place where free expression lives and thrives.

The Law's Responsibilities to Minors

In addition to specifying what children may or may not do, the law also establishes certain responsibilities that the state bears toward children. Since courts and legislatures have embraced the idea that children lack rationality and autonomy, children are owed an extra level of care to allow them to get these skills. The legal approaches to the relationship between government and minors are equally important to our exploration of student speech concerns, as the government's special role of "educator" springs from the doctrines of *parens patriae* and *in loco parentis* as well as the conflict between parent and government regarding the welfare of children under both their care.

Parens patriae, or "father of the country," is a legal doctrine in which the government assumes protective responsibility for those who

1. What Does the Law Say About Children?

are unable to care for themselves.[32] In the particular case of children, it also provides an additional layer of protection for minors when adults who are normally responsible for a child fail in that duty. *Parens patriae* first entered American jurisprudence with *Ex Parte Crouse*[33] to justify the commitment of minors to state-run facilities when parents do not act in their children's moral or physical best interests.[34] *Parens patriae* is perhaps best exemplified by the 1944 Supreme Court decision in *Prince v. Massachusetts*,[35] in which the guardian of a nine-year-old girl was charged with violating child labor laws by having the child sell religious tracts on the streets of Brockton. In response to the guardian's claim that her First Amendment right to religious expression had been violated, the Court noted:

> Acting to guard the general interest in youth's well being, the state as *parens patriae* may restrict the parent's control by requiring school attendance, regulating or prohibiting the child's labor and in many other ways. Its authority is not nullified merely because the parent grounds his claim to control the child's course of conduct on religion or conscience. Thus, he cannot claim freedom from compulsory vaccination for the child more than for himself on religious grounds. The right to practice religion freely does not include liberty to expose the community or the child to communicable disease or the latter to ill health or death. The catalogue need not be lengthened. It is sufficient to show what indeed appellant hardly disputes, that the state has a wide range of power for limiting parental freedom and authority in things affecting the child's welfare; and that this includes, to some extent, matters of conscience and religious conviction.[36]

The concept behind *parens patriae* has justified court decisions to override the wishes of parents and force them to obtain medical care for their children, even if it would allow an adult to forgo the same treatment in the same situation,[37] and to block a minor's ability to purchase indecent materials[38] or hear George Carlin's "Seven Dirty Words" on over-the-air broadcast.[39] In 1997, Congress attempted to push the concept farther to regulate indecent material on the Internet, but failed due to difficulties in simultaneously preserving adult rights.[40] *Parens patriae* may protect children and those unable to care for themselves, but cannot spill over into limiting individual adult rights.

It's not surprising to see *parens patriae* in play when talking about public schools. All 50 states plus the District of Columbia have compulsory education laws[41] to protect minors' ability to get the education they need to prepare for adult life, even over the protests of

Students' Right to Speak

their parents. Compulsory education has been modified, however, to permit parents to choose nonpublic schools for their children (for example, church-affiliated schools or private academies) that meet state requirements.[42]

Parens patriae, as the name suggests, is the government acting as the parent, but when the parent doesn't feel like being replaced, clashes can ensue. While recognizing the importance of parents' rights to raise their children as desired, courts have invoked *parens patriae* to support a public school's choice of curriculum,[43] textbooks[44] or library selections.[45] As the Ninth Circuit put it, "[T]he Constitution does not afford parents a substantive due process or privacy right to control through the federal courts the information that public schools make available to their children."[46]

It's rare, but not unheard of, to see *parens patriae* doctrine give way to parental wishes. If a regulation holds little practical merit, as was the case in *Meyer v. Nebraska*,[47] the courts will accede to the desires of parents. In *Meyer*, parents contested a state statute prohibiting the teaching of a language other than English to children younger than eighth grade. The U.S. Supreme Court saw little value to such a regulation, stating, "No emergency has arisen which renders knowledge by a child of some language other than English so clearly harmful as to justify its inhibition."[48]

A more unique case, and one that has yet to be duplicated, is *Wisconsin v. Yoder*,[49] in which an Old Amish community challenged Wisconsin's compulsory education age of 16. The Amish traditionally educated their children through the eighth grade (age 13–14), and then transitioned the children into apprenticeship roles within their communities to prepare for lives as farmers, craftsmen, and homemakers. The Amish challenged the compulsory law as a threat not only to their religion, but their way of life, claiming exposure to high school life would confuse and alienate Amish teens.

Despite the strong *parens patriae* rationale for keeping children in school, the U.S. Supreme Court found for the Amish. The decision stressed the unique nature of Amish society, its high degree of self-reliance (Amish refuse to accept government programs such as Medicare, Medicaid or Social Security), and its reputation for industriousness, low crime rates and overall self-sufficiency. If the goal of education was to prepare young people for their place in the adult

1. What Does the Law Say About Children?

world, the Amish method was clearly doing so, merely in a smaller world than compulsory education laws generally envision.[50] In subsequent years, non–Amish parents and communities have attempted to invoke *Yoder* to get around compulsory education laws, but with no success.

An alternative to *parens patriae* often used in specific environments like schools, juvenile centers or medical facilities is the doctrine of *in loco parentis*, which allows the government to act "in the place of the parent."[51] Derived from English common law, *in loco parentis* gives an individual or institution the temporary rights of a parent when (and only when) it is assuming the temporary responsibilities of one. This can range from parental figures like legal guardians or foster parents to the more common application to teachers and administrators in public schools.

In loco parentis was used by courts to support the actions of public colleges and universities until the 1960s. Until that point, it was expected that colleges and universities were responsible for their students "from libido to laundry,"[52] and as such, had the ability to enact regulations and restrictions on their students' daily lives to ensure their physical, psychological and moral well-being. As the country began to revise its conception of adulthood, however, *in loco parentis* became problematic for higher education, as the 26th Amendment made most of their students legal adults and there was no parental authority to act "in the place" of.

Dixon v. Alabama State Board of Education[53] was the beginning of the end of *in loco parentis* on public college and university campuses. In this case, six African American students were expelled without notice or charges from Alabama State College in relation to the students' participation in a peaceful sit-in at a whites-only lunch counter. Acting *in loco parentis*, the school claimed it was obligated to remove the threat of lawlessness and rule-breaking from the academic environment. The Fifth Circuit disagreed, stating that more comprehensive due process procedures were required as the relationship between students and the campus was shifting from parent-child to contractual.[54]

In K–12, however, *in loco parentis* remains relevant. *New Jersey v. T.L.O.*,[55] a case involving the constitutionality of an administrator's search of a student's purse for evidence of rule breaking, expanded the idea of a school's rights and responsibilities from merely an extension of parental rights to a unique custodial power that reflects the

Students' Right to Speak

responsibility elementary and secondary schools have for their students' education and safety.[56] Schools had an obligation to provide a safe environment conducive to learning, and could act in the place of parents to ensure both security and order.[57]

Some *in loco parentis* situations have relied on what courts believe parents would want or expect schools to do. In *Bethel School District v. Fraser*,[58] the Supreme Court rested part of its decision to uphold the suspension of a student for making a lewd speech at a school assembly on the idea that parents expect schools to teach their students the "habits and manners of civility essential to a democratic society."[59] This value-based argument also crops up in *Morse v. Frederick*,[60] where the Court upheld the suspension of a student for displaying a banner with a purported pro-drug message in part because of the banner's contradiction of the community values parents expect their children to learn.

Morse also hits on another key element of *in loco parentis*—the safety of children within public schools. The *Morse* decision stated the mission of a school to combat the dangers of illegal drug use was sufficiently compelling to outweigh the First Amendment value of what could be seen as a pro-drug banner.[61] Schools had a duty to protect the safety of their students in a scary new world, enhancing student welfare as a spotlight issue for the courts.

Added to the dangers of drug use were a rash of school shootings and a perceived rise in bullying and harassment that led the Ninth Circuit to conclude, "We live in a time when school violence is an unfortunate reality that educators must confront on an all too frequent basis."[62] Many schools responded to the Columbine High School massacre with zero-tolerance measures,[63] which mollified parents and communities but also led to kindergarteners being suspended for playing cops and robbers during recess[64] and a second-grader suspended for pointing a chicken strip at a teacher and saying "Pow, pow."[65] Schools acting *in loco parentis* have opted to err on the side of caution, moving to suspend or expel students for poems,[66] rap lyrics[67] and pictures[68] suggesting violence against other students or the school.

Bullying was not only an *in loco parentis* safety concern for schools, but also a matter of potential legal liability as well. The *Davis*[69] decision of 1999 not only held that a school's failure to address student-on-student sexual harassment violated Title IX of the Education Amendments of 1972,[70] but also that the school could face financial

1. What Does the Law Say About Children?

damages if the harassment was determined to be severe and pervasive and the school acted with deliberate indifference.[71] Guidance from the Department of Education has encouraged schools to develop policies defining harassment in a much broader way in order to protect themselves from costly lawsuits:

> Harassing conduct may take many forms, including verbal acts and name-calling; graphic and written statements, which may include use of cell phones or the Internet; or other conduct that may be physically threatening, harmful, or humiliating. Harassment does not have to include intent to harm, be directed at a specific target, or involve repeated incidents.[72]

Broadening the definition may encompass more behavior, including constitutionally protected speech, but may also protect students from harm and schools from liability.

Together, *parens patriae* and *in loco parentis* have helped define what the government looks like when it plays the role of educator rather than sovereign/leader.

	Means...	Supports ideas like...	Case Examples
Parens patriae	"father of the country"	Compulsory education Variable obscenity laws	Prince v. Mass. Ginsberg v. New York
In loco parentis	"in the place of the parent"	Curricular decisions Student searches Restrictions on lewd speech	New Jersey v. T.L.O. Davis v. Monroe

Compulsory education laws shaped by *parens patriae* ensure the majority of minors old enough to attend school do so, and most attend public schools. Meanwhile, the compelling interest of protecting student welfare via *in loco parentis* gives the government-as-educator latitude to restrict or regulate the rights of minors. Considering the fragmented nature of American public education, a uniform legal conception of government as educator likely would not have emerged if it were not for these two doctrines.

The Common School Movement Also Leads to Government-as-Educator

The Constitutional Conventions initially debated the idea of a federal educational system from the earliest grades through colleges and universities, but despite the fervent support of such notables as George Washington and Thomas Jefferson, that duty was left to the states.[73] Schooling was uneven in the country for its first 50–75 years, with urban areas offering secondary schools led by trained teachers, and rural areas hiring "itinerant teachers" to stay for a few weeks and hold a school session when enough students and fees were available.[74] Early colleges and universities were often sectarian and intended to train the children of the upper classes to lead the country into "mature and autonomous societies."[75]

By the mid–1800s, prominent academics as well as politicians saw the benefit of a more unified approach to elementary and secondary education. Immigrants began forming insular cultural communities in both cities and rural areas, causing some elected officials to question these immigrants' allegiance to their new country. Education, it was thought, would ground the next generation in the values and cultural ideals of the United States, as well as prepare them for active participation in their civic duties when they reached adulthood.[76] States began to revise their constitutions to provide for the education of all children, regardless of ability to pay, and the federal government provided land grants to every state admitted to the Union after Ohio in 1802 for the support of schools.[77]

The "common school" movement began around 1850, building on the ideas of Horace Mann and his contemporaries to create a model of academic efficiency that trained most students for trade work, while elite students were given a more rigorous curriculum to prepare for professions in medicine or law.[78] This led to a "tracking" system in secondary schools that existed well into the 20th century, in which some students were given courses to prepare them for specific trades, some were given basic academics that would prepare them for lower-level white-collar work or homemaking, and some were given the opportunity to pursue college-preparatory work. Students were not consulted about their tracks—their elementary-level work and testing (often IQ) determined their futures.[79]

A surge in secondary school attendance after World War II forced schools to re-evaluate tracking and adopt more of a one-size-fits-all approach. Soldiers returned from the war looking for jobs, giving employers their pick of highly trained veterans for jobs they previously filled with teenagers. Young people could no longer drop out of high

1. What Does the Law Say About Children?

school and find meaningful employment that would likely last until retirement. In response to these trends, states raised their compulsory attendance ages to funnel students back into schools.

The decision to keep minors in school longer may have solved one problem, but it created others. Teens who thought they were on the cusp of autonomy were forced back into the classroom, creating a disillusioned sub-culture that complicated efforts to maintain order.[80] Schools responded by trying to tighten authority over the academic environment, and the "children's rights movement" hit the courts in response during the 1960s and 1970s. State and federal courts saw a dramatic increase in cases dealing with the constitutionality of school rules and disciplinary actions.[81]

In the midst of the increase in judicial activity, courts displayed a consistent deference to schools when assessing the validity of school rules and school disciplinary actions. Early cases acceded to the locally elected school boards that ran schools and approved regulations:

> The Board of Education has full power in every particular to maintain and govern the public schools of Chicago. It is the controlling and guiding body, caring for its property, regulating the course of study, governing the teachers and providing generally for the educational welfare of the pupils.[82]

Courts refused to debate the "practical wisdom displayed by the school authorities"[83] unless the schools "unreasonably and arbitrarily exercise the discretionary authority conferred upon them."[84]

That deference continues today when courts take up issues involving public schools, though the tone has shifted somewhat from refusing to question the school's authority to refusing to question its competence. Teachers and administrators are increasingly well educated in both the art of education and the science of children's development and as such, it is "not the business of this Court to gainsay the judgments of *experts* on matters of pedagogy."[85] In *Board of Regents v. Southworth*, the Supreme Court refused to declare "what is or is not germane to the ideas to be pursued in an institution of higher learning,"[86] while *Chiras v. Miller,* rejecting the claim made by a textbook author that his book had been unconstitutionally rejected by the Texas State Board of Education because of viewpoint, said states had broad discretionary power "to establish public school curricula which accomplishes the states' educational objectives."[87]

Students' Right to Speak

Judges have declared themselves "incompetent to tell school authorities how to run schools in a way that will preserve an atmosphere conducive to learning,"[88] and have expressed a general hesitancy to contradict school officials' expertise and authority in determining if a students' actions threaten the school environment, whether it is handing out religious-themed candy in the hallways[89] or banning the Confederate flag from school premises in response to violent altercations between white and black students.[90]

When the government acts as educator, then, the courts have given it a little more space and flexibility than when the government acts as sovereign. Judges appear to recognize that government-as-educator is not a typical arm of the state,[91] and the trained professionals within it know far better what is pedagogically sound as well as disciplinarily necessary.[92]

Whether examining the justification to restrict children, to protect children or to empower schools, the recurring theme is the immaturity of youth and the duty to help children rise above their inexperience so that they can become productive adults. That consistency helps us see how the law of children and the law of schools combine to support and uphold each other. Because the Constitution applies to all citizens, regardless of age,[93] those who are not able to defend their own rights must have the protection of the government so that they may grow into adulthood and become active members of our democracy. The most reasonable place for this to occur is public schools, which grew out of the common school movement of the mid–1800s and now educate nearly 50 million students.

But to confuse the idea of "student" and "child" is to confuse a designation made strictly by chronological age and one based on a role that one holds temporarily, then sheds. To understand the complexity of student free speech concerns means we need to shift our focus on that particular role and the environment that makes it so—the public school. Past cases have shown the courts to be extremely reluctant to become involved in what they see as daily operations of academia, with one exception: when constitutional rights are potentially infringed.

2

The Constitution Goes to Public School

When Supreme Court Justice William Brennan reviewed a Pennsylvania law requiring schools to start their days with Biblical verses, he wrote, "Americans regard the public schools as a most vital civic institution for the preservation of a democratic system of government. It is therefore understandable that the *constitutional prohibitions* encounter their severest test when they are sought to be applied in the school classroom."[1]

Some constitutional questions have been dealt with fairly quickly and conclusively: for example, most courts agree that corporal punishment administered by a public school official that meets a "reasonableness standard" does not violate the Eighth Amendment.[2] Questions about public schools and how they interact with speech and press freedoms,[3] religious expression and exercise, search and seizure, due process, and equal protection under the law have involved more complicated discussions.

James Ryan, Dean of the Faculty of Education at Harvard's Graduate School of Education, identified a dual approach to the U.S. Supreme Court's approach to constitutional questions in public schools[4]:

> Student free speech, Fourth Amendment, and due process rights are more limited in the school setting than they are outside of that setting. With regard to this group of rights, the Court has characterized the government as acting in a special capacity-that of educator-and has accordingly given education officials greater leeway to bend constitutional rights in order to achieve certain educational goals. By contrast, student equal protection rights to be free of racial and gender discrimination, or to benefit from affirmative action programs, at the moment appear to be no different within the school setting than they are outside of that setting. The same is true with regard to student free exercise rights.[5]

Students' Right to Speak

Ryan explains this split in the context of the primary concerns of the modern public school: students' academic success and social development.[6] However, exploring the cases that make up the foundation of constitutional law in public schools also reveals a sense of the internal vs. external in play. If a school chooses to regulate speech of its students, search their lockers or discipline them without the benefit of a trial and counsel, those actions remain largely internal to the school. Actions related to race, ethnicity, gender or faith, however, are far less confinable to the school context. They are inextricably connected to the person outside of school as well. Reviewing some key areas of constitutional law in schools helps us see this split in action and lends some insight into the question of student speech and expression.

Religion and the Classroom

The First Amendment begins: "Congress shall make no law respecting an establishment of religion, or prohibiting the free exercise thereof."[7] These two phrases, called the Establishment Clause and Free Exercise Clause respectively, outline two ways in which government and religion intersect. For both, the definition of "religion" is key. While the Supreme Court has yet to offer anything concrete, we do know that in general, religious beliefs are "beliefs which are based upon a power or being, or upon a faith, to which all else is subordinate or upon which all else is ultimately dependent"[8] and not merely a collection of individual philosophical or personal creeds.[9]

The Establishment Clause was created to avoid the state-supported religion from which the colonists had fled, placing Jefferson's "wall of separation between church and state" between matters of government and those of personal faith.[10] The clause also applies to state governments as a result of *Everson v. Board of Education*[11]:

> The "establishment of religion" clause of the First Amendment means at least this: Neither a state nor the Federal Government can set up a church. Neither can pass laws which aid one religion, aid all religions, or prefer one religion over another.... Neither a state nor the Federal Government can, openly or secretly, participate in the affairs of any religious organizations or groups and *vice versa*.[12]

The Free Exercise Clause, on the other hand, allows citizens to profess whatever faith they desire (including none) and worship as they

2. The Constitution Goes to Public School

wish, barring the violation of other laws.[13] Where the Establishment Clause looks closely at whether the government action is advancing a particular religion over others, the Free Exercise Clause asks if the government action is suppressing genuine religious expression of any type. As noted in *Sherbert v. Verner*[14]:

> Government may neither compel affirmation of a repugnant belief; nor penalize or discriminate against individuals or groups because they hold religious views abhorrent to the authorities; nor employ the taxing power to inhibit the dissemination of particular religious views.[15]

Applying the reasoning of these landmark cases, the Establishment and Free Exercise clauses would appear to restrict public schools from giving preferential treatment to one religion over another, and require that schools allow religious expression as long as it does not impede safety or discipline. Subsequent cases bear that prediction out.

On the heels of the *Everson* case, the Supreme Court decided *Illinois ex rel. McCollum v. Board of Education of School District 71*,[16] deeming an Illinois program that allowed area churches to offer religious education in public schools an Establishment Clause violation. Calling the program "beyond all question a utilization of the tax-established and tax-supported public school system to aid religious groups to spread their faith,"[17] the Court acknowledged that while public schools in this country had sectarian roots, today's elementary and secondary public education was strictly secular in its efforts to serve all eligible children, and that secular nature needed to be maintained.

Everson and *McCollum* focused on religious activity in public schools—it did not prevent parents from seeking faith-based education for their children. The *Pierce*[18] decision of 1925 still guaranteed a parent's right to choose private education over public, as long as the school met state criteria. But when parents of public school students demand that public school classrooms conform to religious beliefs, however, courts are not as deferential. In *Mozert v. Hawkins County Public Schools*,[19] the Sixth Circuit refused to direct a Tennessee school district to change its reading program for grades 1–8 based on parent complaints that the mandatory textbook contradicted the parents' religious values. The decision stated that to "tailor a public school's curriculum to satisfy the principles or prohibitions of any religion"[20] would offend the Establishment Clause. As long as the textbook didn't require an affirmation of any belief or participation in any prohibited practice, simply requiring reading the book did not violate the First Amendment.[21]

One issue that has grabbed a lot of Establishment and Free Exercise clause attention has been prayer in the classroom. Our country's educational system has its roots in the church, and an echo of that religious foundation still existed in public school classrooms. The Supreme Court addressed this connection in *Engel v. Vitale*,[22] when it struck down a New York state statute requiring all public schools to begin the day with a religious invocation. Despite the state's argument that the prayer was nondenominational and students could be excused from participation, Justice Black wrote, "[T]he constitutional prohibition against laws respecting an establishment of religion must at least mean that in this country it is no part of the business of government to compose official prayers for any group of the American people."[23]

Engel's concern was about what the Court saw as a state-mandated affirmation of belief—one year later, *School District of Abington Township v. Schempp*[24] explored the individual nature of faith. *Schempp* invalidated a Pennsylvania law that not only required the reading of Bible verses at the start of each school day but also a recitation of the Lord's Prayer. In the decision, Justice Clark focused on the personal impact of the law as he characterized religion as an "inviolable citadel of the individual heart and mind."[25] Where *Engel* argued one prayer could not be forced on a group of students, *Abington* stressed that even one student's personal beliefs could not be trumped by enforced participation in a contradictory statement of faith.

Once mandatory participation was resolved, the Court took on voluntary participation in religious activities in public schools. *Wallace v. Jaffree*[26] dealt with an Alabama statute that called for a period of silence each day for meditation or voluntary prayer. At the time, 25 states permitted or required schools to start each day with a moment of silence, which could be used for prayer, meditation or simple reflection upon the upcoming day.[27]

Unlike most the other statutes mandating moments of silence, the Alabama law specifically included the word "prayer" in the law, and the Supreme Court would not overlook this direct reference to religious activity. The Court stated the word "indicates that the State intended to characterize prayer as a favored practice"[28] and took issue with comments by the law's primary sponsor, who said he had proposed the law

2. The Constitution Goes to Public School

in an effort to return prayer to schools. As such, the Court invalidated the law, claiming it was "not consistent with the established principle that the government must pursue a course of complete neutrality toward religion."[29] Dissents by Justices White and Rehnquist based on the voluntary nature of the law and the multiple purposes to which a student could use that moment of silence, however, left a door open to voluntary opportunities for religious participation in public schools.

The question of religion and voluntary school activity was addressed in *Lee v. Weisman*,[30] in which a parent challenged a school's practice of inviting area clergy to deliver invocations and benedictions at commencement ceremonies. Despite the fact that clergy members were given strict guidelines to keep their comments nondenominational and inclusive, Weisman argued that it was still a "formal religious exercise which students, for all practical purposes, are obliged to attend."[31]

To answer *Weisman*, the Court acknowledged that commencement ceremonies were not required activities, but their status as a rite of passage made them a fundamental part of American education. Students should not have to miss the ceremony to avoid participating in a religious exercise contrary to personal beliefs. The Court suggested students would be under tremendous pressure to participate in the proceedings, even if such participation contradicted their personal faith, and thus created an involuntary participation scenario:

> Of course, in our culture standing or remaining silent can signify adherence to a view of simple respect for the views of others. And no doubt some persons who have no desire to join in a prayer have little objection to standing as a sign of respect for those who do. But for the dissenter of high school age, who has a reasonable perception that she is being forced by the State to pray in a manner her conscience will not allow, the injury is no less real.[32]

Whether student participation is voluntary or required, schools' attempts to bring overt religious practice into the classroom have failed Establishment Clause challenge. As predicted, schools can't appear to favor one line of religious thought over another. When *students* attempt to bring religious practice into schools, however, courts utilize more of a blend of the Establishment and Free Exercise clauses to find the fine line between allowing students to express their personal faith and avoiding the promotion (or appearance of promotion) of that expression.

Widmar v. Vincent[33] explored student religious expression in 1981, when the University of Missouri refused to allow a Christian student group to register as an official student organization, effectively blocking the group from meeting in university facilities and benefiting from other services available to student groups. The Supreme Court rejected the idea that allowing such a group "official" status would contravene the Establishment Clause, as long as the university's policy would allow other religious organizations equal opportunity to gain such status. Justice Powell noted that university students were likely mature enough to understand that the university was not endorsing the organization's message, but merely adhering to its equal access policy for student organizations that met basic criteria.[34] *Widmar* was reinforced by *Rosenberger v. Rector's* argument that "neutral criteria and evenhanded policies" would include, not exclude, religious viewpoints among a "broad and diverse" range of ideas at a public university.[35]

The reasoning of *Widmar* entered high schools in *Board of Education of the Westside Community Schools v. Mergens*,[36] in which a high school student was denied permission to form a Christian student group due to the school's requirement that all student groups have a teacher as an official adviser. The school said assigning a teacher to advise the group would have created an impermissible advancement of religion, and to allow the group to meet without an adviser would be preferential treatment.

The Supreme Court examined this issue within the framework of the 1985 Equal Access Act,[37] passed to officially extend the reasoning of *Widmar* to public secondary schools and ensure groups were not prohibited from using school resources on the basis of religious, philosophical or political viewpoint. Reviewing the law, the Court reaffirmed its constitutionality, stated that it did not violate the Establishment Clause, and subsequently declared the school's refusal to allow the student group to form to be a violation of the Act. Justice O'Connor specifically noted that high school students "are mature enough and are likely to understand that a school does not endorse or support student speech that it merely permits on a nondiscriminatory basis."[38]

Lower courts have used the combination of *Widmar, Mergens* and *Rosenberger* to allow for the passive distribution of religious literature in school hallways[39] and allow students to wear plastic rosaries to school at a time when rosaries were also being used as a gang symbol.[40] In these cases, courts watched closely to ensure students would understand there was no school endorsement or coercion regarding a religious message, determining that even elementary school students could distinguish when a school supported a message from when it was being presented by an outside party.[41]

In the Establishment and Free Exercise Clause cases, the courts have been careful to respect religious beliefs, practices and freedoms, even when doing so runs contrary to the preferred actions of the school. Schools can regulate actions that may appear to endorse one religious idea over another, as well as religious expression that causes harm to other students, but these regulations are pretty analogous to what government can do outside schools as well. Students aren't expected to check their faith, something that is integral to who they are in their whole lives and not just their student lives, at the schoolhouse door. It's not too surprising, then, that government's ability to act on religious expression is largely unchanged as student moves from outside the school to within it.

Overview of Key Cases:

Pierce v. Society of Sisters (1922)	Compulsory education can be fulfilled by religious schools
Everson v. Board of Education (1947)	The Establishment Clause applies to all levels of government; schools cannot aid or prefer one religion over another
Engel v. Vitale (1961)	Schools cannot create a mandatory single prayer for all students
Wallace v. Jaffree (1984)	Daily prayer/meditation statute is unconstitutional because "prayer" promotes a specific religious view
Westside Comm. Sch. v. Mergens (1989)	Noncurricular student groups can meet in public schools as long as all student interests have equal access
Lee v. Weisman (1991)	A denominationally neutral invocation at a school commencement ceremony is still a religious exercise

Equal Protection in Public Schools

Like issues of faith, when courts take up student issues based in race, ethnicity or gender, they do not give public schools more ability to restrict or regulate than they do to other government entities. After all, students don't leave these defining characteristics behind at the start of the school day; issues related to race, ethnicity or gender can't be internalized to the school (it happens here but nowhere else) and

Students' Right to Speak

therefore there is less of an argument to give schools more power to regulate than government in general.

The most famous example of equal protection within public schools is *Brown v. Board of Education of Topeka*,[42] which struck down the "separate but equal" doctrine that emerged out of *Plessy v. Ferguson*.[43] Newly appointed Chief Justice Earl Warren shepherded the court to a unanimous decision in *Brown*, writing in its sole opinion that a reliance on the state of affairs at the time of the nation's founding would not reflect the realities of modern education:

> Today, education is perhaps the most important function of state and local governments. Compulsory school attendance laws and the great expenditures for education both demonstrate our recognition of the importance of education to our democratic society. It is required in the performance of our most basic public responsibilities, even service in the armed forces. It is the very foundation of good citizenship. Today it is a principal instrument in awakening the child to cultural values, in preparing him for later professional training, and in helping him to adjust normally to his environment. In these days, it is doubtful that any child may reasonably be expected to succeed in life if he is denied the opportunity of an education. Such an opportunity, where the state has undertaken to provide it, is a right which must be made available to all on equal terms.[44]

The critical nature of education, and the inherent unfairness of separating children solely on the basis of race, "generates a feeling of inferiority as to their status in the community that may affect their hearts and minds in a way unlikely ever to be undone."[45]

A separate-but-equal approach regarding gender and education was rejected by the Court in *United States v. Virginia*, in which a female student contested the male-only admissions policy of the Virginia Military Institute (VMI).[46] The state had offered to create a parallel program for women, but the Supreme Court determined that separating public programs solely on the basis of gender required a compelling interest that could not be satisfied in any other fashion—and VMI lacked such an interest.[47]

Harms based in gender are a constitutional concern due to the Equal Protection clause and a federal concern due to Title IX of the Education Amendments of 1972.[48] If a student can't get the full benefit of education because of that student's gender, Title IX can trigger an administrative action ranging from a warning to a withdrawal of federal funds, as well as act as the basis for a civil lawsuit.[49] Cases involving teacher-on-student[50] as well as student-on-student[51] sexual harassment

2. The Constitution Goes to Public School

found schools liable not simply because an interruption of educational opportunity occurred, but because the interruption occurred primarily due to the student's gender.

Overview of Key Cases:

Brown v. Board of Education (1954)	Public schools cannot use "separate but equal" to segregate students based on race.
United States v. Virginia (1995)	Public educational institutions must show an "exceedingly persuasive justification" to support a gender-based admissions policy
Davis v. Monroe Board of Educ. (1998)	Title IX requires schools to ensure that students are not prevented from the benefit of public education based on gender

Right to Privacy/Search and Seizure in Public Schools

The judiciary's approach to constitutional rights like protection from unreasonable search and seizure,[52] and due process[53] are addressed differently than equal protection or religious expression. Courts have granted schools greater ability to regulate in these areas as a reflection of the unique needs of the academic environment. While students aren't required to check their citizenship at the schoolhouse door, the approach taken to issues of privacy or due process reflect response to internal actions within the school, not characteristics students carry into the school.

Students' right to privacy over their property and bodies was closely examined in 1985 with *New Jersey v. T.L.O.*[54] A New Jersey high school freshman was accused of smoking in the girls' bathroom and brought to face an administrator. The student denied the allegation, and the assistant vice principal searched the student's purse for cigarettes. He found a pack, but in the process of removing it, found rolling papers, a small amount of marijuana and a list of names that suggested T.L.O. was selling drugs at the school. She was subsequently arrested and charged with delinquency. The student and her mother said the search was unconstitutional—once the administrator found the cigarettes, he had no reason to examine the purse further and thus would not have found evidence of drugs.

The Supreme Court disagreed with the student and her mother. While it held that the Fourth Amendment's prohibition on unreasonable search and seizure applies to searches conducted by public school officials,[55] the Court determined school administrators did not have to satisfy the same standard of suspicion as other government figures. A search conducted on adults or minors off of school grounds must either be backed with a warrant or with a high degree of probable cause. In *T.L.O.*, the Court said a "reasonableness" standard would suffice for schools:

> Determining the reasonableness of any search involves a twofold inquiry: first, one must consider "whether the ... action was justified at its inception"; second, one must determine whether the search as actually conducted "was reasonably related in scope to the circumstances which justified the interference in the first place." Under ordinary circumstances, a search of a student by a teacher or other school official will be "justified at its inception" when there are reasonable grounds for suspecting that the search will turn up evidence that the student has violated or is violating either the law or the rules of the school. Such a search will be permissible in its scope when the measures adopted are reasonably related to the objectives of the search and not excessively intrusive in light of the age and sex of the student and the nature of the infraction.[56]

The Court justified this lower standard for school administrators by citing the need for order and discipline in public schools and anecdotal evidence of rising levels of drug use and violence. The heavy emphasis on the idea of "schools under siege" makes *T.L.O.* appear very result-oriented, focusing on the litany of problems that may be addressed by allowing schools greater leeway in search and seizure.[57] The Court's decision also granted school administrators authority to use this lower standard judiciously, in the best interest of their students and schools.

"Reasonableness" is not without its boundaries, and those boundaries are set in part by the level of invasiveness. For example, searches of lockers or desks, which are technically school property and not highly invasive, require a very low level of certainty of suspicion. They can't be searched on a whim, but courts don't require overwhelming evidence to support the reasonableness of such a search. Searching a student's personal property that is on school grounds, such as backpacks, purses or cars, requires a slightly higher level of certainty to support the reasonableness of the school's action. In recent cases, the

2. The Constitution Goes to Public School

constitutionality of searches of personal electronic devices such as cell phones has hinged on whether the student was breaking a rule by using the phone at the time of the seizure.[58]

Physical searches of students themselves, ranging from a simple turnout of pockets to full-fledged strip searches, are considered the most invasive. Such searches require a degree of justification closest to that for non–school searches to be constitutional. Even these searches, however, are tinged with deference to the school. In *Safford v. Redding*,[59] a 13-year-old girl was forced to strip to her undergarments, shake out the lower band of her bra and pull out the elastic of her underwear to prove she was not carrying prescription and over-the-counter drugs. While the school had reason to suspect her—the student had been in trouble before and other students claimed she was carrying drugs—the invasiveness of the search did not match severity of the danger and it was found to be unconstitutional.[60]

Personal privacy in public schools has also been addressed in the context of drug testing—schools have searched for illicit drugs not only in backpacks and lockers, but also in urine samples. Again, a "reasonableness" standard has been deemed sufficient in light of the rising tide of drug use in public schools, allowing administrators to require student-athletes to submit to random drug testing as a condition of sports participation[61] as well as students participating in any competitive extracurricular activities.[62] Despite concerns for students' privacy regarding their medication history (they had to share the medications they were taking in order to get an accurate urine screening) as well as the invasiveness of requiring them to submit samples of bodily fluids, the Supreme Court upheld random drug testing in both cases "in furtherance of the government's responsibilities, under a public school system, as guardian and tutor of children entrusted to its care."[63]

Overview of Key Cases:

New Jersey v. T.L.O (1985)	A school search of a student may occur if the search is reasonably related to its objective and not excessively intrusive.
Vernonia School District v. Acton (1994)	The interest in preventing drug use and minimally invasive nature of urine screenings justify a school's requirement that athletes submit to drug tests.
Safford v. Redding (2008)	A strip search of a student requires extraordinary justification due to the invasive nature of such a search.

Students' Right to Speak

Due Process in Public Schools

Like privacy, due process has been given different meaning in the school environment, and for largely the same reasons. Prior to the Supreme Court's decision in *Goss v. Lopez*,[64] public schools were not required to offer students due process when handing out discipline. The students in *Goss* had been suspended for 10 days without any idea of the evidence against them, or the chance to tell their side of the story. The Supreme Court deemed that problematic, since states, through compulsory attendance laws, had transformed education into a right that couldn't be taken away without the due process guaranteed by the Fourteenth Amendment.[65]

However, due process in schools didn't have to mirror due process outside schools. A citizen can't be deprived of rights or property without legal considerations like a formal hearing, the right to counsel and the right to cross-examine one's accusers. The Court in *Goss* explicitly noted that schools were not required to provide such procedures to students.[66] Instead, due process in schools is satisfied with oral or written notice of charges, an explanation of evidence against a student and an opportunity to present the student's side of the story.[67] The Court justified this "due process lite" approach on the basis of the school's need for an orderly environment and a desire to avoid further burdening schools with bureaucratic processes.[68] *Goss* was extended to the college/university level in *University of Missouri v. Horowitz*,[69] which held that due process procedures were required for disciplinary measures, but not for academic ones, and was refined by *Ingraham v. Wright*,[70] which determined discipline that did not result in a withholding of education (in this case, corporal punishment) did not require due process.

Overview of Key Cases:

Goss v. Lopez (1975)	Schools must offer students oral or written charges, an explanation of evidence and the opportunity to present their stories if discipline involves removal from school
Ingraham v. Wright (1976)	Corporal punishment does not require due process

Unlike the religion and equal protection clauses, privacy and due process law aren't based in an external trait that the student carries in. Both are centered on the school environment itself and are responses

2. The Constitution Goes to Public School

to actions that occur within the school environment. All four concepts—equal protection, religious expression, search and seizure, and due process are constitutional rights guaranteed to citizens. But we can separate the first two from the second because of the nature of the rights and their grounding within or without the academic environment. It's tough to make an argument that a minor can be treated differently based on race or gender by a school because such treatment is necessary to the academic environment—there's nothing special about a school to support such an argument. A claim to treat due process differently, to adapt it to better reflect the relationship between student and administration and allow it to respond to the specific needs of a public school as opposed to a government courtroom, is a more passable argument. One is external, the other is internal—the more internally the argument can live, the more likely a school will be able to regulate above and beyond the government-as-sovereign.

This difference is instructive as we turn to free speech in public schools. Free speech and free expression emerge from the same amendment, but religious expression springs from the deep and significant faith that is expressly protected by the Constitution. General expression of thought or idea is not similarly treated, and a school's desire to regulate speech is more likely a response to actions occurring in or near the school. We might therefore expect free speech in public schools to be given similar treatment as search and seizure or due process—more deferential to schools and more generosity with the ability to restrict or regulate in the name of order and discipline.

3

You Can't Say That in a Public School— or Can You?

According to the American Heritage Dictionary of Idioms, "out of the mouths of babes" references a passage from the Book of Matthew in the New Testament, and means "[y]oung and inexperienced persons often can be remarkably wise."[1] There's some truth to that old saying, but "the mouths of babes" also historically produce speech that is less than admirable. Public K–12 schools, as government entities that act *in loco parentis* to the children under their care, are caught between the First Amendment's prohibitions on speech regulation and their educational responsibilities. This constitutional clash echoes the concerns voiced in search and seizure as well as due process, where the argument that the school deserves special consideration is largely internal and focuses on responding to in-school situations and preserving in-school order.

Early Speech Cases

Many analyses of student speech in public education start in 1969 with *Tinker v. Des Moines*, but the Supreme Court of Vermont was ruling on student speech more than 100 years earlier. In *Lander v. Seaver*,[2] the Vermont high court considered whether a teacher could discipline a student by whipping him with a small rawhide for calling out "Old Jack Seaver!"[3] as the student passed the teacher's home after the school day was done. The student's father didn't believe teachers should belong

3. You Can't Say That in a Public School—or Can You?

to a class of public employees "vested with judicial and discretionary powers"[4] to administer such discipline. While the *Lander* decision focused on the authority granted public officials, the Vermont Supreme Court did not ignore the power of words, noting, "This misbehavior, it is especially to be observed, has a direct and immediate tendency to injure the school, to subvert the master's authority, and to beget disorder and insubordination."[5] The language was described as "contemptuous" and "insulting" as well as a direct threat to the master's control over the school. The whipping was upheld, and the court indicated its trust in the schoolmaster's "judgment and wise discretion."[6]

The Supreme Court of Wisconsin echoed Vermont in its 1908 decision on *State ex rel Dresser v. District Board of School District 1.*[7] The court upheld the fining and suspension of two students for writing a satirical poem about the rules at their school and submitting it to a local newspaper for publication. The parents of the students claimed in court that the school could only levy these punishments if "the offense was a violation of some rule prescribed by the board, or involved moral turpitude, or was committed during school hours in the school room or in the presence of the master and other pupils."[8] Because the students' actions did not meet any of these criteria, the parents claimed the school overreached in its discipline.

The court disagreed, citing the principal's general charge to take whatever actions necessary to uphold an orderly school environment.[9] As with *Lander*, the decision upheld the ability of schools to punish conduct that occurs outside school hours: "[S]chool authorities have the power to suspend a pupil for an offense committed outside of school hours and not in the presence of the teacher which has a direct and immediate tendency to influence the conduct of other pupils while in the school room."[10]

The Wisconsin Supreme Court indicated written speech such as a poem meant to poke fun at the school could disrupt a classroom or influence other pupils. Perhaps more importantly, the court deferred to schools to decide if the disruption earned a disciplinary response:

> The teachers are especially familiar with the disposition and temper of the children under their charge, and the effect which such a publication would probably have upon the good order and discipline of the school. The school authorities must necessarily be invested with a broad discretion in the government and

discipline of the pupils, and the courts should not interfere with the exercise of such authority unless it has been illegally or unreasonably exercised.[11]

Shifting from humor to something a little more serious, in *Wooster v. Sunderland*[12] a high school senior was expelled days before graduation for making a speech to the student body during which he claimed the chemistry rooms were unsafe and the school did not have the required number of fire exits. He encouraged the Board of Education to put a bond issue in the next election for funds to improve the school.[13]

The Board of Education demanded a public apology and retraction from the student, and when he refused, prevented his graduation. The Board did not argue that the student's language was profane or inappropriate, but rather the content was insubordinate, raised to discredit or humiliate the school.[14] In finding for the school, a California court agreed the speech was intended to belittle the Board and therefore was punishable. It also agreed with the school's initial demand for an apology, deeming it "adequate punishment for the misconduct of the plaintiff," and upholding the expulsion when the student "accentuated his misconduct" by refusing to apologize.[15]

Lander, *Dresser* and *Wooster* were heard in state courts and focused more on disciplinary issues than speech rights. These cases also predated *Gitlow v. New York*,[16] which extended the First Amendment's protection of speech and expression through the Fourteenth Amendment to apply to state government as well as federal government. Thanks to *Gitlow*, when the Barnette family chose to challenge West Virginia's mandatory flag salute in its public schools as a form of unconstitutional compelled student speech, they were able to seek redress through the federal courts.[17]

The Barnettes challenged the law on the basis of their faith as Jehovah's Witnesses and a very strict interpretation of the Second Commandment.[18] They were facing an uphill battle, as the Supreme Court had recently upheld as constitutional a Pennsylvania law requiring a daily flag salute in public schools in the face of a challenge from another family of Jehovah's Witnesses.[19] In *West Virginia v. Barnette*,[20] however, the Supreme Court made a very rare reversal, overruling its previous ruling and creating a new precedent regarding compelled speech. Recognizing that the flag salute is a form of symbolic speech,[21] the Court invoked the "clear and present danger" rule of *Schenck v. U.S.*,[22]

3. You Can't Say That in a Public School—or Can You?

requiring the state to show evidence of a threat that the government is empowered to prevent as rationale for the mandatory salute. Finding none, Justice Robert Jackson suggested that such mandatory affirmations of patriotism have the potential to do more harm than good,[23] and declared:

> If there is any fixed star in our constitutional constellation, it is that no official, high or petty, can prescribe what shall be orthodox in politics, nationalism, religion, or other matters of opinion or force citizens to confess by word or act their faith therein. If there are any circumstances which permit an exception, they do not now occur to us.[24]

Concurrences by Justices Hugo Black, William Douglas and Frank Murphy supported the idea that patriotism and love of country "must spring from willing hearts and free minds."[25] They also cited the turbulent history surrounding the creation of the First Amendment and its protections for speech as well as religious doctrine as proof that the State was never intended to centralize viewpoints or enforce public sentiment over private belief.

Student speech and expression in public schools continued to fly largely under the legal radar until an overall heightened interest in children's legal rights began to grow in the late 1950s and '60s. In 1959, the United Nations issued its Declaration of the Rights of the Child, which stated all children should be given full opportunity to develop "physically, mentally, morally, spiritually and socially" as well as receive education that enables them to "develop his abilities, his individual judgment, and his sense of moral and social responsibility."[26] Through the 1960s and '70s, court cases involving school discipline surged from an average of nine cases a year in the early 1960s to 76 cases a year between 1969 and 1975.[27] Many of these disciplinary cases were related to student speech or expression, as students began seeking a voice on social issues such as racial equality and the war in Vietnam.

Two particular Fifth Circuit cases set the tone for student expression rights within public schools. *Burnside v. Byars*[28] and *Blackwell v. Issaquena County Board of Education*[29] appeared before the Fifth Circuit at the same time to address "freedom buttons" in support of voter registration for African Americans. In *Burnside*, the school banned the buttons after a few students began wearing them, claiming the buttons were non-educational and would likely have a disruptive effect on the school day. Students wearing the buttons after the ban were told to remove them or go home. In all, about 30 students were suspended for one week as a result of the ban. The parents in *Burnside* sued, alleging the school's actions were an abridgement of the First and Fourteenth Amendments, given that the buttons resulted in no more than "a mild curiosity" on the part of the students.[30]

In *Blackwell*, a similar ban on freedom buttons was imposed. Again, some students wore the buttons anyway and were told to either remove the buttons or leave school premises. These students, however, chose to re-enter the school after being ordered home and, in some cases, forcefully pinned buttons to the clothing of fellow students.[31] Each day, greater numbers of students arrived wearing the buttons and a greater number of confrontations occurred between teachers and students as well as students and students in the hallways. By the time of the initial *Blackwell* court filings, the Issaquena County Board of Education had suspended 300 students, some for the rest of the school year.[32] The parents in *Blackwell* alleged violations of the First and Fourteenth Amendments in the creation of the ban and urged the court to overturn the suspensions.

The district courts in both cases found for the schools, and the Fifth Circuit chose to hear *Burnside* and *Blackwell* together due to their factual similarity. While the students argued for a "clear and present danger" approach to speech restriction in public schools, the court instead opted to focus on the legitimate interest of orderly conduct within the school. The Fifth Circuit suggested that free speech did exist within schools, but conclusively stated student speech could be regulated in the interest of discipline.

After establishing that speech regulation hinged on the school's interest in maintaining order, the Fifth Circuit split its decisions in *Burnside* and *Blackwell*. The buttons in *Burnside* had caused very little disturbance prior to the ban, and the Fifth Circuit determined there was little reason to forecast a threat to the orderly functioning of the school if the buttons continued. As such, there was no compelling interest to override the First Amendment right to wear the freedom buttons.[33]

In *Blackwell*, however, the Fifth Circuit saw a legitimate cause for concern. Not only were more students involved, there had been open defiance to school authority prior to the ban. Students were accosting other students; in one example, an older student forced a pin on a younger student and caused the child to cry.[34] While the court acknowledged that free speech was a valuable constitutional right, it found in *Blackwell* "an unusual degree of commotion, boisterous conduct, a collision with the rights of others, an undermining of authority, and a lack of order, discipline and decorum"[35] that was not present in *Burnside*. As such, the court found the button ban a legitimate use of the school's authority, but emphasized "the fundamental requirement that school officials should be careful in their monitoring of student expression in circumstances in which such expression does not substantially interfere with the operation of the school."[36]

Burnside and *Blackwell* were the foundation upon which the landmark *Tinker* decision was built, but these decisions also stood on their own as precedents applied by other courts to student expression issues. Twelve cases used the *Burnside/Blackwell* precedent prior to *Tinker*— five in high schools and seven in college or universities. Only two of those cases (both college/university) found for the students and overturned the school's disciplinary decision.[37]

The Four Supreme Court K–12 Student Speech Cases

From 1969 to 2007, the Supreme Court addressed student speech in K–12 public schools four times. Those decisions, plus lower court interpretations, form the legal guidance available to public schools as they work to balance First Amendment rights of students with disciplinary needs of school. Though the review of cases presented here is not intended to be exhaustive, it will show how the courts have interpreted the ability of the government-as-educator to regulate speech in a way that generally not applied to other government officials.[38]

John Tinker (age 15), Mary Beth Tinker (age 13) and Christopher Eckhardt (age 16), all students in the Des Moines Independent Community School District, decided to wear black armbands to school "to mourn the casualties in Vietnam, support the Christmas truce and oppose the Vietnam War."[39] A friend of Eckhardt's wrote a student newspaper article about the armband plans, which alerted administrators and led to an emergency school board meeting to pass a policy forbidding armbands[40] upon threat of suspension. All three students

Students' Right to Speak

wore their armbands and were told to leave school until they would agree to return without the bands. Instead, the teens remained out of school with their parents' blessing until January 1, the pre-determined end of the protest.[41] They then filed suit in federal court, claiming the suspension violated their First Amendment right to free expression.

The federal district court found for the school, determining the school's actions to be reasonable in an effort to prevent a disturbance of school order.[42] It's an understatement to say that the Vietnam War was a controversial topic by itself, and for those students with family or friends serving in the U.S. military, the subject was personal. The district argued it was concerned not only for the ability of students to learn in the presence of the armbands, but also for the Tinkers' and Eckhardt's safety. Incidents had already occurred: vandals threw red paint on the Tinkers' house, both families received death threats by mail and telephone, and a radio personality offered to lend a weapon to anyone willing to shoot the Tinkers' father.[43]

The Tinkers appealed to the Eighth Circuit, which eventually heard the case *en banc* and affirmed the lower court in a *per curiam* decision.[44] A year later, the Supreme Court agreed to hear the case. In oral arguments, the Court appeared to have *Burnside* and *Blackwell* in mind as Justice Thurgood Marshall asked school board attorney Allan Herrick to explain why "the school board was afraid that seven students wearing armbands would disrupt eighteen thousand."[45]

Ultimately, in a 7–2 decision, the Supreme Court overturned the Eighth Circuit.[46] Writing for the majority, Justice Abe Fortas made a simple declaration of a student's constitutional rights that has found its way into scores of subsequent decisions:

> First Amendment rights, applied in light of the special characteristics of the school environment, are available to teachers and students. It can hardly be argued that either students or teachers shed their constitutional rights to freedom of speech or expression at the schoolhouse gate.[47]

Justice Fortas took particular note of the passive, political nature of the armbands, akin to the "pure" speech at the heart of the First Amendment. The school district had admitted that the armbands were a form of symbolic expression, but had still been singled out from other forms of symbolic expression for restriction. Such an action, Fortas wrote, could not be justified by mere "undifferentiated fear or apprehension of disturbance."[48]

3. You Can't Say That in a Public School—or Can You?

Citing *Burnside,* the Court concluded that a school can't regulate student speech above and beyond the ability of government in general unless the school can show that the expression would materially and substantially interfere with the requirements of appropriate discipline in the operation of the school, or if the expression would collide with the rights of others.[49] This burden of proof on the schools created a presupposition of First Amendment protection for student speech unless the speech causes or credibly threatens such a disturbance.[50]

Justice Fortas also deviated slightly from the prior deference shown to educators and administrators. He wrote:

> In our system, state-operated schools may not be enclaves of totalitarianism. School officials do not possess absolute authority over their students. Students in school as well as out of school are "persons" under our Constitution. They are possessed of fundamental rights which the State must respect, just as they themselves must respect their obligations to the State. In our system, students may not be regarded as closed-circuit recipients of only that which the State chooses to communicate. They may not be confined to the expression of those sentiments that are officially approved. In the absence of a specific showing of constitutionally valid reasons to regulate their speech, students are entitled to freedom of expression of their views.[51]

The Court was by no means united in this decision. Justice Hugo Black's dissent argued strongly that schools, not courts, should be able to determine what is appropriate discipline for their students, and should be able to restrict students from turning classrooms into political platforms.[52] According to Justice Black, the Court's decision to find for the students was "surrender[ing] control of the American public school system to public school students."[53]

Despite Justice Black's concerns, *Tinker* made a bold statement on behalf of student speech rights. Students no longer had to prove their speech deserved protection; schools now had to justify regulation. But *Tinker* also created a new standard—material or substantial disruption—that lacked definition. The passive wearing of armbands was not disruptive, but this yardstick was missing too many inches to be truly effective. Could the disruption of one student's educational experience qualify, or would that be a collision with the rights of another? If a school wished to prevent harm before it occurs, how far would it have to go to prove its expectation of a disruption was reasonable?

Further, *Tinker* mentioned *Terminiello v. Chicago,*[54] suggesting

Students' Right to Speak

when speech provokes a listener to respond with bad behavior, it's the response that should be regulated instead the speech—in essence, avoiding the heckler's veto.[55] Yet, the substantial disruption standard is based on an audience response. Is it right to punish a speaker for the reaction his or her speech creates? Or should the people responsible for the reaction bear the blame for their own behaviors?

A variety of lower court cases illustrated some of these uncertainties during the 1970s and '80s as students came forward with a variety of free speech challenges to school actions. Most of the challenges during the post–*Tinker* time period fell within one of three categories: student publications, racial speech and personal student expression.

Hot on the heels of *Tinker* came *Zucker v. Panitz*[56] and *Baker v. Downey City Board of Education*,[57] both federal district court cases dealing with issues in student newspapers. In *Zucker*, students sued their school when the principal refused to allow them to run an advertisement placed and paid for by a group of students opposed to the Vietnam War. In *Baker*, students protested their suspension for distributing an underground newspaper containing vulgarities and a retouched unflattering photo of President Nixon.

The court in *Zucker* compared the anti–Vietnam ad to the *Tinker* armbands, noting both were passive forms of communication (a student could choose not to read the student paper) that espoused a political viewpoint. The district court also pointed out the student newspaper had traditionally been open for the dissemination of student ideas, so arbitrarily banning some content contradicted its purpose in the first place. Further:

> This lawsuit arises at a time when many in the educational community oppose the tactics of the young in securing a political voice. It would be both incongruous and dangerous for this court to hold that students who wish to express their views on matters intimately related to them, through traditionally accepted nondisruptive modes of communication, may be precluded from doing so by that same adult community.[58]

Baker, on the hand, was distinguished from *Tinker* because the California federal district court in that case found the suspensions were not in response to the students' desire to express an opinion, but rather the method they used to engage in that expression: "profane and vulgar in context as well as out."[59] The court stated the discipline was related to the manner of speaking, and that "First Amendment rights to free

3. You Can't Say That in a Public School—or Can You?

speech do not require the suspension of decency in the expression of their views and ideas."[60]

The Second Circuit handled two cases involving underground student newspapers following *Baker*: *Eisner v. Stamford Board of Education*[61] and *Thomas v. Board of Education, Granville Central School District*.[62] In *Eisner*, students argued against a school policy requiring they get their newspaper pre-approved before distributing on school grounds, calling the policy a prior restraint. The Second Circuit disagreed, finding the policy a reasonable protection against the distribution of material designed to disrupt the school day, though the court cautioned the school district that the policy was impermissibly vague regarding review criteria, time guarantees on review and an appeal process for students who disagree with the result.[63] While the court recognized public schools as "marketplaces of ideas," it gave equal weight to a school's ability to make decisions relevant to the orderly functioning of the school day.[64]

The situation and result were different in *Thomas*, where the student-created, though underground, newspaper was distributed off campus. The newspaper had been patterned after Harvard's "National Lampoon," and was intended to be a satirical look at the school community. A member of the school board saw the newspaper, was offended, and demanded that the students be punished.[65]

The Second Circuit declined to push the boundaries of the district's authority off school grounds. It distinguished the case from *Tinker* because of the off-campus nature of the speech, noting, "We may not permit school administrators to seek approval of the community-at-large by punishing students for expression that took place off school property.... The First Amendment will not abide the additional chill on protected expression that would inevitably emanate from such a practice."[66] The court likened such discipline to punishing a student for "watching an X-rated film on his living room cable television."[67] Further, the court refused to remove the voice of a minor from the community, recognizing that youth must have some opportunity to express views free of school oversight.

The Vietnam War was not the only social issue causing conflict in the 1970s. Passage of the Civil Rights Act and the continued slow desegregation of schools also caused a significant amount of tension in public education, as well as challenges to personal expression.

Students' Right to Speak

Symbols of the South became a common source of contention. For example, a Chattanooga high school student wore a jacket with the Confederate flag on it in defiance of a school rule prohibiting the symbol, and sued in federal court when he was told he could not return to school until he agreed to leave the jacket at home.[68] The Sixth Circuit declared that arbitrary restrictions on student speech would not survive constitutional review, but the increase in racially motivated violence at this school was enough to reasonably fulfill the disruption standard.[69] The Fifth Circuit came to a similar conclusion when African American students at a newly integrated school protested the use of "Rebels" and the Confederate flag for the athletic teams.[70] In upholding the district court's decision to prohibit both the name and the symbol, the circuit court noted that such regulation would not solve racial problems, but was a necessary step toward that goal.[71]

The third category of post–*Tinker* cases involved personal expression by students within the school environment. In *Karp v. Becken*,[72] a group of students planned a walkout to protest the firing of a popular English teacher. The students notified the media about the plan and came prepared with signs, which the vice-principal attempted to confiscate. The leader of the walkout refused to give up his signs and was suspended for five days. He sued in federal court, and the district court found for the school.

In assessing this case, the Ninth Circuit echoed the dissent of Justice Black in *Tinker*, claiming "the reason for his [Black's] concern is amply demonstrated in this case, which presents a conflict between asserted Constitutional rights and good-faith actions by school officials."[73] The court clarified its interpretation of the *Tinker* precedent, that schools not only did not have to wait for a substantial disruption to occur, but could (and should) act to avoid disruption from happening in the first place; and because of the state's interest in orderly education, the standard required to justify intervention is lower than it would be on a street corner.[74] Applying its vision of *Tinker*, the court found ample reason for the school to forecast a disruption due to media interest, dissent among students regarding the walkout's effect on an upcoming athletic award ceremony and the gawker effect of students distracted from their studies to watch. The court also cautioned other courts to be wary of second-guessing the reasonable decisions of school administrators using the benefit of hindsight.[75]

3. You Can't Say That in a Public School—or Can You?

The 15 years following *Tinker* saw multiple cases struggle with figuring out where the precedent applied (on campus versus off) as well as the extent to which speech must be disruptive or reasonably forecast to be disruptive to be restricted or punished. One student speech case in the post–*Tinker* years, however, declined to apply the precedent at all, paving the way for the Supreme Court's next student speech case.

In *Stanton v. Brunswick School Department*,[76] a high school senior alleged a violation of her First Amendment rights when the yearbook committee refused to print her chosen quotation: "The executioner will pull this lever four times. Each time 2000 volts will course through your body, making your eyeballs first bulge, then burst, and then broiling your brains."[77] The student stated she had chosen the quote to highlight her opposition to the death penalty and because she wished to use something meaningful (albeit graphic) rather than sentimental.

Stanton did not cite *Tinker* at all—the court framed the question as "whether or not school authorities could be required to provide a vehicle for the expression and transmission of personally held views on matters of importance to senior students."[78] The court acknowledged that the yearbook was traditionally an open opportunity for students to share their views, and subject only to the clear regulation against speech involving alcohol, sex or drugs.[79] Testimony revealed a secondary regulation against speech in "poor taste," but the court found this to lack the clear definition required to be constitutional. Further:

> The vagueness and uncertainty of the standard is geometrically increased when it is prospectively applied, as was done here, through a period of future years. If the intellectual and ideological ferment of the last four decades of the American social experience teaches anything, it teaches us that whatever may be the accepted meaning of "good taste" on any given day, the content of that meaning does not rigidly abide through time.[80]

While schools may be an ideal place to instill the values of good taste and respectful speech, they could not do so at the expense of an idea's attempt to succeed within the marketplace of ideas, even if that marketplace only encompasses the student body of a single high school. "Taste," the court implied, could not be arbitrarily used to restrict speech.

The question of speech in "good taste" did not end in *Stanton*. It was the basis of the second Supreme Court case involving student speech: *Bethel School District v. Fraser*.[81] In this case, Washington high school student Matthew Fraser delivered a speech at a school assembly nominating a friend for student government:

> I know a man who is firm—he's firm in his pants, he's firm in his shirt, his character is firm—but most ... of all, his belief in you, the students of Bethel, is firm. Jeff Kuhlman is a man who takes his point and pounds it in. If necessary, he'll take an issue and nail it to the wall. He doesn't attack things in spurts—he drives hard, pushing and pushing until finally—he succeeds. Jeff is a man who will go to the very end—even the climax, for each and every one of you. So vote for Jeff for A. S. B. vice-president—he'll never come between you and the best our high school can be.[82]

Fraser had discussed the content of his speech with two teachers prior to the assembly, both of whom warned him he could face negative consequences if he delivered it. After his speech, an administrator informed Fraser that his comments violated the school's student code prohibiting the use of obscene language in school. Fraser was suspended for three days and removed from the list of eligible graduation speakers. He sued in federal district court, claiming a First Amendment violation of free speech by virtue of a vague student policy.

The Washington federal district court and the Ninth Circuit both ruled in favor of Fraser,[83] applying the *Tinker* standard and finding that despite testimony from teachers that younger students appeared confused and bewildered by the speech and one teacher had to deviate from his lesson plan to discuss the speech with his class, there was no material disruption of the academic day. The Ninth Circuit warned allowing the school unbridled discretion over the definition of "decent" speech would "increase the risk of cementing white, middle-class standards for determining what is acceptable and proper speech and behavior in our public schools."[84]

The Supreme Court, however, reversed both lower courts, distinguishing the case from *Tinker* on several counts: the speech was not political, it was not clearly attributable only to the student and it was not passive. By giving his speech at a school assembly, Fraser had a captive audience who could reasonably believe the program had the tacit approval of the school. Though it was a speech for student government office, the opportunity of student government was educational in nature, shifting the core purpose of the speech from political to curricular.[85]

Instead of focusing on the speech and its potential disruptive effect, the Supreme Court examined the role of speech within the

3. You Can't Say That in a Public School—or Can You?

purpose of public schools. The Court cited its own commentary in *Ambach v. Norwick*,[86] that the objective of public education was the inculcation of values necessary to a democratic society.[87] Among these values were the "habits and manners of civility," which not only included a tolerance of a diverse range of viewpoints but also a respect for the sensibilities of one's fellow citizens.[88]

As with *Baker* and *Stanton*, the Court was concerned less with the message than with the way it was presented—the method of discourse was equally as important as the discourse itself. The Court saw no reason why a school couldn't set guidelines to encourage the development of socially acceptable skills in civil discourse, which would omit the use of vulgar or offensive terms. Chief Justice Warren Burger wrote that Congress had rules regarding appropriate speech for members while in session, so it was reasonable to allow schools to do the same.[89]

Fraser established that "the First Amendment does not prevent the school officials from determining that to permit a vulgar and lewd speech such as respondent's would undermine the school's basic educational mission."[90] Unlike *Tinker*, which presupposed speech to be protected unless the school could prove its real or reasonably forecast disruptive effects, *Fraser* allowed for a school-specific categorization of speech that lay outside First Amendment protection: that which was "lewd" or "vulgar."

Justice John Paul Stevens's dissent in *Fraser* offered an interesting deference to student sensibilities on the appropriateness of speech:

> This respondent was an outstanding young man with a fine academic record. The fact that he was chosen by the student body to speak at the school's commencement exercises demonstrates that he was respected by his peers. This fact is relevant for two reasons. It confirms the conclusion that the discipline imposed on him—a 3-day suspension and ineligibility to speak at the school's graduation exercises—was sufficiently serious to justify invocation of the School District's grievance procedures. More importantly, it indicates that he was probably in a better position to determine whether an audience composed of 600 of his contemporaries would be offended by the use of a four-letter word—or a sexual metaphor—than is a group of judges who are at least two generations and 3,000 miles away from the scene of the crime.[91]

There were few cases between *Fraser* and the Supreme Court's next examination of student speech rights, but those few did show that *Fraser's* emphasis on the inculcation of appropriate values found traction in lower courts. For example, a district court in Ohio decided against a brother and sister who wished to attend their high school prom in opposite-gender clothing in violation of the school's dress regulations.[92] The court determined the regulations to be "reasonably related to the valid educational purposes of teaching community values and maintaining school discipline"[93] and deemed the responsibility for "maintaining proper standards of decorum and discipline and a wholesome academic environment is not vested in the federal courts, but in the principal and faculty of the school."[94]

Two years after *Fraser*, the Supreme Court heard *Hazelwood School District v. Kuhlmeier*,[95] creating a third precedent related to student speech. This case began when the editors of the Hazelwood East High School student newspaper *Spectrum* sued their school over the censorship of two articles from their May 13, 1983, issue. The school had a policy of administrator review of the newspaper prior to printing, and during that regular review, Hazelwood East Principal Robert Reynolds felt articles on divorce and teen pregnancy posed problems. Reynolds believed the divorce article included comments made by a student about her father that could be considered libelous, and the teen pregnancy article did not do enough to prevent readers from figuring out the identities of the young women profiled.

Because the issue was due to print in May, with less than a month left in the school year, Reynolds did not feel there was enough time to correct the articles, so he directed the faculty adviser to omit the pages on which the articles appeared. The affected pages included four other articles that weren't problematic. The student newspaper staff claimed a violation of its right to free press, but a federal district court found for the school, determining that regulating a school-sponsored activity merely needed a reasonable justification to withstand constitutional scrutiny.[96] The Eighth Circuit reversed, noting the traditional role the student newspaper had played as an outlet for student expression and student viewpoint.[97]

The Supreme Court decision, penned by Justice Byron White, tossed several new concepts into the issue of student speech rights by offering a precedent with three working parts. In finding for the school, the Court declared student speech regulations need only be reasonable due to the school's educational mission, the newspaper's forum status and the school's "imprimatur," or perception of endorsement.

3. You Can't Say That in a Public School—or Can You?

With a nod to *Tinker*, Justice White affirmed that students do have some First Amendment rights in public schools, but that those rights are not coextensive with adults in other settings.[98] More importantly, "A school need not tolerate student speech that is inconsistent with its basic educational mission,"[99] and the determination of that inconsistency properly lay with schools, not the courts.

The decision then moved out of the realm of school speech and applied a general forum analysis to the *Spectrum* to determine if it was a vehicle created by a government entity (in this case, a public school) for public expression. Government property such as a sidewalk or park is generally characterized as a traditional public forum, where speech regulations must survive a high degree of scrutiny to survive constitutional challenge.[100] When the government property or platform is created for a specific communicative purpose, however, speech can be confined to that purpose. For example, if a public school provides mailboxes for teachers to better facilitate work-related communication, it is allowed to restrict access to those mailboxes from people who wish to use them for communication unrelated to work.[101] Government property that is not inherently open to all or was not created for a broad communicative use is considered a nonpublic forum, and expression in such a forum can be regulated so long as the regulation is reasonable and has a legitimate purpose.[102]

In applying forum analysis to *Hazelwood*, the Supreme Court suggested a range of factors that lower courts could examine to determine the type of forum a specific student media outlet might be. In the case of the *Spectrum*, the newspaper was created in a classroom and overseen by a teacher, suggesting an educational purpose over a communicative one. Further, students creating the newspaper received grades and course credit, and restricted themselves to news of the school and student body.[103] The students' contention that they could "publish practically anything"[104] was not supported by the facts, as the adviser oversaw content and the principal was allowed prior review. As such, the Court found the *Spectrum* to be a nonpublic forum, created specifically to offer an educational opportunity to students that also shared information specific to the student community at Hazelwood East. The newspaper could be regulated as any expression in a nonpublic forum—in a manner that is reasonable and is related to a legitimate—in this case, pedagogical—concern.[105]

Students' Right to Speak

The third element the Court brought into its analysis was the concept of "imprimatur," the school's perceived ownership or endorsement of the speech. By virtue of its financial support of the newspaper, its curricular support of the class and the use of the school's name and logo on the publication, the Court agreed that the average reader could reasonably believe the newspaper represented the school's voice. Justice White clarified:

> The question whether the First Amendment requires a school to tolerate particular student speech—the question that we addressed in *Tinker*—is different from the question whether the First Amendment requires a school affirmatively to promote particular student speech. The former question addresses educators' ability to silence a student's personal expression that happens to occur on the school premises. The latter question concerns educators' authority over school-sponsored publications, theatrical productions, and other expressive activities that students, parents, and members of the public might reasonably perceive to bear the imprimatur of the school. These activities may fairly be characterized as part of the school curriculum, whether or not they occur in a traditional classroom setting, so long as they are supervised by faculty members and designed to impart particular knowledge or skills to student participants and audiences.[106]

Because of these three items—educational mission, forum status and imprimatur—the Court determined the principal did not offend the First Amendment "by exercising editorial control over the style and content of student speech in school-sponsored expressive activities."[107]

Hazelwood's dissent, written by Justice William Brennan and supported by Justices Thurgood Marshall and Harry Blackmun, pointed out what they saw as troubling in the majority's decision: a desire to control curriculum (which he wrote was an unnecessary concern, as *Tinker* would consider student speech interfering with curriculum as a material disruption), an attempt to shield students from objectionable viewpoints (generally considered illegitimate regardless of circumstances) and the school's wish to disassociate itself from student expression (easily handled through disclaimers).[108] Justice Brennan wrote that he was far more concerned about the opportunity presented by student press for young people to exercise the constitutional rights and responsibilities, and felt censorship should only be allowed in the most crucial circumstances. He wrote, "The young men and women of Hazelwood East expected a civics lesson, but not the one the Court teaches them today."[109]

Hazelwood gave schools a third approach to student speech—as

3. You Can't Say That in a Public School—or Can You?

the Ninth Circuit wrote four years after the *Hazelwood* ruling, "[T]he standard for reviewing the suppression of vulgar, lewd, obscene, and plainly offensive speech is governed by *Fraser*, school-sponsored speech by [*Kuhlmeier*], and all other speech by *Tinker*."[110] Post-*Hazelwood* cases used this trio of cases broadly to address issues of student expression.

Hazelwood's "educational mission," for example, provided the basis for upholding the suspension of a high school student punished for wearing a Marilyn Manson t-shirt to school that depicted a three-headed Jesus and the word "Believe" with "LIE" highlighted in the middle of the word.[111] The Sixth Circuit found the principal's assertion that the t-shirt was offensive and contrary to the school's values persuasive, stating, "[W]here [the student's] t-shirts contain symbols and words that promote values that are so patently contrary to the school's education, the school has the authority, under the circumstances of this case, to prohibit those t-shirts."[112]

Hazelwood's use of forum analysis guided a district court in Michigan in the case of a student editor claiming censorship when her school refused to publish an issue of the student newspaper that included an article on a pending lawsuit against the district.[113] Experts deemed student Katy Dean's article journalistically sound, and the *Arrow*, her high school newspaper, was sufficiently independent from the school to distinguish it from the private forum and school imprimatur that marked Hazelwood East's *Spectrum*. As a result, the *Arrow* was treated as a limited public forum, and the government could only impose "reasonable time, place, and manner regulations, and content-based regulations that are narrowly drawn to effectuate a compelling state interest."[114] The district court found the school's refusal to print the article unconstitutional, stating that "if the role of the press in a democratic society is to have any value, all journalists—including student journalists—must be allowed to publish viewpoints contrary to those of state authorities without intervention or censorship by the authorities themselves."[115]

Forum analysis has been applied beyond student publications—*Hazelwood's* introduction of forum into the public educational environment has also been used to assess the constitutionality of restricting the distribution of religious materials in the hallways of a high school[116] or an elementary school[117] as well as a pacifist organization's access to

Students' Right to Speak

students during an annual Career and Youth Motivation Day.[118] In these cases and others, the courts have offered an oddly mixed message of claiming to assess the situation under the special characteristics of the school environment, per *Tinker*, and then applying forum analysis, which is not specific to schools.

In the post–*Hazelwood* era, if *Hazelwood* didn't apply, courts turned to check the applicability of *Fraser*. *Fraser's* restriction on vulgar or inappropriate behavior that is not part of a school-sponsored activity was used to uphold the punishment of a kindergarten student for mimicking the use of a gun during a recess game of "cops and robbers," contrary to recent school policy forbidding speech related to violence or weapons.[119] The student had been ill the day the principal discussed the new policy with his class, but the punishment was still upheld due to *Fraser's* deference toward school officials for determining what is "socially appropriate behavior."[120]

Tinker remained the fallback for whatever did not fit the more specific criteria of *Hazelwood* or *Fraser*. In cases involving personal expression through clothing, as was the situation in *Chalifoux v. New Caney Independent School District*,[121] the court determined a student's request to wear a rosary despite its adoption by a local gang as a symbol of membership was "pure speech" analogous to the passive wearing of armbands, and equally nondisruptive. On the other hand, an elementary student's choice to wear t-shirts bearing slogans criticizing her teacher, the principal and the school after she received a series of poor grades was determined to be disruptive, and her punishment for refusing to stop wearing them was upheld.[122]

Not all disagreement with school policy was punishable. In *Holloman v. Harland*,[123] a student contested his punishment for refusing to recite the Pledge of Allegiance and criticizing a teacher's daily habit of beginning class with a Bible reading. Though Holloman's actions were deemed to be a distraction, the court would not uphold the punishment, stating, "[G]iven the fact that young people are required by law to spend a substantial portion of their lives in classrooms, student expression may not be suppressed simply because it gives rise to some slight, easily overlooked disruption."[124]

Tinker's second prong—intrusion on the rights of others—began to surface after the turn of the century as schools struggled with balancing student expression against the right to an educational environment

3. You Can't Say That in a Public School—or Can You?

free of harassment. This is best exemplified by *Harper v. Poway*,[125] in which a student was disciplined for refusing to remove a t-shirt with the slogan "I will not accept what God has condemned" on a school-approved "Day of Silence" to support GLBT students. Rather than look at the potential for a broad disruptive effect, the Ninth Circuit instead looked at how the message of the t-shirt might affect individual students around Harper. The court noted, "[F]rom first grade through twelfth, students are discovering what and who they are. Often they are insecure. Generally, they are vulnerable to cruel, inhuman and prejudiced treatment by others."[126]

The court determined the school had a right to regulate speech in an effort to protect students from verbal assaults based on such characteristics as race, gender or sexual orientation, but was careful to note that it was not attempting to silence a viewpoint, but rather the method of expressing it. That method of expression tied back into *Fraser's* inculcation of values linked to civil discourse—there was no place in public schools for speech "espousing intolerance, bigotry and hatred."[127]

Another variation of student speech that triggered the *Tinker* precedent was violent speech, especially after the shooting at Columbine High School. In 2001, an emotionally troubled student wrote a poem titled "Last Words," depicting the final thoughts of a fictional student prior to committing a school shooting and suicide.[128] He showed it to an English teacher for feedback, who turned it over to a principal. The student was immediately expelled, Child Protective Services was called and the student was not allowed to return to school without clearance from a psychiatrist. Upon receiving the psychiatrist's positive recommendation, the student returned to school, but the incident remained part of his academic record. His parents sued to have it removed.

The Ninth Circuit supported the school's actions, expressing regret for a new age of school violence but affirming that the risk the poem posed if it wasn't just a piece of creative writing was significant enough to overcome any First Amendment concerns.[129] However, the court didn't support the school's decision to keep a full record of the incident in the student's academic file, which could hurt his chances to join the military after graduation, and granted the parents' request to have that information removed.

Students' Right to Speak

The LaVines' appeal to have the case re-heard *en banc* by the Ninth Circuit on the First Amendment challenge was denied, but with strong dissent by Judge Kleinfeld, who noted:

> The panel decision creates a new First Amendment rule: where school officials perceive a major concern about school safety, they may punish school children whose speech gives rise to a concern that they may be dangerous to themselves or others, even though the speech is not a threat, disruptive, defamatory, sexual, or otherwise within any previously recognized category of constitutionally unprotected speech.[130]

Judge Kleinfeld's words seem slightly prophetic, as two years later, a student was expelled and arrested for "terrorizing the school"[131] when some two-year-old drawings he had made depicting the school under siege were accidentally brought to campus. The student's younger brother had grabbed a sketchpad to use at school that included the drawings, unaware that some pages weren't blank. Despite the age of the sketches and the fact that the student did not himself bring them to school, administrators acted swiftly to remove a perceived threat.[132]

The Fifth Circuit overturned the school's disciplinary actions for several reasons. It first took issue with the drawings being classified as student speech in the first place, as his artwork "was completed in his home, stored for two years, and never intended by him to be brought to campus."[133] Because the court couldn't officially claim the drawing to be student speech, it had difficulty in applying *Tinker*, but determined that even if the disruption standard was applied, the fact that the student never intended to bring the drawings to school outweighed an argument about a potential disruptive effect.[134]

In addition to cases involving violent speech, online speech cases began to appear with some regularity with the turn of the century, and courts struggled with finding the appropriate way to apply *Tinker/Fraser/Hazelwood* to email, social media and blogs. Discussed in greater detail in Chapter 7, courts have taken a variety of approaches to adjusting *Tinker* to fit cyberspeech issues, including examining the "nexus" between the student's speech and the school[135] or the intent of the speaker for the speech to make its way to campus[136] in addition to the actual disruptive effect the speech may have had on the academic environment.[137]

The fourth case heard by the Supreme Court regarding student speech was *Morse v. Frederick*,[138] better known as the "Bong Hits 4

3. You Can't Say That in a Public School—or Can You?

Jesus" case. Frederick, a student at Juneau-Douglas High School, skipped school the day of an all-school field trip to watch the Olympic torch pass through the city. He chose to join up with his classmates, however, and as the torchbearer passed in front of him (along with the cameras of many area media), he and his friends unfurled a 14-foot banner reading "Bong Hits 4 Jesus." Principal Deborah Morse immediately ordered the students to drop the banner, and all students but Frederick complied. Morse confiscated the banner and suspended Frederick for violating a school policy prohibiting advocacy of the use of illegal drugs. The school district, as well as a federal district court, upheld the suspension as part of the principal's right to ban speech contrary to the school's mission to combat drug use.[139]

The Ninth Circuit reversed, deeming *Fraser* and *Hazelwood* inapplicable and finding no evidence of *Tinker's* substantial disruption.[140] The Ninth Circuit determined that Frederick's right to free speech in this situation had been so clear, it also rejected Morse's bid for qualified immunity, a legal protection for government employees from being personally liable when they are acting in their official capacity and when their actions are a reasonable interpretation of the law. Morse appealed to the Supreme Court on both the question of the speech right and qualified immunity, and the Court overturned the Ninth Circuit on both counts.

The Supreme Court declined to address the fact that Frederick had not attended school that day and was technically "off campus," dismissing the argument that Frederick was not engaging in student speech. Instead, the Court focused on the fact that he was in the middle of a school-sanctioned event at the time of the banner, which allowed the principal to act.[141]

Chief Justice John Roberts wrote the majority decision, and centered on the drug issue. Citing several statistics about the rising level of drug use in public schools and the drastic effects such use can have on the physical and mental health of students, he framed the issue as: "whether a principal may, consistent with the First Amendment, restrict student speech at a school event, when that speech is reasonably viewed as promoting illegal drug use. We hold that she may."[142]

The Court relied more on *Fraser* than *Tinker* in this case, arguing that speech promoting illegal drug use contradicts the school's educational mission of inculcating positive values, and while it didn't accept

Students' Right to Speak

the school's argument that *Fraser* stretched to cover all speech deemed "offensive,"[143] it did agree that promoting illegal activity is speech subject to restriction. Chief Justice Roberts found it reasonable to interpret the banner as advocacy of drug use, as Morse did.[144]

Two concurrences in *Morse* are worth a mention. Justice Thomas argued the Court should have gone further and overturned *Tinker*, citing the history of American education and his belief that Founders never intended free speech rights for students in public schools. He also criticized the growing patchwork of student speech law:

> Today, the Court creates another exception. In doing so, we continue to distance ourselves from *Tinker*, but we neither overrule it nor offer an explanation of when it operates and when it does not. I am afraid that our jurisprudence now says that students have a right to speak in schools except when they don't.[145]

On the other hand, Justices Alito and Kennedy wrote a short concurrence stating their expectation that the *Morse* precedent would only be used in incidents of speech related to illegal drug use, and no further.[146] Lower courts, however, have used *Morse* to justify the suspension of student for writing a fictional journal detailing a Columbine-like attack, claiming that the special danger posed by gun violence is similar to, if not greater than, that of illegal drugs in schools.[147]

The four-person *Morse* dissent focused on the message's lack of value, and perhaps more significantly, the ability of students to recognize nonsense when they see it:

> Admittedly some high school students (including those who use drugs) are dumb. Most students, however, do not shed their brains at the schoolhouse gate, and most students know dumb advocacy when they see it. The notion that the message on this banner would actually persuade either the average students or even the dumbest one to change his or her behavior is most implausible.[148]

Morse's emphasis on advocacy of illegal action is reminiscent of *Brandenburg v. Ohio*[149] and the legal definition that case created for incitement. Yet the strict standard of *Brandenburg*, which requires advocacy of a law violation that is directed to "producing imminent lawless action and is likely to incite or produce such action"[150] gives a sense of the careful line the Court in the 1960s felt it had to draw between harmless and harmful speech. The much more lax *Morse* decision creates a *Brandenburg*-lite for schools that is missing the sense of imminent harm that speech regulation outside schools requires in order to act.

3. You Can't Say That in a Public School—or Can You?

Post-*Morse*, student speech cases have continued to struggle with issues with cyberspeech (discussed in Chapter 7), student publications (Chapter 6) and a range of personal student expression. One challenge has been the application of the *Morse* standard, as exemplified by three cases dealing with a bracelet and "boobies."

The Keep a Breast Foundation created the "I [heart] Boobies" campaign to connect with young women and men about breast cancer awareness.[151] The campaign created inexpensive, brightly colored rubber bracelets emblazoned with "I [heart] boobies!" on one side and "Prevention is the Cure. Keep-a-breast.org" on the other. The language of the campaign was specifically chosen "to remove the shame associated with breasts and breast health" and to take a "positive approach to breast cancer dialogue."[152]

The word "boobies," however, caused several schools to ban the bracelets under the *Fraser* "lewd and vulgar" standard. Students in Wisconsin, Pennsylvania and Indiana pushed back against their schools' bans, calling them unconstitutional prohibitions of passive, symbolic speech. In Wisconsin, the school's ban was upheld, as the federal district court in *K.J. v. Sauk Prairie School District*[153] determined that it was reasonable for administrators to decide the word "boobies" was "vulgar and inconsistent with their goal of fostering respectful discourse by encouraging students to use 'correct anatomical terminology' for human body parts."[154]

In the Pennsylvania case, however, the Third Circuit introduced a unique interpretation of *Morse* that led to a different decision on the bracelets. The circuit court in *B.H. v. Easton Area School District*[155] focused on the Alito and Kennedy concurrence in *Morse*, specifically:

> I join the opinion of the Court on the understanding that (a) it goes no further than to hold that a public school may restrict speech that a reasonable observer would interpret as advocating illegal drug use and (b) it provides no support for any restriction of speech that can plausibly be interpreted as commenting on any political or social issue, including speech on issues such as "the wisdom of the war on drugs or of legalizing marijuana for medicinal use."[156]

Because the vote in *Morse* was 5–4, the Third Circuit noted that Alito and Kennedy's support had been crucial to the precedent. As such, the limitations suggested in their concurrence had to be considered in the overall application of *Morse*—an approach sometimes called the "narrowest grounds."[157] Subsequently, the circuit court wrote that

Students' Right to Speak

the *Fraser* approach was modified by *Morse* to only allow the regulation of student speech that was *plainly* lewd (no other possible interpretation) or that was reasonably interpreted as lewd *and* was not plausibly commenting on political or social issues.[158] While "boobies" could be reasonably interpreted as lewd, it was not plainly so. In addition, the bracelets were plausibly commenting on the significant social issue of cancer awareness and support. Subsequently, the Third Circuit found in favor of the students because the school could not satisfy the *Morse-Fraser* combination.[159]

However, later that same year, a federal district court in Indiana dealing with a third "boobies" case noted that courts outside the Third Circuit had not applied the "narrowest grounds" application of *Morse*:

> However, the Seventh Circuit has already expressly rejected the argument that Alito's opinion controls *Morse*. The court found that by "join[ing] the majority opinion [in *Morse*], not just the decision," "Justices Alito and Kennedy made it a majority opinion and not merely ... a plurality opinion." Therefore Justice Alito's concurrence was merely his own "view of the permissible scope of [school] regulation [of student speech]." ... The Seventh Circuit is in good company, as eight other appellate courts have adopted the rule articulated by the majority opinion in *Morse* instead of Alito's concurrence.[160]

The federal court in this Indiana case mirrored the approach taken in Wisconsin, examining if the phrase was reasonably interpreted as lewd or vulgar, though the court did take its analysis one step further and explored the vulgar question in the context of the environment of the school. Noting a record of immature responses to the bracelets, the court upheld the ban based on the school's "reasonable belief that it was lewd, vulgar, obscene or plainly offensive."[161]

The post–*Morse* era continues to see application of *Tinker* to clothing. The Seventh Circuit took up the case of an anti-gay shirt in *Nuxoll v. Indian Prairie*,[162] when a student was disciplined for refusing to cover the second half of the phrase "Be Happy, Not Gay" on a t-shirt worn the day after a "Day of Silence" in support of gay and lesbian students. The court determined the school failed to justify the regulation, claiming the t-shirt's wording was too mild to create an educational disruption.[163]

The Ninth Circuit, on the other hand, upheld a school's demand that students wearing American flag t-shirts on Cinco de Mayo turn the shirts inside out after such shirts the previous year had led to a violent confrontation.[164] Similarly, the Fourth Circuit upheld a blanket

3. You Can't Say That in a Public School—or Can You?

ban on clothing with the Confederate flag on it in a school district that had experienced significant racial tensions.[165] In both situations, the circuit courts accepted a past history of conflict as sufficient toward forecasting disruption that merited speech regulation.

A continued deference has been shown in the lower courts to schools and administrators when speech is regulated under the *Tinker* "material and substantial disruption" standard. For example, a fifth-grade student with a history of behavioral issues was suspended when he turned in a drawing of an astronaut that included a wish to "blow up the school with the teachers in it."[166] While the child's parents established in court that the majority of the class responded to the picture as if it was a joke, the court reflected that "Courts have allowed wide leeway to school administrators disciplining students for writings or other conduct threatening violence,"[167] and that that school reasonably forecasted potential disruptions through a failure to act such as student fear, student copycatting or parental concern.

Applying the Supreme Court Precedents

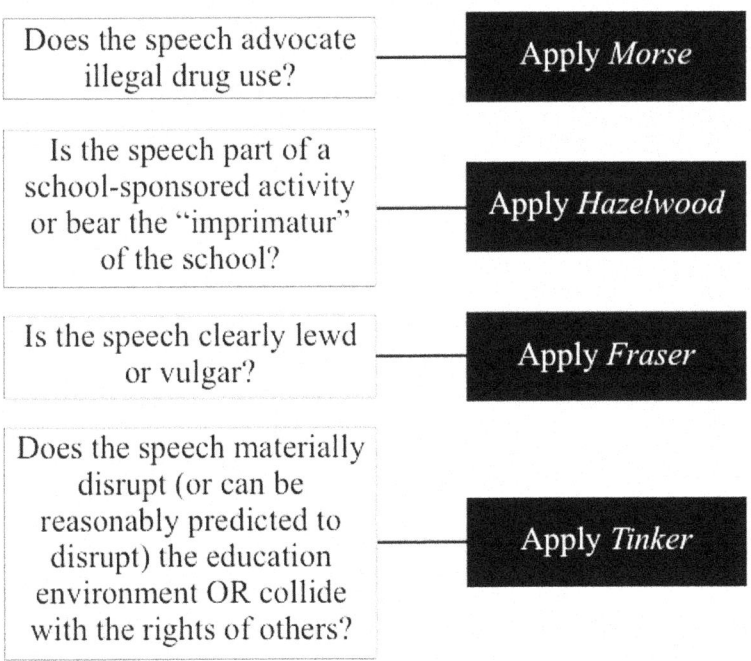

Students' Right to Speak

Overall, the K–12 cases that made their way to the Supreme Court began with a powerful statement that established free speech belonged in public schools unless the schools could find a compelling enough reason to restrict it. This represented a tremendous shift in thinking as the burden of proof moved from student to school. Subsequent cases have narrowed student speech freedoms by creating broad precedents out of very specific circumstances, leading to a somewhat unpredictable approach to student speech in the courts that has not improved as the body of student speech case law has grown. As Circuit Judge Joseph Greenaway, Jr., noted in his dissent in *Easton:*

> [O]ne thing is not open to debate: a school district faced with the same dilemma in the coming weeks, months, or years is given no greater guidance regarding its ability to determine whether a particular message may be proscribed than before the Majority opinion issued.[168]

College/University Student Speech Cases

It's instructive to take a short detour into the realm of student speech cases in public colleges and universities, where most of the students are above the age of majority and enjoy a greater presumption of full constitutional rights. In the words of the Third Circuit:

> Unlike the strictly controlled, smaller environments of public elementary and high schools, where a student's course schedule, class times, lunch time, and curriculum are determined by school administrators, public universities operate in a manner that gives students great latitude: for example, university students routinely (and unwisely) skip class; they are often entrusted to responsibly use laptops in the classroom; they bring snacks and drinks into class; and they choose their own classes. In short, public university students are given opportunities to acquit themselves as adults. Those same opportunities are not afforded to public elementary and high school students.[169]

One body of college/university student speech cases deals with the ability of students to engage in demonstrations or protests on campus. *Hammond v. South Carolina State College*[170] examined the decision of a college to charge more than 300 students with violating the student conduct code by participating in an unapproved demonstration. The federal district court had a problem with the rule requiring public demonstrations to be pre-approved for purposes of protecting "public safety, peace or order," calling it an unreasonable form of prior restraint, and overturned the suspensions.[171]

3. You Can't Say That in a Public School—or Can You?

This is not to say that student protests are free of consequences—*Khademi v. South Orange Community College District*[172] cited *Tinker* in upholding a college's compelling interest in preventing disorder in the academic environment by halting a disruptive demonstration,[173] but finding that line between expression and disruption continues to be a particular challenge. In *Shamloo v. Mississippi State Board of Trustees*,[174] the Fifth Circuit searched for the appropriate balance when taking up the case of two Jackson State University students who were disciplined for participating in unapproved campus demonstrations. In finding for the students, the court noted it was not enough to show some disruption occurred on campus because of the demonstration—some disruption was, in fact, the point of a demonstration. Instead, the court "must also conclude (1) that the disruption was a *material* disruption of classwork or (2) that it involved *substantial* disorder or invasion of the rights of others."[175]

Attempts to corral student protests into pre-approved "free speech zones" in the interest of order have also been met with some skepticism by the courts. In *Burbridge v. Sampson*,[176] students protested the campus's "preferred areas" for demonstrations of 20 students or more, all of which were away from central areas or places where students were likely to gather. The court struck the policy down as both a content-based prior restraint as well as for overbreadth.[177]

College and universities have used *Hazelwood* to bring forum analysis into student speech cases, angling for private forum status based on their creation as institutions designed for the pursuit of knowledge. This argument has had some success. The Seventh Circuit found *Hazelwood*'s use of forum analysis to be appropriate for college publications, as it dealt with an allegation of censorship at a school-sponsored newspaper at Governors State University.[178] The Eighth Circuit used forum analysis to restore a display created by two students to reflect the professional interests of the history faculty at the University of Minnesota at Duluth.[179] Because the display included photographs of faculty with period firearms and other weapons, an administrator felt it created safety concerns.

The university argued the space was a nonpublic forum, subject to reasonable regulation. The *en banc* Eighth Circuit Court accepted the forum argument but rejected the reasonableness of the regulation, calling it an unnecessary form of viewpoint discrimination:

Students' Right to Speak

> To put it simply, the photographs were removed because a handful of individuals apparently objected to the plaintiffs' views on the possession and the use of military-type weapons and especially to their exhibition on campus even in a historical manner. Freedom of expression, even in a non-public forum, may be regulated only for a constitutionally valid reason; there was no such reason in this case.[180]

Perhaps some of the most interesting college speech cases have been related not to the rights of individuals, but to groups. The Supreme Court examined the rights of students groups in *Healy v. James*,[181] in which a group of students at Central Connecticut State College protested the decision of the school to deny them the opportunity to form a local chapter of Students for a Democratic Society (SDS). SDS had a reputation for encouraging destructive demonstrations on other campuses during a time when campus tensions were running high. The Student Affairs Committee had recommended allowing the group to form, but the president overrode that recommendation, denying the group benefits such as access to free meeting space, bulletin boards and the student newspaper.

The Supreme Court considered the denial a form of prior restraint, which was not necessarily unconstitutional, but required a compelling interest to outweigh the students' right to expression. *Healy* began its analysis with its own special turn of phrase that has worked its way into many subsequent decisions: "At the outset we note that state colleges and universities are not enclaves immune from the sweep of the First Amendment."[182] The First Amendment right to expression and association was at issue in *Healy*, and the college had to be able to justify overriding its students' rights.

The Court examined the four reasons given by the college for its decision and found three of them lacking in merit: affiliation with the national SDS group, the president's personal disagreement with the philosophy of the group and the unsubstantiated belief that the group would cause disruption on the campus.[183] A fourth point, however—the students' unwillingness to sign a second statement agreeing to abide by the student code of conduct—was considered worthy of additional investigation:

> Just as in the community at large, reasonable regulations with respect to the time, the place, and the manner in which student groups conduct their speech-related activities must be respected. A college administration may impose a requirement, such as may have been imposed in this case, that a group seeking

3. You Can't Say That in a Public School—or Can You?

official recognition affirm in advance its willingness to adhere to reasonable campus law. Such a requirement does not impose an impermissible condition on the students' associational rights. Their freedom to speak out, to assemble, or to petition for changes in school rules is in no sense infringed. It merely constitutes an agreement to conform with reasonable standards respecting conduct. This is a minimal requirement, in the interest of the entire academic community, of any group seeking the privilege of official recognition.[184]

Healy is a significant case, however, for two contradictory reasons. First, it stated that "the college classroom with its surrounding environs is peculiarly 'the marketplace of ideas,' and we break no new constitutional ground in reaffirming this Nation's dedication to safeguarding academic freedom."[185] Previous academic freedom cases[186] had discussed the value of the college or university environment as a place of unfettered exploration, but in the context of the faculty speech. *Healy* extended this idea to the expression and ideas generated by the students within colleges and universities as well. On the other hand, *Healy* also recognized, similar to *Tinker*, that administrators had a legitimate interest in preventing disruption to the learning environment, even if to do so meant restricting student speech rights.[187] While the Court cautioned that a "heavy burden"[188] lay on the college or university to justify a speech or expression restriction, the case still opened a door to regulation on the basis of maintaining an orderly environment similar to the precedent set by *Tinker*.

Healy was followed fewer than ten years later by the equally important *Widmar v. Vincent*.[189] In *Widmar*, a group of University of Missouri students took their school to court for denial of student organization status because their group dealt with religious topics. The university notified the students that it was forced to deny them organizational status (and the associated benefits of meeting space, printing services, etc.) in an effort to avoid an Establishment Clause violation. The district court found for the school,[190] but the Eighth Circuit reversed.[191]

The Supreme Court deemed the student organization program a type of public forum, meaning regulations had to survive the closest constitutional scrutiny.[192] While it agreed that efforts to comply with one constitutional provision (such as the Establishment Clause) was a significant interest, in this situation it was not compelling enough given the "equal access" policy inherent in the student organization program. All student groups were allowed to apply for official status, with prerequisites focusing on student membership and willingness to comply

Students' Right to Speak

with the student code of conduct, not the specific topic of the group's interest (an element that would skate close to viewpoint discrimination). As Justice John Paul Stevens noted in a concurrence:

> I do not subscribe to the view that a public university has no greater interest in the content of student activities than the police chief has in the content of a soapbox oration on Capitol Hill. A university legitimately may regard some subjects as more relevant to its educational mission than others. But the university, like the police officer, may not allow its agreement or disagreement with the viewpoint of a particular speaker to determine whether access to a forum will be granted. If a state university is to deny recognition to a student organization—or is to give it a lesser right to use school facilities that other student groups—it must have a valid reason for doing so.[193]

If the student activity has a tighter connection with the university, however, the school may assert more control over speech. For example, in *Alabama Student Party v. Student Government Association of the University of Alabama*,[194] the Eleventh Circuit determined a university had the right to place restrictions upon the distribution of campaign literature for student government office, because the university had created the student government program as a "learning laboratory" for those who wished to experience the political process in preparation for a career in public service.[195] Citing *Hazelwood*, the court found that the university only had to satisfy a reasonableness standard when the student speech was a direct part of the learning experience.

Buckley v. Valeo[196] and the range of campaign finance cases that followed it remind us that the U.S. court system recognizes "money talks," and citizens have a right to control what their money says about them.[197] Two significant cases reflecting this point have occurred in the college/university setting—one on behalf of the recipients of university funding, and one on behalf of the providers.

In *Rosenberger v. Rector*,[198] the student group Wide Awake Productions (WAP) sued the University of Virginia for refusing to honor the group's allotted budget by paying invoices for a printed publication discussing issues related to Christian viewpoints. The group had obtained official organizational status and was also designated a "Contracted Independent Organization" (CIO) by satisfying the prerequisites of student membership, full-time student officers, affirmation of non-discrimination and by filing a satisfactory mission and constitution with the university.[199] Only official student groups with CIO status could also apply for funding from the Student Activities

3. You Can't Say That in a Public School—or Can You?

Fund as long as the expense was related to the educational purpose of the university.[200]

WAP's mission—submitted with the group's successful application for organizational status—included the creation and maintenance of a magazine discussing philosophical and religious issues. After the first issue of the magazine was published, however, the university refused to pay the printing invoice, stating the publication was a religious activity and funding it would be a violation of the Establishment Clause. The group appealed through university channels, then to federal district court, claiming that the refusal to fund their publication when the university freely funded others was a form of viewpoint discrimination. Both the district court[201] and the Fourth Circuit[202] found for the university.

The Supreme Court overturned the lower courts, finding the prohibition against publications dealing with religious topics to be viewpoint discrimination. The Court distinguished between a university's control over its own speech and the funding of others' speech:

> It does not follow, however, and we did not suggest in *Widmar*, that viewpoint-based restrictions are proper when the University does not itself speak or subsidize transmittal of a message it favors but instead expends funds to encourage a diversity a views from private speakers. A holding that the University may not discriminate based on the viewpoint of private persons whose speech it facilitates does not restrict the University's own speech, which is controlled by different principles.[203]

WAP's publication had met the desired goal of the Student Activities Fund to forward projects that enhanced the university's educational mission by introducing a discussion of religious, spiritual and philosophical issues.[204] To deny the publication, the Court noted, would mean the university would similarly have to deny any publication dealing with atheism, humanism and many of the classics.[205] By denying WAP solely because of the religious content of its publication, "the neutrality commanded of the State by the separate Clauses of the First Amendment was compromised.... The viewpoint discrimination inherent in the University's regulation required public officials to scan and interpret student publications to discern their underlying philosophic assumptions respecting religious theory and belief."[206]

On the other hand, in *Board of Regents of the University of Wisconsin System v. Southworth*,[207] a student sued the University of Wisconsin to protest the use of his mandatory student fees (paid in addition to his tuition) to support student groups with which he disagreed. Southworth argued such funding amounted to compelled speech and a violation of his right to free association. Both the federal district court[208] and Seventh Circuit[209] were convinced by his argument.

The Supreme Court was not. Just as in *Rosenberger*, the Court deemed the student organizational program to be one meant in its entirety to facilitate diverse opportunities for the many viewpoints of the students attending the university. The precedents cited by Southworth referred to narrow situations involving the use of union dues to pay for political activities,[210] while the student organization program and its method of funding was far broader, "distinguished not by discernable limits but by its vast, unexplored bounds. To insist upon asking what speech is germane would be contrary to the very goal the University seeks to pursue."[211]

The Court agreed that a university the size of the University of Wisconsin would attract a broad range of views and opinions, and it was inevitable that students would disagree with some of the groups that benefited from the student fee fund. Requiring the university to design either an opt-out or opt-in system would be unnecessarily complicated and expensive, and ultimately work against one of the goals of the student organization program, which was to expose students to a broad range of viewpoints and encourage tolerance.[212]

Another hot button issue in college/university student speech is speech codes. Rising in popularity in the late 1980s and early 1990s, these campus-wide policies generally prohibited students from engaging in speech or activities intended to harm another on the basis on that person's gender, race, ethnicity, sexual orientation, creed or age. Speech codes were quickly challenged on grounds of vagueness or overbreadth, as they used terms open to multiple interpretations, like "stigmatize," "victimize" and "interfere with,"[213] or "intentionally demeans."[214] The broad sweep with which these policies encompassed language, and the ensuing chilling effect caused by the uncertainty over what was punishable, led to the policies in both Michigan[215] and Wisconsin[216] being held unconstitutional.

Speech codes were not beyond the requirements of *Tinker* as well. In *DeJohn v. Temple University*,[217] the Third Circuit required Temple[218] to show how the *Tinker* standard justified the university's sexual harassment speech policy, which had been challenged as a restriction of

3. You Can't Say That in a Public School—or Can You?

student speech. A graduate student in military history claimed the policy, which prohibited "expressive, visual, or physical conduct of a sexual or gender-motivated nature, when ... (c) such conduct has the purpose or effect of unreasonably interfering with an individual's work, educational performance, or status; or (d) such conduct has the purpose or effect of creating an intimidating, hostile, or offensive environment,"[219] discouraged him from discussing the role of women in combat with his fellow students, as it might have been construed as intimidating or offensive to the women in his classes. The court accepted his argument, finding Temple's standard of "unreasonably interfering" to be insufficient to meet *Tinker's* material disruption standard.[220]

As with K–12 speech, however, the 1980s and 1990s brought a more school-deferent, less student-protective attitude to the courts. In 1998, a student at the University of Tennessee was reprimanded for refusing to obey a faculty member's rule that first-year dentistry students could not sit in the back row of his lectures.[221] When he sued in federal court, claiming his choice was an expressive act of protest, the Sixth Circuit applied *Tinker* and found for the university, stating his actions were nothing "more than expression of a personal proclivity designed to disrupt the educational process."[222]

The Ninth Circuit applied *Hazelwood* to a case involving the withholding of a master's degree from a student who attempted to deposit a thesis with a "Disacknowledgements" section, insulting the dean of his college, members of the library staff, the regents and the former governor.[223] The court found *Hazelwood* applicable because the thesis was a required part of the curriculum, and as such, the student's department retained a reasonable amount of control over what was acceptable and what was not. While students were encouraged to use the "acknowledgements" section for personal expression, that did not give one free rein to create a nonconforming publication that both insulted members of the academic community and misrepresented the student's adviser and department.[224]

In an interesting trend mirroring the K–12 environment, some universities have attempted to discipline students for online speech. A case in Minnesota's state courts highlights the struggle colleges and universities have experienced in balancing the online speech rights of their students and the concerns of the campus. In *Tatro v. University of Minnesota*,[225] a student in the mortuary science program was

Students' Right to Speak

disciplined in response to several Facebook posts in which she made derogatory comments about the donor body assigned to her for the semester as well as vaguely threatening statements about fellow students. The university informed Tatro she had violated Rule 7 of the anatomy laboratory course, which states, "Conversational language of cadaver dissection outside the laboratory should be respectful and discreet. Blogging about the anatomy lab or the cadaver dissection is not allowable."[226] The department gave her a failing grade in the course as well as required her to take an ethics course, apologize to the department and undergo psychiatric evaluation. Tatro sued, stating she was being disciplined for private comments.

The Minnesota Court of Appeals found for the university, citing *Fraser's* statement about the difference between a student and citizen's right to free speech, *Morse's* concern for a school's responsibility for the safety and welfare of its students, and the applicability of *Tinker's* substantial disruption standard:

> We discern no practical reasons for such a distinction and note that other courts have acknowledged *Tinker's* broad applicability to public-education institutions. We observe, as the Third Circuit did in *DeJohn*, that what constitutes a substantial disruption in a primary school may look very different in a university. But these differences do not per se remove the *Tinker* line of cases from the analysis.[227]

Applying *Tinker*, the court found a very real disruption to the academic environment, as families who had donated bodies of loved ones to the mortuary science program questioned its integrity when they learned of the Facebook posts, and fellow students testified to being genuinely frightened by the offhand comments Tatro made about attacking her classmates with mortuary tools.

The Minnesota Supreme Court upheld the lower court's ruling,[228] but deemed *Tinker* to be inapplicable to the situation: "The driving force behind the University's discipline was not that Tatro's violation of academic program rules created a substantial disruption on campus or within the Mortuary Science Program, but that her Facebook posts violated established program rules that require respect, discretion, and confidentiality in connection with work on human cadavers."[229] The state supreme court's ruling focused on the university's policy requiring that students conduct themselves in a professional manner in relationship to their academic program, deeming that restrictions on a student's non-classroom speech could be constitutional as long as they were "narrowly tailored and directly related to established professional conduct standards."[230]

The adult status of college and university students results in a slightly different approach to regulating student speech. The application—often successful—of *Tinker* and *Hazelwood* to the college and university setting, however, shows us that the core concepts of these K–12 cases are strong. The underlying desire to maintain an orderly educational environment and the ability for a school to control speech that may be attributed to it transcends age in favor of environment. When applied to specific situations, these two motivations play out a little differently. Where K–12 schools seek order to protect safety and welfare as well as inculcate appropriate values per their academic missions, colleges and universities appear to be protecting the orderly environment to maximize students' opportunities to learn and faculty members' opportunities to teach and research. Overall, the courts' treatment of college/university student speech gives us a strong sense of places where the court will not bend—ideas we can rely on as we create solid speech policy for a K–12 level.

State Laws

In response to rulings by the Supreme Court and federal appellate courts, a handful of states have passed statutes safeguarding the right to free speech or press within public schools, as the U.S. Constitution tolerates state laws that grant more freedoms, but not fewer.[231] State statutes are easier to pass than constitutional amendments and can be precisely written with clear definitions to minimize misinterpretation and even anticipate problems, like changing technologies.[232]

As of this writing, nine states have passed some form of student speech or press protection statute, and another two have passed an administrative regulation to the same effect. A brief review of these pieces of legislation, however, reveals a strong emphasis on student press or publications as opposed to speech in general. Sometimes called "anti–*Hazelwood*" laws, it appears these statutes live up to their moniker, addressing the factual circumstances surrounding the *Hazelwood* case as opposed to the broad speech restrictions that arose from it.[233]

Students' Right to Speak

Of the 11 states that have created student speech laws or regulations, Arkansas,[234] Colorado,[235] Illinois,[236] Iowa,[237] Kansas,[238] North Dakota[239] and Oregon[240] worded their efforts to address student press freedoms at the secondary or college/university level. While most of these statutes begin with a general declaration of freedom of speech within the public academic environment, the specifics of the law relate to student control over topic selection and editing in publications, methods of distribution, exceptions for unprotected speech such as libel or obscenity and a prohibition on publications designed to create a material disruption. While these laws provide protection for student press, they are generally not applied to students' personal expression. For example, the Tenth Circuit declined to apply Colorado's Student Free Expression Law to a situation involving a student compelled to apologize for making religious remarks during a commencement ceremony, stating the law was meant to apply to publications only.[241]

Washington's regulation[242] is a one-line statement affirming that students have a right to free speech and press. The remaining three states—Pennsylvania, Massachusetts and California—have written laws or policies that confer protections to a broader range of student speech and expression.

Pennsylvania's policy[243] is detail oriented, and covers "publications, handbills, announcements, assemblies, group meetings, buttons, armbands and any other means of common communication,"[244] with additional clarifications within these categories of expression regarding possible time, place or manner restrictions. Massachusetts' statute,[245] on the other hand, is written broadly to cover the rights of public secondary school students, stating:

> The right of students to freedom of expression in the public schools of the commonwealth shall not be abridged, provided that such right shall not cause any disruption or disorder within the school. Freedom of expression shall include without limitation, the rights and responsibilities of students, collectively and individually, (a) to express their views through speech and symbols, (b) to write, publish, and disseminate their views, (c) to assemble peaceably on school property for the purpose of expressing their opinions.[246]

California has five state laws addressing student speech—one for public community colleges,[247] one for public secondary schools (including charter schools),[248] one for public colleges and universities,[249] one for private secondary schools[250] and one for private colleges and

3. You Can't Say That in a Public School—or Can You?

universities.[251] The California laws, similar to Pennsylvania, spell out a detailed list of protected expression and communication activities. California is also the only state of the 11 to have passed legislation prior to the *Hazelwood* ruling, with initial protections for public community colleges and secondary schools becoming law in 1977.

State legislative responses have been initiated in many other states, but have failed to gain traction at either the legislative or executive level. Gaining support for student speech or press protection laws has proved tricky. In a 1995 survey of individuals involved with attempts to pass student speech legislation, respondents cited a variety of reasons why they felt the attempt failed:

> Fifty-two percent attributed it to "opposition from school administration and school board members." Other responses were "lack of interest among legislators" (48 percent), "lack of support from the professional media" (44 percent), "concern about unregulated high school publications" (36 percent), and "lack of lobbyist activities among supporters" (28 percent).[252]

Jack Nelson's 1974 study of high school journalism, *Captive Voices*, noted a struggle to gain support for student press rights from mainstream media. One Indiana newspaper editor explained that he would not support a student press freedom bill because "All animals walk with assistance before they run. Only poisonous snakes are trusted with a venomous bite from birth."[253]

When we look at these three areas of student speech law—K–12 precedents, college/university precedents and statutory laws—one would hope that a sense of consistency comes through. After all, we avoid running into legal problems best when we know what the law actually is—it's a lot easier to avoid a speeding ticket if you know the limit. The guidance here is murky in part because it's developed in response to the application of law to specific incidents. We can apply those precedents easily to similar situations, but like snowflakes, two student speech scenarios are rarely identical. It's not enough to know that we can justify regulation in the name of order, of academic mission, of safety and of the integrity of the learning environment. We need to understand how those justifications balance against constitutional rights, optimal learning environments and developmental opportunities. A focus solely on law isn't enough to help schools and administrators plot a proactive course. The unique nature of public education calls us to incorporate more.

Students' Right to Speak

Key cases overview:

Pre–1969	*Lander v. Seaver*	Vermont Supreme Court (1859)	Speech can be punished if it "begets disorder an insubordination."
	Burnside v. Byars; Blackwell v. Issaquena County Board of Educ.	Fifth Circuit Court of Appeals (1966)	"School officials should be careful in their monitoring of student expression in circumstances in which such expression does not substantially interfere with the operation of the school."
Tinker	*Tinker v. Des Moines Indep. School District*	U.S. Supreme Court (1969)	"It can hardly be argued that either students or teachers shed their constitutional rights to freedom of speech or expression at the schoolhouse gate." To regulate student speech, school must show that the expression would materially and substantially interfere with the requirements of appropriate discipline in the operation of the school, would collide with the rights of others.
Fraser	*Bethel School District No. 403 v. Fraser*	U.S. Supreme Court (1986)	"The First Amendment does not prevent the school officials from determining that to permit a vulgar and lewd speech such as respondent's would undermine the school's basic educational mission."
Hazelwood	*Hazelwood School District v. Kuhlmeier*	U.S. Supreme Court (1969)	"A school need not tolerate student speech that is inconsistent with its basic educational mission." If a student newspaper is not open to all/created for a broad communicative use, it's a nonpublic forum and can be regulated so long as the regulation is reasonable and has a legitimate pedagogical purpose. The question of this case is if the First Amendment requires a school affirmatively to promote particular student speech that "members of the public might reasonably perceive to bear the imprimatur of the school."
Morse	*Morse v. Frederick*	U.S. Supreme Court (2007)	A school may "restrict student speech at a school event, when that speech is reasonably viewed as promoting illegal drug use."

4

What Is a Student?

When is a door not a door? When it is ajar.[1] When is a student not a student? No clue.

Joking aside, this is a relevant question, especially in the rapidly changing speech environment we find ourselves in today. If we're going to explore the question of student speech, and more importantly, create solid policy that guides teachers and students about its rights and responsibilities, we need begin narrowing in our focus on key details. One such detail is the definition of "student."

Is a student defined by age—for example, a person within the age range of compulsory education? Is a student always a student, or can a person put that designation aside? If so, when? After academic hours have ended, or until promotion, graduation or withdrawal? To create sound policy, we need to resolve some of the inconsistencies regarding "students" and offer a workable definition that students, schools and courts may use in assessing student speech.

A Basic Definition of "Student"

Before we can reconcile inconsistencies in the treatment of the term "student," it is helpful to identify a basic definition from which to begin. It's less pressing to find a common definition for "school," other than to note that we are focusing on public schools (including charter schools)[2] as opposed to private schools, for which there is no direct government actor. Schools are both a physical place and a social construct. Schools consist of buildings, playgrounds, parking lots and other fixed features, but they are also an "idea" of a time and place of learning, which can occur anywhere and at any time, through such varied venues as field trips, athletic or extracurricular events, or online schooling.

The question of when a person is "at school" or not would be relevant if the discussion was about *school* speech. *Student* free speech, however, is more interested in the distinction between the role of "student" and "nonstudent" or "citizen." Education has grown beyond the physical boundaries of the traditional building. For example, in *Morse*, a student who did not report to school at the start of the day but met up with fellow students attending a school-sponsored off-campus event was still considered under school authority. Since geography is no longer a reliable indicator of the extent of a school's authority over speech, focusing on the status of the speaker rather than his or her physical location or proximity to school authority gives a clearer starting point.

Post argued that speech should be evaluated in relation to the purpose of the premises,[3] which would be an intriguing approach should courts consistently agree on the purpose of schools before applying speech analysis. Here, we tweak Post's concept by replacing "premises" with "status," evaluating speech in relation to the purpose of "studenthood." Focusing on status over premises also tilts our analysis more toward speaker than audience, which is consistent with the *Tinker* decision's use of *Terminiello* to warn against regulating student speech based on a "heckler's veto."[4] A "heckler's veto" can be defined as restricting speech because other people respond poorly to it, rather than punishing the responders for their actions.

"Student" is a very simple term for a very complex role. Our friends at Merriam-Webster define it as "a person who attends a school, college, or university" or "a person who studies something."[5] There are procedural definitions, generally used by colleges or universities as well as accountants that are focused on enrollment indicators (like credit or course load). Law takes much of its cue from the Family Educational Rights and Privacy Act,[6] which defines "student" as "any person with respect to whom an educational agency or institution maintains education records or personally identifiable information, but does not include a person who has not been in attendance at such agency or institution."[7] None of these, however, tells us what separates a student from a citizen.

Philosophy gives us quite a bit of description on what is it to be a

4. What Is a Student?

"learner," but not the more focused term of "student." "Learner" and "student" deserve different definitions. Learning never stops—as we take in new experiences and new concepts, we're constantly exploring and cataloguing new information. The idea of student, however, suggests something different, something with structure, purpose or mission: "Students are persons who submit themselves to the acquisition of specific knowledge and skill from instruction, learners are persons who derive meaning and change their behavior based on their experiences. All of us are learners, but only those who submit themselves to deliberate instructional situations are students."[8]

The idea of the submissive student to the learned authority is sometimes called the "transmissive" model of education, but some argue today's educational environment requires a greater degree of flexibility.[9] Teaching is no longer a one-size-fits-all mentality, and not all students succeed in a submissive role. Some students can independently engage in a "deliberate instructional situation" by collaborating with a school as opposed to learning from a single authority figure. A definition of a student, then, needs to include some recognition of a "disciplined and structured" approach to learning over the one-way teacher-student model.[10]

Thus far we know the "how" of a student, but not the "what." Gutmann shines some light on the "what" of a student through her definition of a "scholar": one who examines theories, institutions and widely held beliefs.[11] Her definition applies well, for at every level of education, students are presented with theories, institutions and beliefs, shown the rationale behind them and encouraged to conduct their own assessment.[12] This may be as simple as learning the concept behind addition. It is not enough to tell a younger student that two apples plus two apples equals four apples; teachers want students to replicate that concept and apply it to other quantities of apples. In doing so, students are exploring a mathematical theory and determining whether they agree with the proposed interpretation offered to them.

Adding apples is not a theory with much depth or diversity. We don't expect students to emerge from an exploration of the addition of two and two with the answer of five and argue passionately that their interpretation may have validity. The process, however, remains the same as the more advanced student who may disagree with interpretations of the writings of Shakespeare or the political significance of Kennedy's actions regarding Cuba. As a result, age is not as important as the learning enterprise to an understanding of the "student" in student free speech.[13]

Adding intentionality to Gutmann's process of a scholar allows us to roll in the relationship between the scholar and educational institution.[14] Students have different relationships with their schools at different points in the day; in the classroom the relationship is focused on learning while in hallways or during recess or lunch periods, the relationship shifts to more of a supervisory one. There is also a point at which the relationship is severed either temporarily (such as at the end of daily school activities) or permanently (at graduation or withdrawal). Since the scholar's process is most interested in directed learning, a definition of student would be stronger at times when the relationship between student and school is "disciplined and structured" in the pursuit of learning. Taking this approach allows a shift from geographic emphasis to the connection between student and school at the time of speech.

Putting these ideas together, we can define a student as:

> *Someone who is exploring theories, beliefs or institutions through an intentional and disciplined relationship with a school that is based in such exploration (as opposed to a some other factor, like employment).*[15]

This gives us a valuable starting point toward separating "student speech" from "citizen speech."

The Separation of Student and Citizen

Our working definition of "student" helps us from a broad perspective. Studenthood enters a person's life when he or she begins a relationship with a school (for many, this is kindergarten) and ends when that relationship is officially concluded (graduation or a choice to withdraw). If we accept that as the final word on "student," however, then we're locking people into that status 24/7 for anywhere from 12 to 20 years. At some point during the day, week or year, students need to be able to go back to being citizens and enjoy the broader First Amendment protections offered to all citizens.

4. What Is a Student?

One place we can look for guidance is the common-law approach developed to distinguish between when a public employee speaks "as a teacher" versus "as a citizen." In *Pickering v. Board of Education*,[16] the Supreme Court found a public schoolteacher's dismissal for writing a letter to the editor that was critical of the school board to be a violation of the teacher's right to free speech as a citizen. The court determined that as long as the topic discussed was one of legitimate public concern and the letter did not interfere with the teacher's job performance or the operation of his school, he could not be punished by his government employer for engaging in what would otherwise be constitutionally protected speech.[17] This principle was followed in *City of Madison Joint School District v. WERC*,[18] in which the Supreme Court stated a teacher could not be barred from speaking at a school board meeting about working conditions simply because he was not the designated labor representative. The Court noted, "Where the State has opened a forum for direct citizen involvement, it is difficult to find justification for excluding teachers who make up the overwhelming proportion of school employees and who are most vitally concerned with the proceedings."[19]

While teachers, and all public employees, have a right to speak about issues of public concern without fear of losing their jobs as a result, that right is not absolute. Courts have recognized that government-as-employer still needs to maintain an orderly and effective workplace, and that means having some of the same abilities as private-sector employers to discipline or dismiss employees for engaging in harmful speech. For example, *Mt. Healthy v. Doyle*[20] upheld the termination of a public school teacher when the school was able to prove that the termination was due to the teacher's unprofessional conduct with students, and not a radio interview he had given in which he criticized the school's new guidelines for teacher dress and appearance. *Connick v. Myers*[21] rejected the notion that taxpayer funding automatically confers public interest on every action of a government agency. Myers had been dismissed for insubordination in part for circulating a biased survey suggesting to her co-workers that they were working in a hostile environment. When she claimed the firing was due to protected speech, the Supreme Court declined to get involved in what it said was an internal matter: "[W]hen a public employee speaks not as a citizen upon matters of public concern, but instead as an employee upon matters only of personal interest, absent the most unusual circumstances, a federal court is not the appropriate forum in which to review the wisdom of a personnel decision taken by a public agency allegedly in reaction to the employee's behavior."[22]

The Supreme Court further refined public employee speech guidance in *Garcetti v. Ceballos*,[23] upholding the firing of a Los Angeles County deputy district attorney for issuing a memo to a defendant's lawyer that questioned the legality of a search warrant. The Court added a new first step in the assessment of public employee speech protection. Rather than starting by questioning if the speech involved a matter of legitimate public concern, the Court determined the first analysis should explore if the speech was a direct result of employment, or made as a part of the requirements of the job. If so, "when public employees make statements pursuant to their official duties, the employees are not speaking as citizens for First Amendment purposes, and the Constitution does not insulate their communications from employer discipline."[24]

This brief overview of public employee speech common law shows that a line had to be drawn to distinguish employee speech (which government-as-employer could regulate or use as a basis for discipline or dismissal) from citizen speech. A similar need occurs for public school students. Both teachers and students are in situations in which the government has been granted additional authority to regulate speech in the name of an orderly environment.[25] Both have a status that is hard to shed at the end of the school day: school districts expect or even mandate teachers to model appropriate social behavior both on and off campus,[26] and students have been punished for off-campus speech since a young boy yelled out "Old Man Seaver" while driving his father's cows home well after the school day. Both teachers and students need to explicitly find the line where they might be considered "citizens," or they will remain teachers and students until they graduate or change jobs.

Another similarity between teachers and students in their search for citizen status is the potential benefit the community stands to gain if both groups are allowed to freely speak about conditions within our schools. Students, like teachers, have insights that may be very useful to those who do not attend school but have a vested interest in its functional operation, such as parents, community members or taxpayers.

4. What Is a Student?

Consider the historical case of *Wooster v. Sunderland*,[27] in which a student spoke out about safety dangers in science classrooms and the lack of adequate fire exits, and was subsequently denied the opportunity to graduate. Consider the more recent case of the Fairmont State University student newspaper, whose adviser was fired after the newspaper reported on the university's failure to address black mold in dormitories.[28] Such speech is vital not only to the student body, but also to all those who might be impacted by an incident resulting from these deficiencies.

Students deserve a student/citizen separation, perhaps even more than public employees, who can choose to work for the government. Compulsory education laws require students to attend an educational institution, and for the majority of K–12 students, their attendance is at a public institution. As a result, students find themselves compelled to submit to the government-as-educator for a substantial part of their daily lives. They shouldn't be denied the opportunity to lay their student status aside and speak about issues relevant to their world, much of which relates to school and school activities, without fear of disciplinary action from the school.

What Makes a Student a Student from K to PhD

Another consideration that needs to be resolved in order to adequately separate student speech from citizen speech is the broad continuum of education. We need to determine how age factors into our concept of studenthood and student speech.

Courts have had difficulty determining how speech precedents created in the context of one level of education can be applied to another. A common concern is application of precedents created in the K–12 context to college/university settings. In *McCauley v. University of the Virgin Islands*,[29] the Third Circuit declined to assess a contested university student speech code on the basis of *Tinker* because "there is a difference between the extent that a school may regulate student speech in a public university setting as opposed to that of a public elementary or high school."[30] The court went on to discuss what it perceived to be fundamental differences between K–12 and college/university:

Students' Right to Speak

> We reach this conclusion in light of the differing pedagogical goals of each institution, the *in loco parentis* role of public elementary and high school administrators, the special needs of school discipline in public elementary and high schools, the maturity of the students, and, finally, the fact that many university students reside on campus and thus are subject to university rules at almost all times.[31]

Because universities emphasized the pursuit and questioning of truth, while K–12 schools focused more on the inculcation of democratic and societal values, the Third Circuit found that university students required more opportunity for speech than their younger counterparts.

The Third Circuit has also distinguished between elementary and secondary public school environments. In a concurrence in *Seyfried v. Walton*,[32] Judge Max Rosenn noted:

> [T]he court can take judicial notice of the progressively higher levels of intellectual and emotional development of students in the later grades of secondary school. As a result, more deference should be shown school authorities' curricular decisions regarding a grade school, and perhaps junior high school students, in the face of a challenge that a particular point of view has been excluded. High school students, in contrast, are at an age approaching both adulthood and franchise.[33]

More than 20 years later, the Circuit reaffirmed the elementary-secondary distinction in *SG v. Sayreville Board of Education*,[34] stating, "For our purposes, it is enough to recognize that a school's authority to control student speech in an elementary school setting is undoubtedly greater than in a high school setting."[35]

In contrast to the separation espoused by the Third Circuit, some courts have embraced the applicability of speech precedents created at one level of education to another. Just three years after the *Tinker* decision, the Supreme Court applied the "material disruption" standard in *Healy v. James*,[36] dealing with a public college's decision to deny official student status to a proposed chapter of Students for a Democratic Society. A concurrence by Justice Rehnquist explicitly notes the *Tinker* decision supports the idea that "the constitutional limitations on the government's acting as administrator of a college differ from the limitation on the government's acting as sovereign to enforce its criminal laws."[37] *Tinker* has also been applied in *DeJohn v. Temple University*[38] to assess the constitutionality of a speech code designed to prevent sexual harassment.

The *Hazelwood* precedent has also "trickled up" to college and

4. What Is a Student?

university student speech, especially when such speech can be tied to a curricular aspect of the school. A year after the *Hazelwood* decision, the Eleventh Circuit used it to support the University of Alabama's regulation of campaign literature related to student government elections,[39] stating the school had a legitimate pedagogical concern behind regulating the distribution of student flyers and timing of debates.

In the Tenth Circuit, *Hazelwood* was used to uphold a university's requirement that a theater student perform assigned pieces as written, even if they included profanities that the student claimed her religion prohibited her from saying.[40] The court explained:

> Moreover, it is apodictic that public school students do not "shed their constitutional rights to freedom of speech or expression at the schoolhouse gate." At the same time, however, the Court has emphasized that "the First Amendment rights of students in the public schools are not automatically coextensive with the rights of adults in other settings, and must be applied in light of the special characteristics of the school environment." Nowhere is this more true than in the context of a school's right to determine what to teach and how to teach it in its classrooms.[41]

Cases involving student speech as part of extracurricular activities, which may have a more tenuous connection to curriculum, have been treated inconsistently by the courts. When Kentucky State University chose to withhold distribution of its student-produced yearbook because of administrator objections to some editorial and design decisions, the Sixth Circuit re-heard the case *en banc* specifically "to determine whether the panel and the district court erred in applying *Hazelwood*—a case that deals exclusively with the First Amendment rights of students in a high school setting—to the university setting."[42] The *en banc* court found the principles of *Hazelwood's* forum analysis to be appropriate, regardless of the different educational level.[43]

Hosty v. Carter[44] addressed the application of *Hazelwood* to a university student newspaper as a vehicle of student speech. In exploring the constitutionality of the school's prior review policy, the circuit court held the *Hazelwood* precedent meant: "Whether *some* review is possible depends on the answer to the public-forum question, which does not (automatically) vary with the speakers' age."[45] While the court eventually determined that the student newspaper was a designated public forum that was not open to a *Hazelwood*-style content restriction,[46] it granted Dean Patricia Carter qualified immunity, stating, "Even if student newspapers at high schools and colleges operate under different constitutional frameworks, as both the district judge and our panel thought, it greatly overstates the certainty of the law to say that any reasonable college administrator had to know that rule."[47] By asserting that student newspapers at the college/university level can be subjected to the same speech analysis as their K–12 counterparts, the Sixth Circuit offers support for the idea of a single concept of "student" for purposes of student speech.

Going in the other direction, over the past few years several courts have affirmed the idea that precedents created at the high school level can apply to the elementary levels as well. Cases involving religious speech,[48] personal speech,[49] and violent speech[50] have prompted district and circuit courts to declare that the *Tinker* precedent is fully applicable to younger students as well as older. The Third Circuit commended the use of the precedent, noting, "[O]ur prior precedents seem to recognize that the *Tinker* test has the requisite flexibility to accommodate the age-related developmental, educational, and disciplinary concerns of elementary school students,"[51] and the Fifth Circuit noted, "It is difficult to identify a constitutional justification for cabining the First Amendment protections announced in *Tinker* to older students."[52]

From a strictly legal perspective, it's uncertain if all students are students, or if some kind of age consideration requires unique definitions. Reviewing the cases that suggest different rules for different grade levels supports their assertions with discussions of maturity/cognition, differences in educational environments, and the need for disciplinary authority. To resolve the uncertainty, we explore these factors to see if they change dramatically enough from one level of education to the next to justify a split.

Exploring the different levels in K–12 education is tricky, as not all school systems "break" at the same time. Elementary schools, middle schools, junior high schools and senior high schools differ in their grade breaks across the country. This inconsistency alone suggests that the same definition of "student" can be applied from kindergarten through senior year—if there truly was a difference in maturity, environment or disciplinary needs at certain points in a student's career, then all schools would break at the same spots to reflect the need for change.

To test the idea that all students are students, we examine the biggest challenge to that argument: the break between high school and

4. What Is a Student?

college/university. If we can make the argument that the experience of being a student doesn't change significantly from high school to college, then our definition of student can certainly withstand any other grade breaks. By exploring maturity/cognition, environment, and discipline at a substantial educational transition, we see there are more similarities than differences as students progress through their educational journeys. That shows education is built around a continuum rather than a series of discrete learning levels, and as such, we can consistently apply our definition of student across the board and separate it from citizen speech.

From K to PhD: Cognitive Capacity and Maturity

If the cognitive ability to learn fundamentally changes when a student moves from high school to post-secondary, then a unified definition of student can't be justified. Research in neuroscience over the past 30 years, however, shows that the transition stage between secondary education and undergraduate education is blanketed by an extraordinary time in cognitive growth. In other words, to the brain, age is just a formality.

Prior to the 1970s, neuroscientists believed the brain developed the most rapidly and actively in the first year or two of life, but didn't undergo any further substantive changes.[53] Specifically, it was believed that myelination ("white matter"), which increases the speed of transmission of electrical impulses from neuron to neuron, didn't occur after infancy in the frontal cortex. Advances in MRI technology, however, show this process occurs during adolescence as well. During the teenage years and early 20s, the speed of the human brain undergoes another upgrade, specifically in an area responsible for linking ideas and concepts to create a greater understanding of the world.[54]

Recent research also shows a surge of synapse creation ("grey matter") during puberty, with a subsequent strengthening of some neural connections and pruning of others. This also occurs in the frontal lobes, where many of the executive functions are carried out, such as decision-making, memory, impulse control and selective attention.[55] The surge of synaptic activity in the frontal lobe creates "noise," which can interfere with some of these executive functions, hence the bad decisions made by teenagers. After the growth of grey matter, the brain selectively prunes back the synapses that aren't as active, reducing the "noise level." The net result of these studies suggests that maturity, or a level of mastery over executive function, may occur later than the end of adolescence or after the age of majority.[56]

While this may explain some of the interesting behaviors of adolescents or young adults, it also suggests a heightened opportunity for learning. The surges in speed and growth the brain experiences in the first year of life as well as in the teen years and early 20s are largely experience driven. For infants, that experience is almost entirely in the hands of parents; thus the emphasis on reading to babies and showing them images that stimulate thinking. For young adults, that experience may be impacted by parents, friends, schools, communities and the young people themselves. The strengthening and pruning of synapses is guided by the activities in which the person engages, leading both brain and behavior to become more specialized.[57]

Our newer understanding of the human brain shows we have an exciting new window for explosive learning. The combination of myelination and synaptic growth means young people in secondary schools and colleges and universities are thinking faster and are open to new direction as they begin to create neural patterns that will take them into adulthood. We don't have a set age at which this process starts and ends, but we can say with some certainty that begins prior to age 18 and ends after age 18. This new opportunity for creating new patterns of thinking and behavior therefore bridges K–12 and college/university education, supporting the idea of an education continuum.

From K to PhD: The Social Student

Our definition of a "student" also looks at a relationship with a school, which is procedural and social. Students' social maturity plays a factor in the rationale of courts to apply or not apply precedents formed in one environment to another. This makes social development a factor worthy of analysis. As with cognitive research, however, there is a lot of overlap in the buffer zone of the transition from secondary and undergraduate education that makes it difficult to justify separate definitions.

The experience of "the student" past the most basic grades has

4. What Is a Student?

changed dramatically in the past century, and subsequently so has the social development of the students. When Dewey wrote in 1916 that students were "candidates to enter society,"[58] he was on the front edge of a massive growth in high schools across the country. From the early 1900s to the 1940s, high school enrollment surged from roughly 10 percent of those old enough to attend to 65 percent.[59] Not all students finished high school, and many high schools had a dual-track program meant to prepare a small group of students for post-secondary study and the rest for a practical career or homemaking. Jobs lured the young men away from a high school degree; jobs or marriage and babies drew away the young women.

After World War II, however, teenagers found it more difficult to compete against returning GIs for good-paying jobs. Changes in labor laws and a surplus of well-trained applicants predisposed employers against hiring teens. At the same time, the perception of the value of a high school diploma began to rise, and parents adopted the belief that a person with a high school diploma had more career opportunities than a person who did not.[60] By the late '60s, completing a high school degree became such an expectation that not having one was considered a sign of failure.[61] This remarkable change in public perception over a short 20–30 years funneled a generation of teenagers into a holding pattern of high school that, for many, their parents did not experience, making the transition of values from one generation to the next more difficult and creating a new worldview for young adults.[62]

Move forward another 30 years, and adolescent education transformed yet again. The high school diploma expectation was replaced by post-high school education of some kind. A 1992 survey, for example, showed only 5 percent of high school students planned to end their education after the twelfth grade.[63] There's good reason to pursue education past high school, as the data on earning potential show a college degree is the key to economic opportunity. Over a lifetime, people with bachelor's degrees earn 84 percent more on average than people with only high school degrees.[64] Even attending college without earning a degree results in a 15 percent increase in lifetime earnings over a high school diploma alone.[65]

Let's contrast, then, the high school student of 1915 to 2015. The 1915 student might or might not attend high school, might at any time leave high school for a job opportunity that could become a lifelong career from which he could eventually retire, and could realistically look forward to marrying, starting a family and purchasing a home within the next 10 years. The 2015 student sees dropping out of high school as "failure," knows that there are limited job opportunities for a person lacking a high school degree and virtually none that could translate into a solid career, sees post-secondary education as a necessity for career success (if he desires it) and therefore high school as a requirement.

One result of this shift in student life is a sense of extended adolescence, or a prolonging of the time between "childhood" and "adulthood." Sociologists anticipated this development as early as the 1930s, when Dr. Charles Beard noted to the National Education Association: "The period of youth is prolonged by the restriction of opportunities to enter upon life work."[66] Twenty years later, in a report to the Office of the National Committee on the Employment of Youth, Kenneth Clark observed that advancements in industrial technology combined with a longer life span was creating a "vestibule" stage of adolescence, during which youth had expectations of greater independence but were being shut out of participation in the economy and our political life.[67]

Today, the transition to adulthood remains a topic of sociological interest. A 2005 study stated that age range of the transition from childhood to adulthood runs from the late teens through the mid- to late-20s and beyond.[68] Moving away from one's parents is no longer a chief indicator of independence and adulthood, as many young people move away to attend post-secondary education, yet do not consider themselves "adults." Instead, financial independence appears to be the key for self-identifying as an adult.[69]

Clark University Professor Jeffrey Arnett's work supports the idea that financial independence, along with making independent decisions and accepting responsibility for one's own well-being, is becoming a key criterion for adulthood.[70] He suggests a new developmental stage between adolescence and adulthood, termed "emerging adulthood," that begins in the late teens and extends into the mid–20s.[71] During this stage, young people have some independence in their own decision-making, but there is less societal expectation of responsibility than there is for adults. Emerging adults are faced with a breadth of life choices and opportunities, but are not pressured to commit to a certain path. Arnett notes that "emerging adulthood" is a subjective

4. What Is a Student?

stage with which an individual may or may not self-identify: "There are 19-year-olds who have reached adulthood—demographically, subjectively, and in terms of identity formation—and 29-year-olds who have not."[72]

Today's young people, then, "seem simultaneously like both sophisticated adults and immature children."[73] The greater economic and social forces that have kept young people in an academic setting for longer periods have given rise to a student culture all its own.[74] The sociological mindset of the vestibule adolescent, emergent adult, or whatever term one applies, exists across the barrier that courts would erect between K–12 students and college/university students.

From K to PhD: Educational Institutions Evolve

From the biological and social development of the students, we turn to the sociology of the school itself. One argument for different treatment of K–12 and college/university student speech revolves around the differences in the nature of the academic institution as supporting a greater need for free speech in one than the other. Do the environments, or "school-worlds,"[75] warrant the difference in approach to free expression?

Justice Thomas reflected on the school environment in the early days of the country in his concurrence in *Morse:*

> During the colonial era, private schools and tutors offered the only educational opportunities for children, and teachers managed classrooms with an iron hand. Public schooling arose, in part, as a way to educate those too poor to afford private schools. Because public schools were initially created as substitutes for private schools, when States developed public education systems in the early 1800s, no one doubted the government's ability to educate and discipline children as private schools did. Like their private counterparts, early public schools were not places for freewheeling debates or exploration of competing ideas. Rather, teachers instilled "a core of common values" in students and taught them self-control. Teachers instilled these values not only by presenting ideas but also through strict discipline. Schools punished students for behavior the school considered disrespectful or wrong. Rules of etiquette were enforced, and courteous behavior was demanded. To meet their educational objectives, schools required absolute obedience.[76]

But that was 200 years ago—today, the academic environment in public schools looks very different as the environment adapted to

Students' Right to Speak

compulsory attendance laws and subsequent increases in enrollment. Sociological studies of public high schools in the 1960s and '70s showed public schools to house a student subculture that encouraged exploration of identity and alternatives to lifestyle choices of their parents.[77] The schools' approach to education observed in these studies, on the other hand, countered the student subculture and student-driven exploration with a one-way, vertical approach to teaching: knowledge flowed down from the teacher to the students rather than between teacher and student or student and student. Cusick's study of a public high school noted that separation of teacher from student was even reflected in the physical properties of the school:

> They [classrooms] are all arranged on the principle that the teacher is the one who has the knowledge and skills and therefore has the front desk, and student, the seekers after the same sets of knowledge and skills, sit in five or six rows of metal and plastic desks facing the teacher and waiting to be instructed.[78]

The school's design, both physical and curricular, reflected elements of Justice Thomas's "iron hand," yet the interactions occurring between students and teachers, and among students with each other, revealed a student need to push boundaries, explore alternatives and take more control over their own learning process. Schools and communities interpreted this as rule breaking and defiance to authority, and sought to quash it rather than use it.[79]

Meanwhile, the Soviet Union sent an object into space before the United States and Japanese students began to outstrip American students in math and science. Parents clamored for more intellectual rigor at all stages of education. Educational funding from both the state and the federal government began to tie itself to numbers of students served as well as performance outcomes. All of these elements led schools to begin to change their approach to students, to try to make schools a place where young people wished to be and to apply themselves.

The direction of education became less vertical and more horizontal, with give and take in the classroom as well as the curriculum. Powell, Farrar & Cohen called this the "shopping mall high school," a place with many options from which students could choose, but designed ultimately to try to keep students mentally (or at least physically) engaged with the institution for as long as possible.[80] Some students actively "shopped" the curricular and extracurricular offerings placed before them by the school, while some merely wandered the

4. What Is a Student?

halls.[81] The shopping-mall approach granted students a greater degree of autonomy over their own education than they had previously enjoyed, which benefitted top-tier students but was less useful to the "unspecial."[82] It was also a new paradigm for teachers, who had administrators, parents and now students advocating for classes and services that would meet their specific needs. In the words of one teacher:

> Higher standards, more elective, back to basics, fund the arts, post the 10 commandments, zero tolerance, crack down, ease up, too much homework, much more rigor, I'll sue, but the state says, give my kid another chance.[83]

What we see from this analysis is a gradual growth in student-driven education occurring before students reach college or university, where such student involvement is taken for granted. In response to demands for a more effective educational system, public K–12 schools turned to a more college/university style model that allowed students more autonomy and encouraged them to engage more with their own education by getting actively involved with their curricula and classrooms. This subtle alignment with elements of post-secondary education implies a similarity between educational environments that contradicts those who believe the two are radically different.

Bringing It All Together

We've identified the problem: defining student so that we can define student speech. Doing so will allow us to separate it from citizen speech and give schools a concrete place to start in creating proactive student speech policies.

What is a student?: Our working definition is "someone who is exploring theories, beliefs or institutions through an intentional and disciplined relationship with a school that is based in such exploration."

Is "student" broadly applicable? Our analysis says yes. The definition captures a broad range of educational learning, and perhaps more importantly, acknowledges that the student experience is not a series of jumps from level to level. Rather, it's a continuum that adapts to the changing needs of the learner. Looking at the break between high school and college, for example, reveals far more similarity than difference. Cognitively, there is a surge in learning potential that overlaps high school years and college years. Developmentally, students are in a time of exploration of self-knowledge and community that lingers

Students' Right to Speak

between childhood and adulthood. And their "school-worlds" have remarkable similarities in autonomy and attempts at engagement.

Remember the comments of Judge Max Rosenn in *Seyfried v. Walton*[84]:

> First, the court can take judicial notice of the *progressively higher levels of intellectual and emotional development of students in the later grades of secondary school*. As a result, more deference should be shown school authorities' curricular decisions regarding grade school, and perhaps junior high school students, in the face of a challenge that a particular point of view has been excluded. High school students, in contrast, are at an age approaching both adulthood and franchise.[85]

Judge Rosenn is suggesting that we look at education as a progression rather than a static environment. There is layering naturally embedded in the process of education through the use of grade levels, with each grade tasked to attain a certain level of knowledge. Grades aren't the same as age—if a student has not mastered the educational goals of a grade, he or she is retained until that mastery is completed. Thus our continuum of education is based on what makes a student a student, not what makes a child a minor.

As they advance through the grades, students are progressively faced with more complicated concepts that lend themselves to more questions. If we can make the continuum argument bridge high school to college, which we do through our exploration of cognition, socialization and environment, then we certainly can establish it exists in the K–12 levels as well. The educational journey is a series of measured steps, not giant leaps. Our definition of student allows schools and courts to reflect the continuum in its application—we can look at how a student explores, the types of theories or beliefs being examined and the nature of the relationship with the school at the student's point in the continuum. As such, we can respect the different needs of different students without having to redefine "student." We can apply this definition across the board.

How do we connect this to student speech? Student speech is speech not only spoken by a student, but that also impacts his or her studenthood. The speech must have some connection to the exploration, the intentionality, or the relationship with the school in order to classify it as student speech that is under a school's authority to regulate.

The definition focuses on the speaker and the speech, rather than the geography of the speech, its medium or its audience, which helps

4. What Is a Student?

us retain the "student" in student free expression. Emphasizing the connection to studenthood as opposed to broadly incorporating everything that may be tangentially related to the school also keeps the focus on the student rather than the school. Incorporating the aspect of "impact" is not only a nod to *Tinker*, but it also keeps the burden on schools to prove that the expression is so significant that it merits regulation, as opposed to merely distasteful but otherwise meaningless to the learning process.

This definition also respects the continuum of education, because the nature of exploration, intentionality and school relationships change over time. With each successive grade, the opportunity for speech and expression freedom grows. As Gutmann writes:

> As students develop with age a greater effective capacity for justice, teachers should give them more freedom of speech and encourage them to use that freedom of speech in responsible, constructive ways, to learn from each other, and to develop mutual understandings of each other that would otherwise be inaccessible, or at least less accessible.[86]

Allowing a steady growth of speech freedoms fits in with what we know about brain development as well. Remember that research found synaptic strengthening to be *experience-driven*, not passively reinforced. Just as parents are told they must talk to their infants and encourage response as opposed to placing them in front of a passive source of sound like television, so too do we need an experiential approach to learning during the second burst of synaptic growth. Students may be able to memorize and recite information, but this does not mean they have accepted the intended lesson or absorbed its practical applicability. Learning, as Roe notes, "is an interactive process, not an inculcative one,"[87] and expression can be a valuable tool in the process:

> The learning process, in which students advance from an insufficient, formative level of knowledge to a higher level by formulating and reformulating their thought structures, is essentially an expressive act. Conceptual development involves *actual contribution by the learner* because developing one's cognitive structures is a more active process than creating mental lists of received opinions. Students learn by working with ideas, attempting to fit them into their cognitive structures, and reformulating those structures as necessary.[88]

What Roe seems to suggest, and the research in neuroscience appears to support, is the value of the idea of "teachable moments." Imagine if Matthew Fraser, instead of being suspended, had instead been redirected to better understand the impact of his sexually suggestive speech through guided discussions with other students or research into the difference between effective and ineffective uses of humor. Consider if the students at Hazelwood East had been called to the principal's office and told that together, they needed to find a quick and effective solution to the perceived problems in the article. Perhaps if the discussions that emerged out of the court activity between Amanda Tatro and the University of Minnesota had instead occurred after the first complaint made about her Facebook postings, she might have had a greater appreciation for the impact of her words and the likelihood of their misinterpretation. Learning by doing, meeting speech mistakes with more speech when it is possible, allows cognitive structures to adapt to these new lessons at a time when the brain is highly receptive to learn.

As students are promoted from grade to grade based on their mastery of the knowledge sets,[89] a continuum approach suggests they should gain freedoms. If their speech is called into question by their school, it can be assessed per the expectations of their grade level, thus acknowledging that what is suitable for a tenth-grader is not always right for a third-grader, without having to create a separate concept of student in order to ensure appropriate content for all.

Separating Student Speech from School Speech

In defining student speech, however, we must be sure to recognize the completely independent category of school speech—speech that directly comes from the school, its teachers or the district. A school has a right to maintain control over its own expression and should not have to surrender its voice to the free expression rights of students. Items like curriculum, even when it requires the input of student expression, still remains school speech over which the school maintains control.

A school can present messages and require students to repeat them to ensure the messages have been received, but cannot force students to personally endorse these messages or adopt values with which they disagree.[90] If a school chooses to relax its authority over an aspect

4. What Is a Student?

of curriculum, that aspect may become a form of student expression worthy of protection. For example, if an English teacher assigns a one-page essay on any topic in order to assess core writing skills, with no other parameters, the teacher's requirements regarding writing quality and grammatical accuracy are elements of the school's expression, but the topic is the student's expression. Regulating the topic after it has been freely given to students requires a higher level of scrutiny than the reasonableness standard suggested for curricular speech in *Hazelwood*. If, on the other hand, the teacher assigns a paper on representations of the Reconstruction by Mark Twain in accordance with the curricular goals of the class, the topic of the paper, in addition to its mechanical accuracy, is considered school expression and student free speech guidance wouldn't be in play. In this manner, schools' authority over their own expression, especially as it's conveyed through curriculum, is protected.[91]

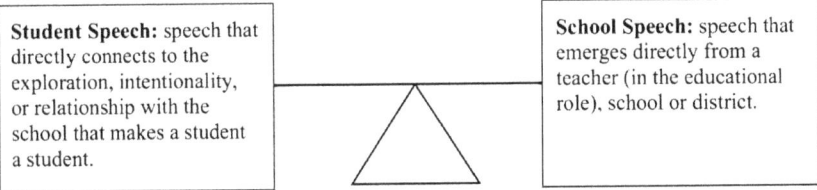

Student Speech: speech that directly connects to the exploration, intentionality, or relationship with the school that makes a student a student.

School Speech: speech that emerges directly from a teacher (in the educational role), school or district.

Defining "student" and "student speech" and separating these concepts from school speech gives us a valuable starting point. The goal isn't to limit students or schools in their ability to speak or regulate, but rather to create more visible borders to these concepts that allow for a greater degree of predictability for students and schools alike. The cores are clear but the edges are fuzzy—strong definitions begin to solve that problem.

5

Why Free Speech for Students at All?

Defining the "what" behind student speech is an important first step. To create solid policies that respect both student and school, however, we need to know the "why" behind student speech as well. "Why" is grounded in law, history, sociology, philosophy and more—it's the foundation that gives form and function to student speech policies. Policy that reflects the comprehensive "why" of student free speech may very well head off problems before they are created. And ultimately, that is a win for schools and students alike.

What Existing First Amendment Philosophy Says About Youth and Schools

The concept of free speech and expression, and the United States' embodiment of free speech within the First Amendment, has filled many an impressive and expensive hardcover book. While some prominent free speech theorists have touched on the applicability of their particular theories to children or academic speech, that discussion is generally brief and dismissive.

Free speech theorists have cited a lack of rationality, autonomy or maturity as reasons to withhold from children the same full free speech protections offered to adults. For example, John Mill wrote of his free expression theory:

> It is perhaps hardly necessary to say that this doctrine is meant to apply only to human beings in the maturity of their faculties. We are not speaking of children,

5. Why Free Speech for Students at All?

or of young persons below the age which the law may fix as that of manhood or womanhood. Those who are still in a state to require being taken care of by others must be protected against their own actions as well as against external injury.[1]

A century later, First Amendment theorists like Scanlon, Richards and Garvey picked up on Mill's maturity argument and extended it into more modern approaches to free speech. Scanlon focused on autonomy, or the ability to bring independent judgment to bear when weighing competing opinions and expressing one's own.[2] A person who lacks that degree of independence, like a child, lacks autonomy and therefore needs protection from potentially dangerous speech.

Richards, along with Scanlon, extended Mill's concern for maturity not only to speakers, but also to audiences. He noted:

> In deriving the principle, we observed that the value of free expression turned on the existence of developed capacities of rational choice. Thus, the principle is not intended to apply to persons presumably lacking rational capacities, such as children. In addition, the liberty of communication was so interpreted that the liberty of expression correlates with the liberty of others to choose to be or not to be an audience. It follows, therefore, that there should be not constitutional objection on free expression grounds to the reasonable regulation of the distribution of obscene materials to children.[3]

Autonomy and rationality arguments popped up in Supreme Court decisions such as *Ginsberg v. New York*[4] and *Tinker v. Des Moines*,[5] where the Court justified the idea of restricting minors' ability to engage in speech or receive speech because "a child—like someone in a captive audience—is not possessed of that full capacity for individual choice which is the presupposition of First Amendment guarantees."[6]

Garvey, on the other hand, called out his colleagues for the lack of philosophical underpinnings for expression rights of minors. He noted other writers casually accepted "the broad ground that children lack the human characteristic of a capacity for rational choice, on which fundamental rights, in their guide as general moral rights, depend."[7] Garvey questioned whether this automatic assumption held minors back from attaining rationality and autonomy, in essence creating a self-fulfilling prophecy. Writers in other areas of the academy have written along the same lines. For example, the work of Jürgen Habermas and his concept of the public sphere recognized social interaction within communication in the public sphere was not only a learning opportunity, but also an opportunity for personal growth.[8] In other words, if you hold people back from interaction, they won't learn how to do so and therefore will be unable to interact.

More recent examinations of First Amendment theory's applicability to youth and schools pick up on this concern about assumptions. Roe wrote that belief in the "*supposed* incompetence" of the young people who make up the classroom's captive audience has justified many restrictions of student speech.[9] Dailey took issue with the concept of "autonomy," arguing that theorists have poorly defined this term by failing to reflect the constant state of change and cognitive growth experienced by children that creates conditions of autonomy worthy of First Amendment recognition.[10] Gutmann more explicitly built on the development argument, stating, "As children mature, however, the paternalistic ground for denying them the same free exercise rights as adults gradually erodes."[11]

The combination of rationality, autonomy and maturity, considered by general First Amendment theorists as crucial for meaningful engagement with, as well as reception of, expression and ideas, is one aspect of free speech theory that has been applied to the worlds of minors. Another aspect is the value of free speech to individual growth. As Emerson noted, "Freedom of expression is essential as a means of assuring individual self-fulfillment."[12] Baker's liberty model of free expression says each individual requires a "realm of liberty" within which to experience the process of self-realization, suggesting that such an experience is one that involves growth, learning and change.[13]

The process of self-realization, however, is not just another way of describing maturity. Self-realization focuses on the whole person and his or her journey toward understanding self and belief. It's more than critical thinking or reflections on public opinions, but discovery of one's intellectual, emotional, philosophical and spiritual self. It is a deeply personal and significant process that requires the ability to engage in a certain amount of free thought and testing of that thought with others through expression. If we create policies that give no freedom for questioning, we risk stymieing this process.[14]

In addition to autonomy/maturity and self-realization, a third element of free speech theory raised during discussions of student speech rights is the role of free expression in a democracy. A country that claims to be self-governed is expected to allow meaningful expression to enter the public sphere. In the words of Meiklejohn, "Far more

5. Why Free Speech for Students at All?

essential, if men are to be their own rulers, is the demand that whatever truth may become available shall be placed at the disposal of *all* the citizens of the community."[15] Meiklejohn didn't mean that all people should have equal opportunities to speak, but rather that all things worth saying be said.[16]

Ensuring all worthy ideas get a chance to be heard, however, assumes an audience capable of examining arguments with a critical eye and making intelligent decisions based on those examinations,[17] even if that decision is to turn away. Capacity for critical decision-making could potentially justify the idea that children or students do not have the right to choose to speak or not speak as well as hear or not hear.

In the words of Sunstein, however, "only tyrannies force people to read or watch."[18] Despite the fact that most public K–12 students have not reached voting age, they are still members of a democracy and need to learn how to navigate its expectations. The argument that children or students do not need full protection to both share and hear all that must be said because they can't vote[19] falls into the trap of the age-based restriction, as it assumes that once a person gets beyond the required age, he or she will somehow magically acquire knowledge and skills. Active preparation is necessary. Gutmann notes that free speech must be taught and practiced within the schools for students to understand that "freedom and responsibility are two sides to the same coin of democratic citizenship."[20] Even the Supreme Court has suggested that greater freedom to express and hear a range of ideas is a necessity, as it teaches students how "to live in a pluralistic society, a society which insists upon open discourse towards the end of a tolerant citizenry."[21]

If our focus was strictly on children, our argument might end here, but our focus is on students. Instead of age, we need to think about speech in relation to the role of the active learner. There is some recognition of this relationship from writers who look at the nature of the government authority—the public school.[22] Commentators using this approach have examined the inherent values of speech within the educational setting, generally within the context of academic freedom. While looking at free speech as it relates to the public school is helpful in our exploration of student speech rights, that discussion has generally centered more on the schools, teachers, and classrooms than the students. For example, Byrne noted universities foster a "careful and critical" manner of discourse essential to democratic society,[23] while Berlin discussed the need for open discussion to seek answers raised in the course of education.[24] Roe likened the "cognitive classroom" to a marketplace of ideas, albeit tempered by curricular values,[25] which Redish and Finnerty determined must be substantially related to the educational process to be valid interests to override free speech.[26]

While First Amendment theory and theorists have not completely ignored free speech as it applies to students, they have not pursued the issue broadly. Robert Wheeler Lane took a slightly pessimistic view in his summary of the situation:

> We witness significant conflict in the claims and assumptions underlying free speech and public education, however. For example, free speech presumes a high degree of rationality, while public education presumes a child's rational capacity requires considerable development. While free speech presumes an independent citizenry, public schooling typically minimizes student autonomy. Finally, free speech reflects substantial distrust of government authority, but public education rests upon a broad grant of state power to control and direct the intellectual and moral development of the nation's youth.[27]

Examining past theorists' discussion of student speech gives us a good path to follow for a greater understanding of practical approaches. Theory is often not thought of as pragmatic, but it offers us something that a strict interpretation of law can't—an exploration of the question: Why? Why should student speech have First Amendment protection? Why is it special, if at all?

Key Values Served by Student Speech

Tinker offers us a tantalizing concept, that "public school student speech has First Amendment protection unless..." rather than "Students have free speech only when...." The first statement presumes protection, while the second statement suggests regulation as a norm except in certain circumstances. But for that presumption to have foundation, it needs values—something to tie it to our overall understanding of the constitutional right to free expression guaranteed all citizens under the First Amendment. Four values emerge to create that tie:

5. Why Free Speech for Students at All?

Education's role in democracy	Socialization into communities
The right of self-realization	Effective, participatory education

Value 1: Education's Role in Democracy

There is some general agreement that democracy involves placing power in the hands of the people rather than a hereditary ruler. After that, interpretations differ, and with that range of perspectives on what democracy means comes a similar range of interpretations of the role of free speech within a democracy. For example, Baker put forward three conceptions of democracy: elitist (in which the citizenry's primary role is to put people with specialized knowledge and skills into leadership roles), liberal pluralist (in which every person has an equal voice, and those aggregated voices create law and policy) and republican (which assumes all citizens would come together to deliberate and find unified solutions that advance the common good).[28] Within each of these concepts, free speech and press had a different role to play.

A common theme among the various perspectives on democracy is the important role communication plays within it, ranging from interpersonal sharing of ideas and opinions to the informative function of the media.[29] Freedom of speech, expression, and the press, guaranteed by the Constitution, allows communication to take place with minimal interference from the government. Free speech is not an absolute, but the closer speech or expression comes to supporting the functioning of democracy, the greater its protection.[30]

Elementary/secondary education in the newly formed United States emphasized skills in discussion and debate about public affairs in an effort to prepare students for their upcoming roles in a democratic society, especially for wealthier families or those in more urban areas.[31] Thomas Jefferson, an ardent supporter of education, strongly advocated for a widely available system of education that would

Students' Right to Speak

empower students "to discharge their duties as citizens while maintaining a vigilant watch against the tendencies of government to encroach on human liberty, including the liberty of free inquiry, thought and speech."[32] As the years passed and education grew into the institution it is today, the emphasis on the necessary role education plays in preparing citizens for their roles in a democracy has remained constant.

In fact, some have called the preparation for democratic participation "the primary task of American teaching,"[33] a sentiment echoed by the Supreme Court. In *Brown v. Board of Education of Topeka*,[34] the Court called education "the very foundation of good citizenship"[35] to support the rationale for extending equal educational opportunities regardless of race. *School District of Abington Township v. Schempp*[36] called public schools "a most vital civic institution for the preservation of a democratic system of government,"[37] and *Ambach v. Norwick*[38] declared a teacher's work "crucial to the continued good health of a democracy."[39]

Justice Felix Frankfurter further lauded the work of teachers:

> To regard teachers—in our entire educational system, from the primary grades to the university—as priests of our democracy is therefore not to engage in hyperbole. It is the special task of teachers to foster those habits of open-mindedness and critical inquiry which alone make for responsible citizens, who, in turn, make possible an enlightened and effective public opinion.[40]

Schools are charged to prepare students for democratic participation, but what does that entail? Studies of curricular decisions suggest preparation for democratic participation begins with reinforcing the concept that democracy is a preferable method of governance, and citizens should want to participate within it. For example, a 2000 study of high school social studies textbooks showed a prevalent use of what the authors called "the language of democracy," or a celebration of the civil and political rights that are hallmarks of American democratic life.[41] Civic voluntarism studies indicate two main factors that boost participation in civic life are the perceptions that one has the ability and the desire to take part in political life. Both of these perceptions can be reinforced through a democratically focused education.[42] Put simply, democratic values in education appear to begin with teaching students to value democracy.

When John Tinker, one of the Tinker children from the landmark

5. Why Free Speech for Students at All?

1969 case, was interviewed as an adult about his role in the case, he noted, "We can't have a democracy without kids learning in school what freedom and democracy are all about."[43] While this may be true, schools are conflicted if it is more effective to instill participatory and democratic values through instruction or experience. It's an understandable concern that students who spend a majority of their time in an environment in which their rights are restricted and their teacher's rights to regulate are expanded may become alienated from civic participation.[44] But there is equal concern that allowing students unfettered freedom will infringe upon constitutional rights of peers, such as the rights to privacy or equal protection. This concern over conflicting rights has especially played out in student press cases, where students have argued that the experience of journalism is a valuable opportunity to engage with a crucial tool of democracy.[45]

Encouraging participation over observation feeds into the self-governance aspect of democracy. Meiklejohn wrote that free speech and expression protected the ability of the people to self-govern, as it opened doors for freely sharing information on issues and allowing people to form their own judgments.[46] The goal is to enhance the public debate, not necessarily just for purposes of voting, but to help all citizens feel engaged in the leadership of their country.

The right of free speech is interwoven into educating for self-governance through the concept of teaching the "skills and virtues of deliberation" in the marketplace of ideas.[47] The idea of the marketplace of ideas is often attributed to a dissent written by Justice Holmes in *Abrams v. United States*[48]:

> But when men have realized that time has upset many fighting faiths, they may come to believe even more than they believe the very foundations of their own conduct that the ultimate good desired is better reached by free trade in ideas—that the best test of truth is the power of the thought to get itself accepted in the competition of the market, and that truth is the only ground upon which their wishes safely can be carried out. That at any rate is the theory of our Constitution. It is an experiment, as all life is an experiment.[49]

The concept of the "marketplace" helps balance out what might otherwise be seen as a simple majority approach in American democracy. The marketplace gives equal access to voices, loud and quiet, for critical examination by an engaged public.[50] The inherent question in applying the marketplace concept to education is whether this "public"—students—can fulfill their role in the metaphor as rational, critical consumers who can hear all views, consider them and make informed personal decisions.

The Second Circuit declared public K–12 schools to be "undoubtedly a marketplace of ideas,"[51] while the Third Circuit has claimed education is responsible for "exposing young minds to the clash of ideologies in the free marketplace of ideas"[52] and "teaching our citizens-in-training how to appropriately navigate the 'marketplace of ideas.'"[53] Further, exposure to the marketplace, as well as the opportunity to participate in it, doesn't hinge on students' chances for success in getting their ideas accepted:

> [T]he First Amendment declares that the highest interest of the people is best served if government is required to stay its hand and permit her (the student), and millions like her, to take upon their personal risk the ability of their ideas and convictions to survive and propagate in the marketplace of ideas. It is a matter of little moment, in the larger sense, whether she fails in that endeavor; it is of vital moment that she and her idea not be denied, by the instrumentalities of the political establishment, the *opportunity to succeed* in that marketplace. It is, indeed, of paramount importance to the public interest that she have that opportunity.[54]

Others, however, argue against the concept of a marketplace of ideas in education. Rauch asserts that giving all voices the same opportunity in an educational environment would suggest all ideas have the same intellectual authority,[55] even if they don't. The Flat Earth Society is an organization of people who believe that the Earth is a flat disk,[56] despite significant evidence to the contrary, and a true marketplace of ideas would allow this group the same authority as NASA to voice its opinion. Would we want that approach in the classroom?

Several commentators insist that the marketplace metaphor simply doesn't work or belong in schools, as curricular decisions necessarily steer students away from some ideas in favor of others.[57] Stewart claims it is almost irresponsible of schools to allow for a heavy marketplace of ideas presence, as it would force students to "relive the competitions of the past," instead of learning what has been accepted through old debates and exploring the new.[58]

The Seventh Circuit once drew a distinction between elementary and secondary schools, claiming, "The 'marketplace of ideas,' an important theme in high school expression cases, is a less appropriate description of an elementary school, where children are just beginning

5. Why Free Speech for Students at All?

to acquire the means of expression."[59] But 12 years later, the same circuit court (different judges) folded high schools in with elementary, stating "The contribution that kids can make to the marketplace of ideas and opinions is modest."[60]

If we're discussing student speech—and we are—then the marketplace of ideas has its place in our discussion, because the true marketplace of ideas within an educational environment doesn't exist in the act of initial curriculum transmission (which is still primarily a one-way process initiated by teachers and administrators), but in the discussion that happens after the initial transmission occurs. The questions asked by students, the opinions students offer in response to both the teacher and each other and the conclusions students create on their own about the material presented to them are aspects of the marketplace of ideas at work, and these aspects are important both to the educational process as well as the development of maturing minds.

Too many theorists conceive of the marketplace of ideas as specifically and strictly the public sphere of political discussion, which can easily lead to people believing the contributions of ineligible-to-vote students are, in the words of the Seventh Circuit, "modest." This is too narrow an interpretation of the concept of the marketplace, which is a place for the exploration of all ideas, the sharing of opinions and the testing of truths to allow individuals to form their own perception of the world around them. The questions and opinions offered by younger students may be less complex than those of older students, or unrelated to the political or civic issues of the day, but the offerings of younger students are no less important to *their* marketplace of ideas, helping them develop and learn.

If we accept the premise that the marketplace model has a place in education, then schools are charged to ensure that students know how to work within the marketplace. This involves both the ability to present and support an argument as well as listen to opposing opinions with an open mind. As early as the 1930s, observers expressed concern that education was too sanitized to prepare students for the clash of ideas and opinions that made up the public political sphere:

> If we are to train our children to face controversial issues, we must let them have some experience in being citizens and not merely subjects in the schools. No wonder we turn out such bad citizens from high schools and colleges when

Students' Right to Speak

students are so often penalized for nonconformity and so generally deprived of any voice in the discussing the issues of their own world.[61]

Any three-year-old can contradict—students need to learn how to discuss. Schools offer an opportunity to teach students the sort of debate that sustains the political process, whether it is engaging multiple perspectives, critically understanding a specific argument or evaluating the factual as well as emotional elements embedded in a public policy issue.[62] Learning how to debate also teaches respect for dissent, helping students learn to acknowledge that opposing opinions can still be rational or have merit.[63] Shielding students from controversial issues or conflicting opinions holds them back from obtaining the skills they need to embrace the full rights and responsibilities of citizenship.

Modern education is still guided by John Dewey's belief that the aim of education is "to form the citizen, not the man."[64] While democratic values and the concept of the marketplace speak strongly to the *rights* inherent in American democracy, it is citizenship that speaks to the *responsibilities* of a person within such a society. The Education Commission of the States frames the distinction between rights and responsibilities as the difference between civic education, which is knowledge about democracy and democratic processes, and education for citizenship, which gives student the opportunity to acquire a "democratic self."[65]

These different elements and perspectives help us craft the first value in support of student free speech. American public schools are institutions of democracy, intended to prepare students to not only understand the political institution that governs them (and in turn, over which THEY govern), but also to participate within it. Education plays a significant role in preparing people to accept the rights and responsibilities of citizenship. More importantly, it plays a critical role in nurturing a desire to engage in those rights and responsibilities.

To cultivate a desire to engage in the rights and responsibilities of democratic citizenship, students need to be able to form opinions about the civic lives around them so they may act in accordance with their own personal values. To form such opinions, students need the freedom to both hear and share various perspectives on the issues that are related to where they are in their civic lives. The first value to protect student free speech is therefore:

5. Why Free Speech for Students at All?

Value 2: Socialization into Communities

"Community," or the larger public within which people live, is a very broad term. One way we can wrap our head around community is by using collective identity theory, which studies an individual's "perception of a shared status or relation."[66] Belonging to a larger group comes with responsibilities to adhere to the social norms of the group, to act appropriately with fellow members of the group and to contribute to its overall wellbeing.

Among society's behavioral expectations is the concept of civility, or "the fostering of moral codes and ... the kind of life, the manners, even the modes of making a living that we hold up for emulation."[67] Civility, according to Arkes, is more like a moral imperative, which makes legal regulation of actions such as speech in the name of civility a potential clash between personal freedoms and communal good.[68]

Public discourse, however, is a substantial component of collective identity, as our ideas and how we choose to share them gives the community shape and boundaries. Government regulation of speech in the name of civility may have a ripple effect on the formation of communal identities,[69] and as such, when the Supreme Court has dealt with "uncivil" words, it has attempted to pair the incivility with clearer, direct harms in order to justify regulation. For example, in *Chaplinsky v. New Hampshire*[70] the Court felt the harm in what it called "fighting words" was the risk of those words creating a breach of the peace or even bodily harm, not the mere incivility of the language used. The limited value such speech might have had to the community was outweighed by the social interest in preventing a provoked attack.[71] In

109

Students' Right to Speak

contrast, in *Terminiello v. Chicago*[72] an angry and offensive race-based rant made to a large audience was not direct enough to justify the charge of disorderly conduct or a breach of the peace, and thus the speech, while disagreeable, was not constitutionally punishable. The court noted:

> Accordingly a function of free speech under our system of government is to invite dispute. It may indeed best serve its high purpose when it induces a condition of unrest, creates dissatisfaction with conditions as they are, or even stirs people to anger. Speech is often provocative and challenging. It may strike at prejudices and preconceptions and have profound unsettling effects as it presses for acceptance of an idea.[73]

Speech may make us uncomfortable, but the Court has shown itself very hesitant to regulate solely in the name of civility when it cannot find a more tangible harm directly attributable to the speech. Even blatant profanity can get a First Amendment umbrella, as seen in *Cohen v. California*.[74] The Court determined the granddaddy of all profanities emblazoned on a jacket in a statement regarding the draft may have been uncivil and offensive, but it was not dangerous. Because it lacked that sense of a direct, tangible threat to the well-being of the community, the Court was unwilling in the name of civil discourse *alone* to restrict speech.[75]

Schools have been identified as valuable tools for enhancing a sense of community among students and preparing them for appropriate behavior within their larger societies. The Common School movement, aimed at providing an educational experience to all school-aged children regardless of ability to pay, gained traction in the mid- to late-1800s in part due to the desire to more quickly integrate the children of immigrants into American culture and society, "instructing them in respect of the spirit and practices of American institutions."[76] Education brought diverse elements of the relatively new country together and gave them a common foundation. More than just preparing students for the role of American citizens, they were also preparing them to be members of American communities.

Research appears to indicate that faith in schools' socialization abilities is justified. A 1960s study of public schools and public school students found public education to be an effective instrument of political socialization in terms of both democratic values and civic involvement.[77] This may be why some efforts at significant social

5. Why Free Speech for Students at All?

change have been initiated in schools, such as advancing the civil rights movement through desegregation of public schools. As society has become increasingly pluralistic, and diversity has become celebrated rather than discouraged, schools are still the principal instrument for preparing students to interact appropriately in both a global and local environment.

Despite broad agreement that schools should be a place where students acquire appropriate socialization skills to prepare them for their lives after formal education, there is no consensus on what skills take precedence. Items with faith-based foundations have been rejected due to Establishment Clause concerns, but more doctrine-neutral values like honesty, diligence, respect for the law, and personal responsibility have been accepted as relatively uncontroversial.[78] Due to the local nature of schools, elements that reflect the particular values of an individual community have also been accepted as appropriate elements of socialization.[79]

The discussion gets more complex as schools attempt to steer students toward socially appropriate behaviors as opposed to values. The vagueness of "socially appropriate" has led to cases such as *SG v. Sayreville Board of Education*, in which the Third Circuit upheld the suspension of a kindergarten student for using his fingers to mimic a gun during a game of cops and robbers on the playground, deferring somewhat uneasily to the school's interpretation of "appropriate."[80] Courts are more comfortable when their decisions result in upholding a behavior or value with which few generally disagree, such as tolerance, fairness or equality. For example, in *Harper v. Poway*, the Ninth Circuit stated it did not see a viewpoint discrimination issue with restricting an anti-gay t-shirt, as there was no need "to provide equal time for student or other speech espousing intolerance, bigotry or hatred."[81]

The heart of judicial activity regarding student speech as an element of socialization into general society, however, lies in *Bethel v. Fraser*.[82] The Supreme Court upheld the student's discipline despite the fact that his speech didn't satisfy the *Tinker* standard, because it was the responsibility of schools to inculcate the "habits and manners of civility,"[83] which per the court's definition didn't have to include "the use of vulgar and offensive terms in public discourse."[84]

But what qualifies as "vulgar" or "offensive" for purposes of student speech? A case preceding *Fraser* noted, "If the intellectual and ideological ferment of the last four decades of the American social experience teaches anything, it teaches us that whatever may be the accepted meaning of 'good taste' on any given day, the content of that meaning does not rigidly abide through time."[85] Justice Stevens's dissent in *Fraser* pointed out that standards of offensiveness vary by generation, and a student would likely have a much better sense of what his peers would find offensive than "a group of judges who are at least two generations and 3000 miles away from the scene of the crime."[86]

The "I [heart] Boobies!" cases have brought a little more clarity to the *Fraser* precedent by reaffirming that student speech can be regulated if it can be reasonably interpreted as vulgar. Such interpretation is allowed to take the grade level and maturity of the audience for the vulgar speech into consideration.[87] However, as discussed in Chapter 3, we do have a split among courts on how much a school can restrict speech that is reasonably interpreted as lewd or vulgar but also has political or social value, as was seen in *B.H. v. Easton Area School District*.[88]

Whether speech is plainly lewd or just reasonably interpreted as so, there does seem to be at least a baseline agreement that such language is not a part of a civil society—the same civil society schools are preparing students to join. This goes beyond democratic values and touches on all aspects of a student's potential future life, such as how he interacts with neighbors, community members, employers or customers. Thus when a student lampoons her principal on social media with crude, sexual language, the underlying rationale for why such speech should fall under a school's authority may be a concern that the student might not otherwise learn the inappropriateness of such discourse and the harms it may cause in the future.[89] When courts uphold disciplinary actions for students wearing t-shirts that mock religion,[90] attempting to distribute newspapers featuring stick figures in sexual positions,[91] or writing racially inflammatory rap lyrics,[92] a similar concern for ensuring appropriate future discourse with community members may be at the root of the court's action.

We can get a better idea of how socialization into community impacts student speech by exploring the ways in which schools attempt to approach social skills, ranging from teaching solely by example to outlining a very specific value code as part of the mandated curriculum.[93] Between these two extremes are more moderate measures that seek to

5. Why Free Speech for Students at All?

teach students how to assess their own value systems without stating a "right" answer, or that take an intellectual approach to the work of great philosophers and the rationale they presented for declaring actions "right" or "wrong."[94] Whatever the process, teaching civility creates a huge opportunity to either protect or restrict speech in the name of socially appropriate behavior.

Students can acquire social skills in many environments, and schools provide an excellent one in which to both gain and practice such skills. At the heart of the process of socialization into community should be instilling the ability to simply talk to others in a manner that is appropriate to the situation. No person spends an entire day in one social context—one may start the day with family, interact with community during travels to and from work, spend several hours among co-workers, supervisors, customers or clients, and end a day with friends or peers. Each of these situations calls for different types of public discourse, which means that the goal of socialization into community calls for *more* experimentation with speech, not less.

The public school student audience is generally based on geography, meaning a student's enrollment in a school is largely based on how closely he or she lives to it. Unless a community is extremely homogeneous, schools will naturally pull together students with a range of backgrounds, personalities and beliefs. These differences aren't discarded at the schoolhouse gate, and represent another aspect of socialization within the students' peer group. A school's mission to prepare students for the diversity of opinions that exists in modern society means that students need to be free to express their differences, at the very least within the horizontal relationship of student to student.[95]

In addition to the peer relationships they experience with their fellow students, students are also gradually becoming aware of the layers of society that surround them and need the freedom to explore the type of speech each layer requires. They need the opportunity to try and the opportunity to fail so that they may learn through personal experience as well as the experience of others.

Communities benefit from a greater freedom of speech to socialize, as their value systems and modes of communication are enhanced by new ideas. In the spirit of Justice Stevens's dissent in *Fraser*, when two generations separate a speaker from a regulator, there is a possibility that innovation is being suppressed because it is unfamiliar. Just as

Students' Right to Speak

obscenity and indecency are evaluated per community standards, a similar consideration must be given to the sense of appropriateness in public discourse of students based on their intended audiences and messages.

We can see the concept of the continuum of education and its connection to speech rights in this value, as younger students have smaller and more uniform socialization opportunities, resulting in less boundary pushing and more consistency. As students' worlds get larger, so too must their ability to engage in speech and expression that allows them to discover the nature of appropriate speech to appropriate situations. The second value to protect student free speech is therefore:

Education's role in democracy	Socialization into communities
Speech and expression by public school students needs First Amendment protection because it helps students achieve a significant goal of modern education: to cultivate the drive and ability to engage in the rights and responsibilities of citizens in an American democracy.	Speech and expression by public school students needs First Amendment protection to allow students to experience the different levels of appropriate public discourse necessary for socialization into community.
The right of self-realization	Effective, participatory education

Value 3: The Human Right of Self-Realization

Hand in hand with speech's role in fostering collective identity and socialization is knowledge of self. The opportunity to experience self-realization and confidently embrace independence is no small thing in Unites States society—the image of the "rugged individualist" has played a prominent role in our national narrative, though historians have challenged this depiction as an unfair misrepresentation of early U.S. community.[96]

Mill said the freedom to express and experience ideas was a necessary part of "the privilege and proper condition of a human being."[97] Freedom allows individuals to experience current truths as well as discover new ones, especially truths that are particular to one person.

5. Why Free Speech for Students at All?

Lack of freedom means people repeat the experiences of the past and are not pushed to try new ideas or grow.[98]

Subsequent theorists have looked at the role of free speech in enhancing autonomy—the ability to define one's own beliefs based on a critical examination of the available information.[99] Autonomy not only confers a sense of personal achievement and satisfaction, but also allows people to take responsibility for their own actions and decisions. Denying access to ideas or beliefs hinders the development of autonomy—not only do people need to express and hear a full range of ideas in order to be prepared for a role in democracy and society, they also need that freedom to gain confidence in their own decision making. After all, if you don't know yourself, how do you know that you are making the decisions that are right for you?

Whether we examine the value of free speech to self-realization from a broad "self-knowledge" angle or a more narrow sense of "autonomy," self-fulfillment supports student free speech in part because it focuses on the speaker and his/her decision to engage in speech. It also fits because self-knowledge is not something we are born with, but rather something we come to learn through many means, including formal education. The journey toward self-realization is part of the student experience, for as Gutmann noted, "children do not leave their souls behind when they go to school."[100]

How students pursue their personal growth is where the value of self-realization begins to intersect with free speech. Beard called for education to "stimulate the more imperial gifts of imagination, originality and invention by which the treasures of mankind are enlarged and enriched."[101] To develop ideas that are new to the human experience, such as imagination and creative thought, students need the freedom to think, explore and express. The right to free speech becomes less "constitutional" and more "human," and is reflected in statements of the rights and freedoms of college/university students[102] as well as secondary school students[103] issued in the late 1960s.

As with other key aspects of development, students learn how to appropriately make decisions by actually making decisions.[104] The experiential value of doing as opposed to observing is key, and students understand the difference. In a 2009 study of high school journalists, respondents "always discussed their work in high school journalism with a sense of personal purpose and fulfillment," and had a lot of satisfaction with the contributions they felt their work made to their school and greater communities.[105]

The value of self-realization is a bit of a double-edged sword, however, as student speech can curb as well as enhance the pursuit of personal understanding. Constitutional law is an exercise in balancing, weighing compelling interests to support or restrict legal rights. One might argue the same balancing act applies to human rights such as equality or dignity. A very real example of this conflict is the regulation of bullying—such speech is one student's expression of personal belief and values, while it also creates a "climate of fear and disrespect" for the subject of the expression.[106] In response to bullying in public schools, new attention has focused on the *Tinker* precedent's regulation of speech that "collides"[107] with the rights of other students. The Third Circuit has noted "there is no constitutional right to be a bully,"[108] and the Ninth Circuit has declared anti-gay speech to "strike at the very core of the young student's dignity and self worth."[109]

Yet regulating free speech to protect general "rights" has the potential to be wildly ineffective or overreaching. In the search for a line between unpleasant speech and unacceptable speech, Denning and Taylor pose the following concerns:

> [W]hat *are* the "rights" of public school students vis-à-vis the expressive activities of their classmates? A right not to be gossiped about? Criticized? Ridiculed? Federal law does obligate schools to protect against certain types of harassment, but to convert that ambiguous language from *Tinker* into an anti-bullying exception stretches that language too far.[110]

Current First Amendment law and theory recognizes some basic human rights outweigh the compelling interest inherent in free speech, such as the right to personal safety from true threats, the right to personal privacy and the right to reputation. In *Jones v. State of Arkansas*,[111] the Supreme Court of Arkansas upheld a disciplinary action taken against a student who shared violent song lyrics with another student that closely reflected a current argument the two shared. The court used a "true threats" analysis to trump student speech precedent. Aligning approaches to student free speech with non-student First Amendment doctrine when it is possible and appropriate makes sense, in an effort to ensure a level of consistency in the balancing of free speech issues against other basic rights, so long as the same standards are applied as they would be outside the school environment.[112]

5. Why Free Speech for Students at All?

Self-fulfillment, self-realization, self-awareness—no matter how you phrase it, the idea is as old as Shakespeare ("To thine own self be true"[113]) and older. It is a human right that transcends politics or dogma, and is a lifelong journey. During the student years, when one is actively engaged in opening one's mind to new experiences, the opportunity to advance one's self-realization is heightened. To take full advantage of that opening, a student needs the ability to freely express and share ideas among his or her peers and within his or her communities.

Learning more about the impact of speech firsthand will help students learn how to use it more responsibly. By holding true to the same human rights conditions that govern non-student speech, free student expression can also help students grow through the understanding of consequences, protecting the vital speech right along with the privacy and safety of others. We grow through experiments, we grow through mistakes, we grow through witnessing the mistakes of others—but we do not grow when we are held back and forced to retrace the steps taken by those afraid to see us walk a different path. The third value to protect student free speech is therefore:

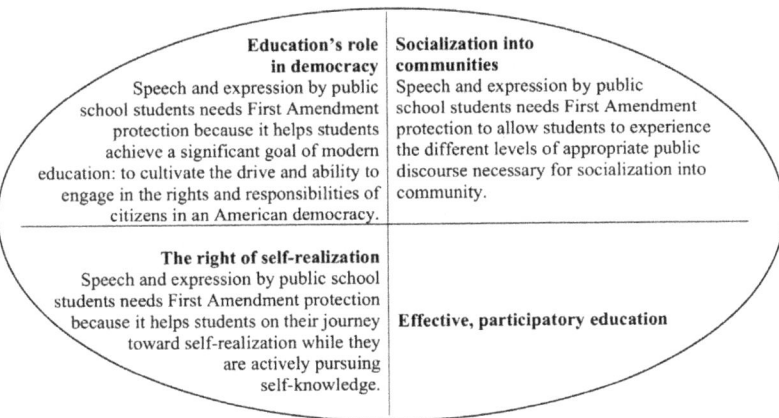

Value 4: The Goal of an Effective, Participatory Education

A student, per the definition previously laid out, has an active affiliation with a school. To reference a "Monty Python" sketch, however, a cheese shop with no cheese can hardly satisfy its customers.[114] A

Students' Right to Speak

school that can't provide education fails to hold up its end of the social contract between student and school. If a student wishes to be a student, he or she needs a school that can truly be a school. Student free speech plays a role in the ability of a school to provide an effective, participatory educational experience, and must be examined for the contributions it can make to the educational environment.

Tinker's attention to a "material and substantial" interference is an excellent starting point for the discussion of student speech and an effective educational environment. *Tinker* speaks specifically to the importance of maintaining "the work of the school,"[115] suggesting it is not the school administrators, their discipline or their authority that is being protected, but rather the actual processes of providing education to students and moving knowledge forward in general.

Based on Justice Fortas's opinion, we see that students are both contributors to the work of the school as well as recipients of it:

> School officials do not possess absolute authority over their students. Students in school as well as out of school are "persons" under our Constitution. They are possessed of fundamental rights which the State must respect, just as they themselves must respect their obligations to the State. In our system, students may not be regarded as closed-circuit recipients of only that which the State chooses to communicate. They may not be confined to the expression of those sentiments that are officially approved.[116]

If schools do not have complete authority over students, then students must have a certain degree of autonomy and can be active participants in the work of the school. If students may not be regarded a "closed-circuit recipients," then there must be give and take. *Tinker* contributes much more than "substantial and material disruption" to the conversation about student speech rights; it explicitly integrates students into the educational process and makes regulation of their speech possible only when such speech blocks students from receiving the benefit of their own work. *Tinker* does not balance school/teachers versus students, but student opportunity to speak against student opportunity to learn.

Ryan suggests education is an interest that by default will trump student speech rights:

> [E]ducating students is sufficiently important to justify truncating constitutional rights that interfere with that goal. For example, if forced to choose between ensuring that students are able to learn the lessons teachers have selected for them and allowing students full freedom to speak and select their own lessons, I would argue that the former objective should prevail.[117]

5. Why Free Speech for Students at All?

Ryan's example is not quite exact, as he contrasts school speech (curriculum) against student speech. A better approach may be one offered by Richard Roe, in which he distinguishes between student speech that intercepts the school's curricular message and student speech that contradicts the school's curricular message.[118] When students contradict curriculum by presenting alternate views, they are engaging in the truth-testing process that is at the heart of education. When students intercept curriculum through speech to the point that they are blocking their own education, the speech becomes an interference that warrants regulation.

Another way to conceptualize *Tinker's* view of disruption is something that substantially stands in the way of students' participation in the education that makes them students in the first place. Unfortunately, this description is still somewhat broad. Would a disruption of one student's experience qualify, or does the educational disruption need to be more widespread to be substantial?[119] The Seventh Circuit suggested that indications of a school experiencing a material disruption might include "a decline in students' test scores, an upsurge in truancy, or other symptoms of a sick school."[120] Other courts have declined to offer as specific a conceptualization of disruption, perhaps because of the difficulty of drawing a bright line between student speech and negative outcomes on the educational environment.[121]

Instead of Roe's "contradiction" and "interception," consider "disagreement" (which offers a less confrontational subtext) and "blocking" (a more straightforward way to describe the prevention of education) to create more useful guides for school and courts than "material disruption." To examine these concepts in action, let's look again at *Healy v. James*,[122] in which the Supreme Court analyzed Central Connecticut State College's rationale for refusing to allow a group of students to form a chapter of the Students for a Democratic Society (SDS). The college's arguments that: (1) the national SDS organization had an unsavory reputation, (2) the president disagreed with SDS's philosophy and (3) the university believed (without evidence) the local chapter would be as disruptive as chapters at other colleges and universities were rejected by the Court. A fourth argument, that the students were unwilling to sign an additional measure pledging their commitment to abide by campus rules and conduct regulations (none of which were found to have constitutional problems), was found to be compelling by the Court.

The college's first three arguments attempted to establish the

Students' Right to Speak

presence of an SDS chapter as a danger to others students' ability to learn. The Court rejected these arguments as unfounded; there was no proof that allowing the petitioning students to form a local chapter of SDS would mean their chapter would be as disruptive as other chapters had been across the country. It didn't help the college's case that the president was so personally opposed to the mission of the national organization—ultimately the attempt to deny the local SDS chapter failed First Amendment challenge because the college appeared to be attempting to restrict *disagreement* speech, not *blocking* speech.

The fourth argument offered by the college was the students' refusal to sign an additional pledge to adhere to reasonable student conduct rules. Here, we see a more plausible argument for a potential disruptive effect on the learning environment. The students claimed they declined to sign the pledge out of principle, as no other group had been asked to do so. Principle or no, the Court agreed the college had a right to be concerned when the group refused to reaffirm their commitment to the student code of conduct. That act of refusal in and of itself was a form of *disagreement* expression, but the plausible *blocking* impact of a group that refused to commit to following school rules gave the fourth argument enough strength to allow the Court to find in favor of the college.

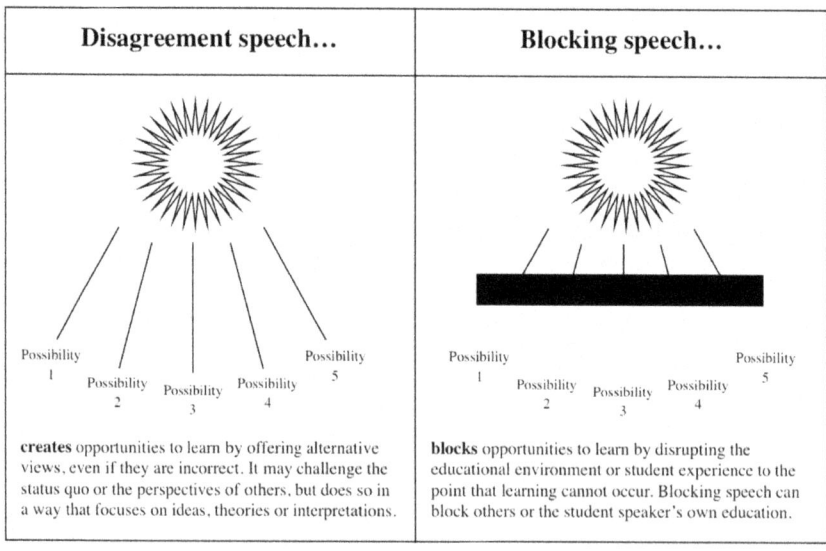

Disagreement speech...	Blocking speech...
creates opportunities to learn by offering alternative views, even if they are incorrect. It may challenge the status quo or the perspectives of others, but does so in a way that focuses on ideas, theories or interpretations.	**blocks** opportunities to learn by disrupting the educational environment or student experience to the point that learning cannot occur. Blocking speech can block others or the student speaker's own education.

5. Why Free Speech for Students at All?

The *blocking* of education doesn't necessarily have to be of others' education. We can also assess if a student's free speech blocks his or her own education. An example of this can be seen in *Settle v. Dickson County School Board*,[123] in which a high school freshman was assigned to write a research paper on any topic as long as that topic was pre-approved by the teacher. The student chose a topic and received the necessary approval, but changed her mind mid-assignment and selected a new topic without seeking permission from her teacher. The teacher refused to accept the assignment, deeming the new topic (the life of Jesus Christ) unsuitable.

This case is a blend of school speech and student speech—the assignment itself was part of the curriculum, and the rationale for requiring a pre-approval of topics was tied to the curricular purpose of the assignment.[124] The student argued that the refusal to accept her new topic was a content-based regulation of her personal speech. Looking at the *Settle* situation from the perspective of an orderly, participatory education, however, we see that in pursuing the topic of her own choice, the student was circumventing curricular standards put in place to make the assignment a meaningful educational experience. If we view this situation strictly through a student speech lens, the student was blocking her own education through her own speech.

Situations in which students use speech to disagree with their schools have been regulated in the name of disorder and discipline, but such regulation isn't always in line with the First Amendment. In *Karp v. Becken*,[125] a student was suspended for participating in a demonstration over the lunch period protesting the firing of a popular English teacher. While the Ninth Circuit had some concerns about the disruptive effect of a demonstration, the court found that the student was engaged in a constitutional protest and overturned the suspension.

When the government serves in a special capacity, such as educator, the expectation of a level of authority appears to be greater. Public education moves in several directions; in the younger years, it is vertical, with a top-down emphasis of transmitting information. As students move through the grades and greater opportunities are made available to them, education takes more of a diagonal nature, allowing for more give and take between teacher and student while still recognizing the responsibility and authority of the teacher/school.[126]

Accepting the argument that school authority is a necessity in order to provide an orderly, participatory education, however, has the potential to take students entirely out of the participatory process of education and recast them as passive recipients. A significant amount of speech within the academic environment is already controlled, as there is a finite amount of time to teach a potentially infinite curriculum. Teachers and administrators make countless decisions about what information to present, and how to present it, in an effort to ensure curricular standards are met. Students are taught one version of the facts, regardless of subject, and due to time constraints or the wishes of the district, might not be exposed to any other possible interpretations. Students are then tested on these facts and lose points if they suggest other possible answers might be correct,[127] which teachers state is as it should be, as they would not be able to effectively do their jobs if they could not penalize incorrect responses or substandard assignments.[128]

Because of the sheer amount of content control that already exists in the educational setting in the name of an effective education, we must be cautious when administrators seek to extend the ability to regulate further in the name of authority or discipline. General First Amendment theory references the chilling effect when speech is over-regulated or vaguely regulated. In a study of urban high schools, sociologist Michelle Fine called vague content-related speech regulation "silencing" and noted its power to undermine educational empowerment.[129] In one of the earliest student speech cases, a student was denied his high school diploma for making a speech about safety concerns in science classrooms and the auditorium, not because his facts were incorrect or his mode of speaking was inappropriate, but because the school believed he "intended to discredit and humiliate the board"[130] by raising the issue in the first place. Sometimes, school authority needs to be challenged, and as we've seen in teacher speech cases, it's often the people within the educational institutions who are best positioned to do so.[131]

We know government-as-educator has greater ability to regulate some of the constitutional rights of students, but the role of educator also confers additional responsibilities. The doctrine of *in loco parentis* recognizes that while schools don't have the same authority as parents when students are in their care, they have a comparable ability to take appropriate action to safeguard students and the educational environment, including regulating student speech that is threatening or dangerous.

5. Why Free Speech for Students at All?

Harmful speech has been seen as open to regulation as a part of the human condition. Mill wrote, "The only purpose for which power can be rightfully exercised over any member of a civilized community, against his will, is to prevent harm to others"[132] and Justice Abe Fortas noted dissenters should enjoy full protection under the Constitution unless the means of their dissent might cause physical injury to others.[133] Emerson's lengthy treatise on free expression also allowed for regulation of speech that qualifies as incitement or true threats.

Combine a pre-existing acceptance for the regulation of threatening or harmful speech with the added responsibility government-as-educator accepts for the safety of students, and we can see why schools are wary of the sticks and stones of student speech. Then add public perception regarding the safety of schools in a post–Columbine world, and the most off-hand comment can lead to suspension, expulsion or even arrest.

Schools, courts and speech commentators use the public perception that schools are dangerous places to justify the restriction of student rights, including speech. Yet, according to the National Center for Education Statistics (NCES), crime within secondary schools has decreased by nearly half from 1999 to 2011.[134] Perhaps even more importantly, students' perceptions of their own safety while at school improved between 1995 and 2011, from 12 percent reporting a fear of attack or harm at school to 4 percent.[135] These statistics aren't meant to minimize the crimes that have occurred on school grounds—but the NCES data do suggest that schools aren't the crime-ridden places courts would have us believe that they are, and that students are not nearly as afraid of their schools as nonstudents appear to be.

The value of an orderly and participatory education allows another opportunity to ensure alignment with nonstudent free speech doctrine, by reinforcing the idea that speech satisfying the definition of true threats, fighting words or incitement enjoys less constitutional protection. Fear does not enhance the learning process, and student speech that causes real, plausible fear of tangible harm intercepts a student's ability to learn.

In the *Jones* case mentioned earlier, the state of Arkansas heard from a student who felt concerned for her safety after a peer, with whom she'd had a falling out, gave her rap lyrics written from the point of view of a person about to violently attack a former friend. The circumstances were too similar, and the speaker had a history of aggression.

Students' Right to Speak

The entire educational environment was not impacted, but his speech blocked her ability to learn to a dramatic degree. In another Arkansas case, a student was pulled out of his class and questioned by several administrators after turning in a variety of disturbing writings to his teachers. When he claimed in court that this treatment was a violation of his right to free speech, the federal district court determined that "The First Amendment does not require a 'wait and see' approach when it comes to the safety of students"—in other words, the potential for actual violence created a blocking potential that clearly outweighed any potential free speech concern in play.[136]

More difficult are cases involving speech that is teasing, taunting or bullying without crossing the line to true threats or incitement. The anti-gay t-shirt cases give us examples of student speech that may be seen as intimidating or abusive by GLBT students, but the courts have deemed them not so dramatically abusive that these t-shirts would without question block the targeted students' abilities to participate in their education. There is also a degree of personal tolerance involved—what one person finds offensive, another may be able to ignore. We can't allow the most thin-skinned students to set the bar for speech that blocks education. The fourth value to protect student free speech is therefore:

Education's role in democracy	Socialization into communities
Speech and expression by public school students needs First Amendment protection because it helps students achieve a significant goal of modern education: to cultivate the drive and ability to engage in the rights and responsibilities of citizens in an American democracy.	Speech and expression by public school students needs First Amendment protection to allow students to experience the different levels of appropriate public discourse necessary for socialization into community.
The right of self-realization	**Effective, participatory education**
Speech and expression by public school students needs First Amendment protection because it helps students on their journey toward self-realization while they are actively pursuing self-knowledge.	Speech and expression by public school students needs First Amendment protection so students can fulfill their role in a participatory and orderly system of education. When student speech "dissents," it needs more protection, but when student speech "blocks" education, the school has a responsibility to act.

5. Why Free Speech for Students at All?

Of the four values that provide the foundational support for student free speech, the fourth value is the only value that expressly promotes regulation in some instances. Student free speech is important to an orderly and participatory education, however, because it allows a student to participate in that education—an expressive action in and of itself. In essence, this fourth value protects the other three values. The relationship among the values more accurately looks like this:

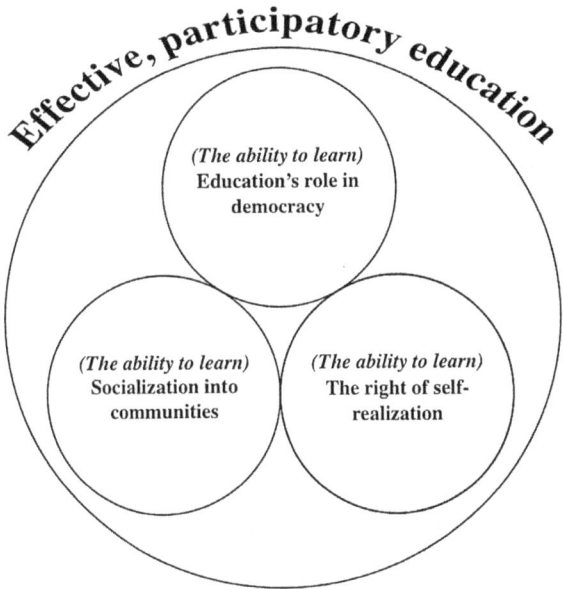

To recap, the four main values that support public student free speech are:

1. Speech and expression by public school students needs First Amendment protection because it helps students achieve a significant goal of modern education: to cultivate the drive and ability to engage in the rights and responsibilities of citizens in a U.S. democracy.
2. Speech and expression by public school students needs First Amendment protection to allow students to experience the different levels of appropriate public discourse necessary for socialization into community.

3. Speech and expression by public school students needs First Amendment protection because it helps students on their journey toward self-realization while they are actively pursuing self-knowledge.
4. Speech and expression by public school students needs First Amendment protection so students can fulfill their role in a participatory and orderly system of education. When student speech "dissents," it needs more protection, but when student speech "blocks" education, the school has a responsibility to act.

Forged from history, philosophy and the law, these four values give us a set of assumptions with which to support the concept of a positive protection of student free speech. Values give us a sense of a common language, or an agreed-upon starting point. As we dive into some of the thornier problems within the larger realm of student speech, such as student publications or cyberspeech, a shared set of core values just may get us to the adaptable, applicable solutions we seek.

6

A Foot in Both Worlds
The Special Case of Student Newspapers

Administrators at Rochester High School in Michigan had a problem. The student newspaper, *The Talon*, had tackled some challenging topics over the academic year, including stories on hookah use and sex. The newspaper ran a photo of students making a hand gesture with a double meaning, and an advertisement from a local pregnancy center. Parents were complaining, the district was concerned—the school felt the need to act.

And act it did, by creating prior review policy for the *Talon*. When students cried foul, the district publicly supported the policy, calling it a good move for the school as a whole. As *Talon* editor-in-chief Danielle Kullman told the Student Press Law Center, the district's secondary school executive director of curriculum and instruction told a *Talon* staff member "that she'd rather our paper report on all of the good things going on in the school rather than like, be a journalism class."[1]

Undoubtedly, the topics of sex or drugs are challenging for teens, which is probably why the newspaper selected them in the first place. Those topics can certainly be mishandled, which could potentially lead to a disruption in the academic environment.

Yet, prior review (the demand to review materials for suitability before distribution) may lead to prior restraint (censorship or mandatory content changes), which touches on a fundamental principle for the First Amendment. In the 1931 *Near v. Minnesota* decision, the Supreme Court vigorously protected freedom of the press from government censorship, noting, "The exceptional nature of its [the First

Students' Right to Speak

Amendment] limitations places in a strong light the general conception that liberty of the press, historically considered and taken up by the Federal Constitution, has meant, principally although not exclusively, immunity from previous restraints or censorship."[2] Subsequent cases have continued to support the idea that prior restraint or censorship by a government body on the press must meet the most stringent standards to survive constitutional challenge.[3]

The Court has also acknowledged that censorship is not only a harm in and of itself, but can also make other problems worse. In *Nebraska Press Association v. Stuart*,[4] the Court examined the constitutionality of an injunction preventing media from reporting on a high-profile murder trial in an effort to preserve the accused's right to an impartial jury. The Court questioned if the injunction would actually work:

> Finally, we note that the events disclosed by the record took place in a community of 850 people. It is reasonable to assume that, without any news accounts being printed or broadcast, rumors would travel swiftly by word of mouth. One can only speculate on the accuracy of such reports, given the generative propensities of rumors; they could well be more damaging than reasonably accurate news accounts.[5]

We might apply that same reasoning to the *Talon*—students are likely discussing sex and/or drugs, so is it truly effective to muzzle the outlet that has some kind of professional commitment to telling an accurate story?

The answer isn't that simple. K–12 student publications are valuable outlets for student expression as well as direct, hands-on opportunities to engage with the constitutional right to free press, but they also live within the school and are often generated in a classroom environment. As such, student publications like newspapers and yearbooks have one foot in the student speech world and one in the school speech world. In this chapter, we look at that unique split and how to apply what we know about student speech and press toward a thoughtful examination of the rights of student publications

A Brief Discussion of a Free Press

Attempting to capture the breadth and depth of the wide-ranging discussions on free press is a book altogether. It's worthwhile, however,

6. A Foot in Both Worlds

to briefly recap the why a free press is seen as so important that it needs a constitutional amendment to protect it.

"Congress shall make no law ... abridging freedom of speech, or of the press"[6] deliberately creates two freedoms, not one. In doing so, the founders suggested that there was something different about the press that couldn't be protected by freedom of speech alone. Otherwise, the sentence ends up being redundant—you have freedom to speak, and also to speak. Justice Potter Stewart wrote that in creating the Free Press clause of the Bill of Rights, the founders showed they envisioned the press as more than a forum for the marketplace of ideas.[7] Instead, the constitutional guarantee of a free press was intended "to create a fourth institution outside the Government as an additional check on the three official branches."[8] In essence, the Bill of Rights did what the Constitution did not: created a nongovernmental check on the work of elected officials by removing the ability to censor the watchdogs.

A great deal of the conversation about the constitutional necessity for a free press is tied to the needs of healthy democracy. If people are to make smart decisions about their elected officials, they need to know what those officials are doing. Reporters are the eyes and ears into our democratic world, and are tasked with finding and sharing the information we all need.[9]

If the media actually fulfills that role is quite another question. Because the press has fiercely maintained its right to constitutional freedom, it has lacked the "check" that it provides to the other three branches of government. In the 1940s, a group of journalism professionals and academics came together to take a serious look at their own field. The group, called the Hutchins Commission, determined that freedom of the press was under threat in part because of the press's own practices, and developed a set of principles to reaffirm journalism's commitment to accuracy, objectivity and serving society.[10]

Another concern for freedom of the press is the impact of the market. Modern media means big business—the largest media companies in the United States have annual earnings in the billions. In his exploration of the role of the press in a democratic society, Baker wrote that any form of democracy should have a legitimate concern that "the lure of profits or the competitive forces of the market could cause the press to short change its democratic role."[11] Moreover, consolidation of media ownership has narrowed the range of voices and opinions available in the marketplace of ideas; one study suggests six media companies control roughly 90 percent of the media in America.[12] If we accept the idea that the press serves as a fourth branch of government, then this consolidation results in what Baker termed "inadequate pluralism."[13]

As the internet creates a new world of opportunity for the press, these questions of representation, dedication and professionalism remain constant, as does the core idea that the press allows the people an opportunity to learn, to speak and to debate the ideas of the day. It may not play out in practice as nobly as it does in concept, but the principle of a free press remains vigorous today.

The Student Press in Public Schools

Student newspapers have been present in public high schools since the turn of the 20th century, with recorded mentions of student journalism at Decatur (Illinois) High School and Rockford (Illinois) High School in 1892.[14] High school student newspapers picked up momentum in the 1910s and 1920s, but were primarily seen as a vehicle for school spirit and a valuable tool for public relations. There was minor pushback from students who wished to engage in more journalistic writing, but by and large most student newspapers were seen more as social clubs and opportunities to obtain leadership skills as opposed to informative media outlets.[15]

The 1960s and 70s saw some perception changes about student newspapers in public schools. The *Tinker* decision suggested schools had less power to regulate student media speech, but many students still saw student newspapers as administrative mouthpieces of the "establishment."[16] Writing did start to turn away from gossip and novelty stories, however, and student journalists began to tackle more newsworthy work focusing on topics most relevant to them. The last quarter of the 20th century and the beginning of the 21st continued that trend—a 1993 study of 233 student newspapers found that 37 percent of content covered school-related events and news, followed by sports, editorials and features.[17]

Research into student media found other benefits as well. A 1976

6. A Foot in Both Worlds

study, for example, found that public high school students who engaged with their student newspaper were better media consumers overall than students who didn't.[18] The project used the student newspaper as the main source of examples and content for a semester-long course in media literacy. Students who participated in the project had "increased knowledge of the location of certain news items, ability to distinguish news articles from editorials, understanding sources of news and understanding news values."[19]

A series of studies during the past 30 years have established a correlation between participation in high school journalism and overall academic performance. A 1987 JEA report found that students who had been on a staff of a high school newspaper or yearbook had higher ACT composite scores and college freshman GPAs than students who had not participated in a publication.[20] An overview of similar studies in the 1990s and early 2000s reveal similar findings—higher grade point averages, higher test scores and more media literacy.[21] A 2009 study evaluated a group of high school publications students against non-publications students on 17 academic criteria:

> Nine of the areas involved high school and collegiate grades while eight of the areas involved scores on standardized tests taken either in high school or college. The journalism students had statistically significant higher scores in 14 of the 17 comparisons.[22]

Experience with high school journalism may do more than simply improve test scores; a 2011 project suggested that working on a student newspaper enhanced students' civic engagement and connection to communities.[23] Through focus groups with student journalists from 19 different schools, Clark and Monserrate found students infused their work with a high degree of purpose and responsibility, and as such:

> [H]igh school journalism experiences may serve less as a location for learning about politics as traditionally conceived, or even as pre-professional preparation for aspiring journalists, and more as an important avenue of socialization into an awareness of one's role within a larger collective.[24]

We can see that student press has benefits for both student journalists and student readers, helping them academically, socially and civically. If the constitutional freedom of the press was intended to give citizens an essential tool to be better citizens, we can see how student press gives students an essential tool to be better students. If constitutional freedom of the press is intended to ensure a voice of the people and help them explore ideas, we can see how the student press can fill the same role within the academic environment. And if constitutional freedom of the press can only be overridden when a highly compelling interest is at stake, then it stands to reason that freedom of the student press should only be restricted in a comparable fashion.

The Current Legal Approach to Student Publications

We covered *Hazelwood v. Kuhlmeier*[25] in Chapter 4, but to recap in case you skipped directly to this chapter: this case dealt with the decision of a high school principal to cut two pages out of the student newspaper due to concerns over libel and invasion of privacy. The student staff sued, claiming a violation of freedom of the press, and the U.S. Supreme Court found for the school. Writing for the majority, Justice Byron White stated that "educators do not offend the First Amendment by exercising editorial control over the style and content of student speech in school-sponsored expressive activities so long as their actions are reasonably related to legitimate pedagogical concerns."[26]

Within this statement is a concept worth discussing with a little more depth. "School-sponsored expressive activities" is essential to application of the *Hazelwood* precedent, as it is what defines and separates this speech from the student speech generally governed by *Tinker*. The Court noted that when student expression occurs as a result of the school's "name and resources,"[27] the school has a right to disassociate itself from speech that could reflect poorly upon it or is inconsistent with its basic mission to educate. When the student newspaper occurs in a class and is overseen by a teacher paid to teach or advise the newspaper, when it is paid for primarily from school funds and when it bears the school's "imprimatur" or mark[28] (for example, if the school's name is incorporated into the newspaper's name), the degree of association is strong enough to empower the school to act.

6. A Foot in Both Worlds

This approach has a non-educational equivalent in law: forum analysis. Just because government creates a place where communication can occur doesn't mean the public has carte blanche to use it. *Kincaid v. Gibson*[29] provides insights on the three types of forums:

Type	Definition	Example	Can be restricted based on content if ...
Traditional public forum	"a place which by long tradition or by government fiat has been devoted to assembly and debate"	Park, sidewalk	Restrictions are narrowly drawn to serve a compelling interest.
Limited (designated) public forum	An opportunity to speak that is made available "to the public at large for assembly and speech, for use by *certain* speakers, or for the discussion of *certain* subjects."	Municipal auditorium, Student center meeting rooms	Restrictions are narrowly drawn to serve a compelling interest OR if content is not appropriate to the purpose of the forum.
Nonpublic forum	Anything not fitting the two categories above; a place not opened to public expression.	Government office buildings, public hospitals	"so long as the distinctions drawn are reasonable in light of the purpose served by the forum and are viewpoint neutral"[30]

The application of forum to student newspapers looks at policy and practice to see how free students are to speak within the forum of the student newspaper. Courts look at elements like district policy, school codes of conduct, and syllabi or course descriptions for "policy," but also at how those policies were followed (or not followed) for "practice." For example, in *Hazelwood*, the school's established prior review policy and consistent practice of allowing the principal to read the paper before publication as well as demand changes overrode that students' unfounded belief that "they could publish practically anything."[31]

We can also see the analogy between forum analysis and *Hazelwood* in the Court's requirement that a school's regulation of school-sponsored student expression be "reasonably related to a legitimate pedagogical concern." This is the "reasonable manner" standard of the nonpublic forum—therefore, if a student newspaper is considered school-sponsored under the *Hazelwood* analysis, it is a nonpublic forum open to a reasonableness standard that is connected, in some way, to the school's basic educational mission.

All this legal language is well and good, but how does it play out in the real world? Application of *Hazelwood* in cases dealing with student newspapers gives us some good ideas. We focus on the states that do not have state laws created to counter the *Hazelwood* decision (or in California's case, that predated *Hazelwood*). In those eleven states, the state law is paramount: a California court in *Leeb v. DeLong*[32] stated, "The broad power to censor expression in school sponsored publications for pedagogical purposes recognized in *Kuhlmeier* is not available to this state's educators,"[33] and an Iowa state court similarly noted that "section 280.22 prohibits school officials from exercising prior restraint of student publications to the extent allowed under *Hazelwood*."[34]

Courts look seriously at the school-sponsored/imprimatur element before applying *Hazelwood*. Three cases involving independent or "underground" newspapers highlight this examination. The Ninth Circuit refused to apply *Hazelwood* to a case involving five students disciplined for circulating an "unauthorized student-written newspaper" at a student event on school grounds because the school could not establish that anyone would reasonably believe the publication was officially connected to the school or reflected its views.[35] The circuit court, along with the Seventh Circuit[36] and the state of Oregon,[37] agreed that regulation of underground newspapers with no reasonable connection to the school should be guided by *Tinker*, not *Hazelwood*.

When publications are more clearly connected to the school, courts begin to explore the nature of that connection to determine if the publication is school-sponsored or bears the school's imprimatur. Financial support is not enough—in *Romano v. Harrington,* a federal district court did not accept the school's argument that analysis could end at who funded the newspaper.[38] Instead, the court asked "the question of whether, at the time of the events in question, the contents of *The Crow's Nest* might reasonably be perceived to bear Port Richmond High's imprimatur is a genuine trial-worthy issue."[39] Two years later, a federal district court in Michigan also refused to settle the school-sponsored/imprimatur question solely on financial support, but went on to explore the stated purpose of the publication, its pedagogical goals and its facial connection to the school through its name and mission statement.[40]

The Sixth Circuit used *Hazelwood* to create a list of "intent factors" to evaluate a student publication and the applicability of the precedent.

6. A Foot in Both Worlds

Cases like *Kincaid v. Gibson*,[41] *Draudt v. Wooster*[42] and *Dean v. Utica*[43] have explored the following to figure out forum:

Cases have explored:	A limited public forum would more likely:	A nonpublic forum would more likely:
if the students produced the newspaper as part of the high school curriculum	Be an extracurricular activity or loosely affiliated, optional course	Be a class that fulfills a degree requirement
if students receive credits and grades for completing the course;	Not offer credits or grades	Offer credits and grades
if a member of the faculty oversaw the production;	Have a faculty member in a strictly advisory role	Have a faculty member integrally involved in editorial decisions
if the school deviated from its policy of producing the paper as part of the educational curriculum;	Identify the newspaper as something other than a class or educational offering	Primarily identify the newspaper as a curricular opportunity
the degree of control the administration and the faculty advisor exercise	Vest editorial power and decision-making in students	Allow the faculty adviser and administrators prior review and restraint as requested
applicable written policy statements of the board of education.[44]	Have limited forum status officially stated in district policy	Have policy that permits administrator review and/or restraint

For example, the *Arrow*, the student newspaper at issue in *Dean*, was created in a classroom by students who earned grades and credit for their work from a faculty adviser. These elements, similar to the situation in *Hazelwood*, suggested that the *Arrow* was a nonpublic forum. However, the newspaper's history of allowing students to repeat the course for credit ("the Court presumes, for example, that the course description for calculus does not state that 'students may take this class for credit more than once.'"),[45] acceptance of outside letters to the editor and guest columns, and lack of significant involvement in editorial decisions by the adviser or administrators led the court to call the *Arrow* a limited public forum.[46]

Policy is one thing, but "actual practice speaks louder than words in determining whether the government intended to create a limited public forum."[47] In *Draudt*, the federal district court noted "although the Board policies give editorial control to the advisor, the advisor testified that in practice, the students exercise much of the editorial control of the *Blade*. Importantly, the student editor, rather than the advisor, determines the content of the newspaper."[48]

The approach taken in the Sixth Circuit and its lower courts has not been universally adopted by other federal courts. The Second Circuit Court instead chose to focus primarily on policy when analyzing a school's decision to censor a student newspaper cartoon depicting stick figures in sexual positions,[49] rather than distilling some form of intent from practice.

If the student newspaper is found to be a nonpublic forum/school-sponsored, courts also need to look at the reasonableness standard to ensure that a school's actions are related to a legitimate pedagogical purpose. While the courts prefer to defer to the schools when it comes to what is good (or not) for education, that doesn't mean that a school can justify its own regulation simply by saying "because we said so." We can see this in *Desilets v. Clearview Regional Board of Education*,[50] when the New Jersey State Supreme Court deemed a middle school's decision to censor movie reviews of R-rated movies as unconstitutional. The justification—that R-rated movie reviews posed a danger to student health[51]—was a problem for the court:

> The foregoing does not mean that the school had no legitimate pedagogical concerns over the publication of articles dealing with R-rated movies or, indeed, did not in fact have an educational policy dealing with that subject. Rather, the record suggests only that such a policy, if it exists, is vaguely defined and loosely applied and that its underlying educational concerns remained essentially undefined and speculative.[52]

While we have a strong handful of cases to help us understand how courts apply *Hazelwood* to conflicts involving student newspapers, we know that just as many (if not more) situations never make it to a courtroom. A search of the Student Press Law Center's website[53] for just the first five months of 2015 reveals a California high school newspaper censored for reporting on an athletic director's resignation,[54] a Virginia high school reporter censored for investigating student use of concentrated marijuana,[55] a Michigan high school newspaper facing prior review for running a photo of a condom-wrapped banana,[56] and other similar situations. While it's highly possible that none of these situations will engage lawyers, judges and court dates, the fact that they occur incurs a cost. We have angry and

6. A Foot in Both Worlds

confused students, frustrated and confused teachers, beleaguered and confused administrators and bewildered and confused parents.

The Proactive Approach for Student Publications

The central theme to this book is that the more we understand the many working pieces that go into student speech, the better prepared we'll be to create solid, proactive policy that honors both student speech rights and an efficient and effective educational environment. This concept applies to student publications as well.

Student publications play an equivalent role within academic environments as the professional press within communities—to inform a public and give people the tools to be better participants within their society. For the professional press, we see this through a democracy lens, to prepare citizens to better engage with their civic lives. For the student press, we need to see this through an educational lens—to prepare students to better engage with their student lives.

If we reflect back to Chapter 4 and its definition of a student— "someone who is exploring theories, beliefs or institutions through an intentional and disciplined relationship with a school that is based in such exploration"—then we can tease out the role of student press as to prepare students to better engage with the exploration of theories, beliefs or institutions through an intentional and disciplined relationship with a school. Wordy? Yes, but useful nonetheless. Once we acknowledge the "why" of the student press, then we can better determine the best way to approach proactive policy.

The more pressing challenge with student publications is the separation of student speech from school speech. We can see this play out with the concept of forum in the student press cases that have made it to courtrooms. We know that schools have a right to control their own speech, and that curricular decisions are considered school speech. We know that a school can surrender control over curricular decisions to students—for example, allow them to select the topic of a paper or the subject of a performance—and when that happens, those decisions have been treated as student speech. However, even in those situations, the school retains the authority to define what a good learning

opportunity is—or isn't—and has the responsibility to act to ensure that students can learn.

To approach student press policy, then, we need to think about addressing the three Ps of student newspapers: professionalism, platform and practice.

Professionalism, the First P: What Does It Look Like, and Is It Expected and Protected?

Effective journalism needs quality in order to do its job. This quality comes in the form of writing mechanics as well as ethical standards, as can be seen through professional journalism associations such as the Society of Professional Journalists.[57] The *Hazelwood* decision also recognized that quality writing and reporting is a reasonable expectation for schools to have for their student newspapers:

> Hence, a school may in its capacity as publisher of a school newspaper or producer of a school play "disassociate itself," not only from speech that would "substantially interfere with [its] work ... or impinge upon the rights of other students," but also from speech that is, for example, ungrammatical, poorly written, inadequately researched, biased or prejudiced, vulgar or profane, or unsuitable for immature audiences.[58]

Professional journalism also adheres to existing laws, like libel and invasion of privacy. Freedom of speech and press commentators have consistently said that speech can be regulated to prevent harm to others,[59] and such an expectation of the student press only further connects it to its non-educational counterparts.

Professional expectations for student journalists should be clear and objective. In *Dean v. Utica*, a principal censored a student's article on a pending lawsuit against the school district because the principal believed the piece lacked quality.[60] Yet in federal court, the director of the journalism department at Michigan State University stated that "the journalistic quality of Dean's story is excellent for a high-school publication, and meets all of the standards for a college newspaper."[61] Such praise for the student's work cast doubt on the principal's decision to censor.

6. A Foot in Both Worlds

Platform, the Second P: Evaluating Type, Creating Content, Making Decisions, Accepting Consequences

In both mainstream press and student media, we need to deal with the issue of funding. When the bottom line becomes more important than the core purpose, we see mainstream media drift away from its democratic ideals and focus on the sensational, pop culture, and news of the weird in order to retain readers and advertisers. In student media, the question of funding threatens to define a student newspaper more than the journalism does.

To keep student media focused on its core purpose, we need to be wary of conflating "who pays" with "who decides." The publication's platform, or environment in which it is created, needs to be defined by more than simply who pays the bills so that students understand both their opportunities and responsibilities as a newspaper staff. We can better create that definition by getting away from the financial and instead focusing on who produces the content and who makes the important decisions that lead to content being created and published. The Supreme Court holds editorial independence in high regard, as noted in *Miami Herald v. Tornillo:*

> The choice of material to go into a newspaper, and the decisions made as to limitations on the size and content of the paper, and treatment of public issues and public officials—whether fair or unfair—constitute the exercise of editorial control and judgment. It has yet to be demonstrated how governmental regulation of this crucial process can be exercised consistent with First Amendment guarantees of a free press as they have evolved to this time.[62]

Platform is an element that can allow a school to give its student newspapers a lot of freedom or a lot of regulation—this definition creates the analogy to forum that will set limits around a school's ability to constrain its student newspaper. A common concern for schools is that surrendering control to the students to make editorial decisions means blindly accepting the consequences should those decisions turn out badly. That isn't a given, however. In *Yeo v. Town of Lexington*,[63] a parent sued a school after the student newspaper and yearbook rejected an ad that he wanted to place. Because the school was able to establish that students were solely responsible for editorial decisions (including decisions to accept or reject ads), Yeo could not claim that his ad was

Students' Right to Speak

censored by a state actor—it wasn't the school that turned him down, but rather the student staff.[64] Our takeaway from this is that courts can honor a school's decision to invest editorial decisions in its student staff and apply consequences appropriately.

Practice, the Third P: Trust, Test, Evaluate

Put your money where your mouth is. Talk the talk, walk the walk. Write checks your ... you get the idea. If policy and practice don't match, confusion ensues. At its most basic, that's what puts any free speech or press case into the courts—either policy and practice don't match, or someone has a fundamental misunderstanding of policy.

If policy is created thoughtfully and platform defined clearly, then practice shouldn't be a problem. Where we tend to see practice fail to meet policy is when schools rethink policy in response to a specific situation. Sticking with policy when an incident pushes the edges of it takes trust, in the policy itself as well as teachers and students.

Trust in your policy. If a situation arises that tests it, see it through and evaluate if changes are needed after the situation is over.

As we think about student press, the words of Justice Abe Fortas in *Tinker* rings true:

> Any departure from absolute regimentation may cause trouble. Any variation from the majority's opinion may inspire fear. Any word spoken, in class, in the lunchroom, or on the campus, that deviates from the views of another person may start an argument or cause a disturbance. But our Constitution says we must take this risk, and our history says that it is this sort of hazardous freedom—this kind of openness—that is the basis of our national strength and of the independence and vigor of Americans who grow up and live in this relatively permissive, often disputatious, society.[65]

Allowing a free and vigorous student press can create risk, but such a "hazardous freedom" comes with reward as well. It plays a healthy role within the educational environment as well as offers a valuable training tool for the rights and responsibilities of citizenship that wait beyond graduation. It's good for students both as media creators and consumers, and in this increasingly hypermedia-driven world, training in both media production and consumption is becoming more and more valuable.

6. A Foot in Both Worlds

There are many excellent resources to begin your student publication policy journey:

- Journalism Education Association: http://jea.org/
- Nearly every state has a state scholastic journalism association: http://jea.org/home/people/scholastic-media-associations/
- Student Press Law Center: http://www.splc.org/
- National Scholastic Press Association: http://studentpress.journ.umn.edu/nspa/
- FIRE (Foundation for Individual Rights in Education): https://www.thefire.org/
- National School Board Association: http://www.nsba.org

As schools consider how to approach this specific intersection of student speech and school speech, the three P's can be a helpful guide toward creating clarity, protecting press rights and giving schools the tools they need to continue the work that they do.

7

Facebook and Twitter and Texting, Oh My! Cyberspeech

According to the Pew Internet Project, 74 percent of all internet users were on some form of social media in 2014.[1] That number rises to 90 percent when looking just at adults aged 18–29.[2] It's been estimated that there are more than 152 million blogs on the internet worldwide.[3] And 182.9 billion emails were sent or received each day worldwide in 2014.[4] To put it simply, a lot of us use the web to communicate. Why, then, is regulating that online speech so difficult for public schools?

Part of the challenge lies in the "schoolhouse gate" imagery from *Tinker* that frames student speech. When speech and its consequences occur on school grounds or at time during which a school is clearly in authority, the question of the school's ability and responsibility to act is clear. When the speech occurs off school grounds, outside school hours and with personal technology, however, the question becomes more complex.

The solution isn't to back away and claim no authority in issues of student cyberspeech—not only do the consequences of such speech often have very real impact of academic settings, but the public education mission of developing both the academic and social student means that there are teachable moments when online speech creates harm. The solution isn't to regulate all student cyberspeech either—schools aren't prepared to police their students' actions 24/7, and there are likely very few who would want to do so.

Another challenge is fear: fear by parents, fear by schools and fear by communities swept up in high-profile stories of cyberbullying, sexting and short-term thinking with long-term consequences. Such fear can lead to hasty solutions like zero-tolerance policies and social media surveillance that give a false sense of security while teaching nothing.

Our goal here is to determine how we can align cyberspeech with student speech in general, while still accounting for the unique nature of online communication and its impact on the educational environment. There is clearly no magic solution that perfectly satisfies school needs and the right to free speech—and even if there were, it would be outdated before this book made it to readers. If we think about cyberspeech broadly, however, we can start to address these questions and get on the path to good policy.

On-Campus vs. Off-Campus Speech

Prior to *Tinker* and its emphasis on the "schoolhouse gate" as a boundary of school authority, courts found the location of student speech to be a less persuasive reason to remove students from school authority. The Wisconsin Supreme Court upheld the suspension of two young women for writing a poem poking fun at the rules of their school and taking it to the local newspaper for publication, noting, "[S]chool authorities have the power to suspend a pupil for an offense committed outside of school hours and not in the presence of the teacher which has a direct and immediate tendency to influence the conduct of other pupils while in the school room."[5] A few years later the Connecticut Supreme Court supported a school's decision to spank two boys as punishment for harassing younger female students as they walked home after the school day.[6] The proper test, the court stated, was not where the offense occurred, but "its effect upon the morale and efficiency of the school, whether it in fact is detrimental to its good order, and to the welfare and advancement of the pupils therein."[7]

After *Tinker* and the children's rights movement, courts were divided on how (or if) to apply location to the question of school authority over student speech. On one hand, a student suspended for calling his teacher a "prick" when passing him in a shopping mall on a Sunday was denied relief by a federal district court in Pennsylvania, which deemed such an insult in a public place a matter for school discipline as a way to maintain authority.[8] A federal district court in Maine, however, overturned the suspension of a student who gave his teacher "the finger" in the parking lot of an area restaurant: "The conduct in question occurred in a restaurant parking lot, far removed from any school premises or facilities at a time when teacher Clark was not associated in any way with his duties as a teacher."[9]

We'll find more guidance, however, from cases in which speech or expression was created off campus but found its way on to school grounds. *Thomas v. Board of Education*[10] dealt with four students who created a satirical off-campus newspaper patterned after the *National Lampoon*. The students tried to keep the newspaper off of school grounds but were unsuccessful, and the students were suspended after a school board member saw a copy and demanded that administrators take action.

The Second Circuit overturned the suspensions, strongly condemning the attempt by the administrator to "extend his dominion"[11] beyond the schoolhouse gate. Noting the clear intent by the students to keep the speech off campus, the court wrote:

> It is not difficult to imagine the lengths to which school authorities could take the power they have exercised in the case before us. If they possessed this power, it would be within their discretion to suspend a student who purchases an issue of National Lampoon, the inspiration for Hard Times, at a neighborhood newsstand and lends it to a school friend. And, it is conceivable that school officials could consign a student to a segregated study hall because he and a classmate watched an X-rated film on his living room cable television. While these activities are certainly the proper subjects of parental discipline, the First Amendment forbids public school administrators and teachers from regulating the material to which a child is exposed after he leaves school each afternoon.[12]

More than 20 years later, federal courts echoed the decision in *Thomas* when dealing with created-off, found-its-way-on campus student speech. One case dealt with school discipline for an unflattering "Top Ten" list created off-campus by a student about an athletic director, which a friend had copied and brought to school.[13] Another tackled a suspension for a sketch by a student depicting an attack on a school, which had been created at home two years earlier and mistakenly brought to school by the student's younger brother.[14] In both these cases, the court declined to allow the school authority over the speech because it was "not exactly speech on campus or even speech directed at campus."[15]

These examples, while helpful, don't get at the breadth and reach of cyberspeech. After all, the only people who saw the offending list or the frightening sketch were the few people who managed to get their hands on a physical copy. Cyberspeech can be shared with an infinite number of people. It's time, then, to look at how the courts have dealt with student cyberspeech (so far).

Cyberspeech and Students

Cyberspeech and students is a partnership that rivals peanut butter and jelly. One perfect place to see this is Beloit College's annual "Mindset List." Published at the start of every academic year since 1998, the list features aspects of life incoming freshmen have always taken for granted that their parents (or faculty) may not. The 2018 list began with this introduction:

> The College class of 2018, starting their first year on campus this fall, arrives with a grasp of their surroundings quite distinct from that of their mentors. Born in 1996, they have always had The Daily Show to set them straight, always been able to secure immediate approval and endorsement for their ideas through "likes" on their Facebook page, and have rarely heard the term "bi-partisan agreement." ... The digital technology that affords them privacy from their parents, robs them of their privacy amid the "big data" of the NSA and Google. How will the absence of instant on-line approval impact their performance in the classroom and work place?[16]

For the most recent generation, online speech is neither a novelty nor an alternative for communication. It is a standard tool for both interpersonal and mass communication, a way to share lives and feelings as well as learn about the world. The speed with which the Internet became a daily part of American lives, however, is a challenge for those tasked with creating and upholding policy and law. Courts were hearing cases about dial-up chat rooms while students were flocking to Facebook on their cell phones. The gulf between the speed at which technology advances and the speed with which the law can address it continues to widen.

As stories of teens committing suicide as a result of online harassment continue to make national headlines, parents and community

Students' Right to Speak

members have demanded "something" be done by *someone*. The logical "someone" seems to be the schools, which is often the force that brings victim and attackers together. Regulating cyberspeech, however, is still a regulation of speech or expression, and schools need to tread carefully to ensure that they are not creating a First Amendment conflict. There is no separate Bill of Rights for the internet, and contrary to the Marshall McLuhan axiom, the medium is not *always* the message.[17]

The First Amendment applies to all media, from the moveable-type presses that issued the first copies of the Bill of Rights to tweets discussing the merits of reality television.[18] In *Reno v. ACLU*, the Supreme Court determined the Internet was more like a newspaper than an over-the-air broadcast station in terms of constitutional protection of speech from content-based regulation by the government, even when the reason for such regulation is to protect children.[19] *Reno* reaffirmed that restrictions of otherwise protected speech had to be finely honed to achieve their goal but go *no further:* the government's attempt at shielding children from sexual material that didn't quite rise to the level of "obscenity" resulted in adults losing access to material they had a right to view.[20]

Reno acknowledged the power of the Internet to serve as a marketplace of ideas for many voices, fulfilling an important role in our modern democracy. What we can take away from this case as we look at regulating cyberspeech is that the Internet is not in and of itself enough of a reason to justify regulation. The Supreme Court has refused to treat it differently than print media, even to protect children from pornography, and subsequently we shouldn't treat it differently when exploring the limits of protection for student speech.

As with print or broadcast speech, just because one has the freedom to say something does not mean that person is free from the consequences of the speech. While some schools have attempted to impose prior restraint on students[21] or faculty[22] regarding their online speech, far more common are situations involving school discipline after cyberspeech has occurred. When these situations reach courtrooms, judges have been faced with a question that has yet to find a single answer: can a school punish a student for speech created off-campus, during non-school hours and in a forum that is not owned by the school? Or is such speech the concern of law enforcement and the courts?

7. Facebook and Twitter and Texting, Oh My! Cyberspeech

The challenge within this question isn't the time or place of speech, but rather the manner in which it is delivered, consumed and shared. The accessibility of online speech to virtually any person and at any time, with possible ripple effects to the school environment, has transformed it in many an administrator's eye into a school issue subject to regulation or discipline. In a sense, we're revisiting the cases of *Dresser*[23] or *Fenton*,[24] when the idea that speech that *might* be overheard by other students and *might* undermine the authority of school officials is more than enough reason for a school to step in and discipline a student, up to and including expulsion.

The Supreme Court has yet to weigh in on student online speech, and lower courts have taken a variety of approaches to the question. A California federal district court summed up the three main approaches taken by lower courts this way:

> First, the majority of courts will apply *Tinker* where speech originating off campus is brought to school or to the attention of school authorities, whether by the author himself or some other means. The end result established by these cases is that any speech, regardless of its geographic origin, which causes or is foreseeably likely to cause a substantial disruption of school activities can be regulated by the school.
>
> Second, some courts will apply the Supreme Court's student speech precedents, including *Tinker,* only where there is a sufficient nexus between the off-campus speech and the school. It is unclear, however, when such a nexus exists. The Second Circuit has held that a sufficient nexus exists where it is "reasonably foreseeable" that the speech would reach campus. The mere fact that the speech was brought on campus may or may not be sufficient.
>
> Third, in unique cases where the speaker took specific efforts to keep the speech off campus, or clearly did not intend the speech to reach campus and publicized it in such a manner that it was unlikely to do so, the student speech precedents likely should not apply. In these latter scenarios, school officials have no authority, beyond the general principles governing speech in a public arena, to regulate such speech.[25]

We could simplify these three approaches to:

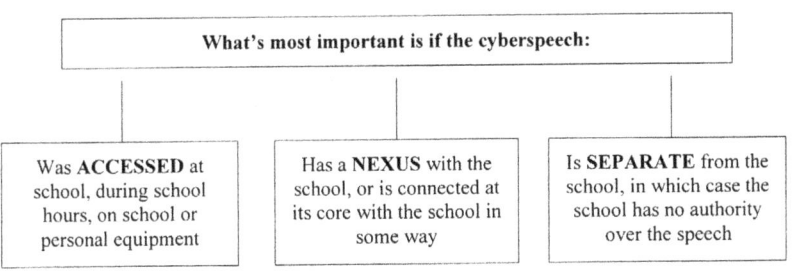

Students' Right to Speak

Exploring each approach independently gives us better insight on the concerns of schools, students and the courts.

1. *Accessed at school:* The rationale behind this argument is speech that is created off school grounds but is accessed on school grounds can be regulated by the school if it meets the *Tinker* disruption standard. From a common-sense perspective, this seems right. Once the questionable speech is accessed on school property during school hours, it is essentially re-spoken at the school, making it the same as on-campus speech. The application of this approach by the courts is often accompanied by one refinement: the likelihood or reasonable expectation of the speech finding its way to school grounds.

The question of likelihood/expectation is a good one. Schools, as we've noted, are charged with preparing students to enter a civil society, one that has many layers. By exploring the likelihood of a student's off-campus speech to make it on campus, we can see if the student is acknowledging the many layers of his or her society by attempting to keep speech in one layer. Online speech platforms can make that attempt very visible, through the deliberate selection of audiences for any specific expression. If a student is making a good-faith effort to keep speech off campus, then he or she may have a reasonable expectation that it will stay off campus. Allowing for that expectation to be a part of the analysis means we're giving students a chance to apply a valuable aspect of their social education.

However, a mere privacy setting won't do. Action and intent need to match, and lack of awareness of the actual effect of audience filters is a little like ignorance of the law: it doesn't shield a person from consequences. Take, for example, *J.S. v. Bethlehem*,[26] in which a student was suspended for creating a website that solicited donations to have a teacher murdered. The site included a lot of profanity and a clear desire for the teacher's death. When she learned of the site, the teacher experienced anxiety to the point of illness, leading her to leave her job before the end of the school year. The case was appealed up to the Pennsylvania Supreme Court, which determined the speech to be within the school's authority because it was accessed by the student and shown to others while on school property. Further, the nature of the site brought the "likelihood" element into play:

7. Facebook and Twitter and Texting, Oh My! Cyberspeech

Importantly, the web site was aimed not at a random audience, but at the specific audience of students and others connected with this particular School District; Mrs. Fulmer and Mr. Kartsotis were the subjects of the site. Thus, it was inevitable that the contents of the web site would pass from students to teachers, inspiring circulation of the web page on school property.[27]

The resulting disruption for the teacher, the teacher's classes (which had to be covered by substitute teachers) and the school environment as a whole was determined to satisfy the *Tinker* test, and the school's decision to punish the student was upheld.

Threatening speech tends to draw school attention and court support. Like *J.S., D.J.M. v. Hannibal Public School District #60*[28] dealt with violent statements made by a student, in this case via instant message to a friend. The student's repeated references to firearms and the deaths of classmates led the friend to notify school administrators, and the student was suspended. While the student claimed he was joking, the Eighth Circuit believed "it was reasonably foreseeable that D.J.M.'s threats about shooting specific students in school would be brought to the attention of school authorities and create a risk of substantial disruption within the school environment."[29]

In a less threatening case, the Wilson twins of Lee's Summit, Missouri were suspended by their high school after creating what they called a satirical website that included "a variety of offensive and racist comments as well as sexually explicit and degrading comments about particular female classmates, whom they identified by name."[30] Because the site was aimed specifically at their peers at their high school, the Eighth Circuit said it was highly likely the site could reach the school and was therefore open to school discipline.[31]

We see social media appear under the access approach to off-campus speech in *Kowalski v. Berkeley County Schools*.[32] Kowalski had created a MySpace discussion group dedicated to offensive and hateful speech about a fellow classmate. She was identified as the group's creator and suspended after the targeted student's parents complained to the school. The Fourth Circuit refused the off-campus argument, noting:

> Kowalski indeed pushed her computer's keys in her home, but she knew that the electronic response would be, as it in fact was, published beyond her home and could reasonably be expected to reach the school or impact the school environment. She also knew that the dialogue would and did take place among Musselman High School students whom she invited to join the "S.A.S.H." group

and that the fallout from her conduct and the speech within the group would be felt in the school itself. Indeed, the group's name was "*Students* Against Sluts Herpes" and a vast majority of its members were Musselman students.[33]

However, even if the access approach is being used, it's important to note that it is used in tandem with the *Tinker* standard. If the school can't show the substantial disruption (real or reasonably forecast), then the school has no standing to discipline. Take, for example, *R.S. v. Minnewaska Area School District*,[34] in which a sixth grade student was given detention for expressing her dislike for an adult hall monitor on her Facebook wall, and then suspended for posting "I want to know who the f%$# [sic] told on me."[35] The federal district court saw no disruption, real or potential, in the Facebook posts of a preteen who stated she "hated" a school employee and wanted to know who had told administrators about her postings. Subsequently, the school's actions were deemed unconstitutional.

2. *Nexus with school:* The nexus approach is similar to the access approach, but instead of exploring the speech's presence on school grounds (or likelihood of appearing on school grounds), it looks specifically at the connection between the speech and the school. If the speech was created with the intent of intersecting with the school (or can be reasonably interpreted as doing so) and satisfies the *Tinker* standard, then a school's regulation can be considered constitutional.

A good example of the nexus argument in action can be seen in *Doninger v. Niehoff*.[36] Doninger had called her school administrators "douchebags" in a blog post after the school cancelled an event she had helped plan. She encouraged other students and parents to call the school and complain, resulting in a rush of phone calls and emails to the school's main office. As a result, Doninger was banned from running for student government and her name blocked from a list of potential graduation speakers.

The nexus, the Second Circuit noted, was evident when you in that "Doninger's blog post directly pertained to an event at LMHS, that it invited other students to read and respond to it by contacting school officials, that students did in fact post comments on the post, and that school administrators eventually became aware of it."[37] The disruption was in the volume of phone calls and emails that demanded responses from administrators. Subsequently, the Second Circuit upheld the school's disciplinary measures.

7. Facebook and Twitter and Texting, Oh My! Cyberspeech

The nexus approach has also come into play with threatening speech. In *Wyner v. Douglas County School District*,[38] a student was suspended after posting to MySpace a variety of statements suggesting he was planning a school shooting. He claimed the posts were a joke, but the Ninth Circuit upheld the school's discipline, stating, "Given the subject and addressees of Landon's messages, it is hard to imagine how their nexus to the school could have been more direct."[39]

3. *Separate from school:* Of the three approaches, the idea that cyberspeech is by definition not student speech is the least used. Here we have no discussion of *Tinker* because there is no need.

In *Emmett v. Kent School District*,[40] a senior at Kentlake High School created a website to showcase the mock obituaries he and his fellow classmates had written for a school project. The site included disclaimers that it was not an official site for the school and that it was for entertainment purposes only. The student encouraged readers to suggest who should "die" next and be the subject the next fake obituary. An area television news station learned of the site and ran a story on it, characterizing it as a "hit list." The student was emergency expelled "for intimidation, harassment, disruption to the educational process, and violation of Kent School District copyright,"[41] though the expulsion was modified to a five-day suspension.

After a quick review of the three Supreme Court precedents guiding student speech (this case pre-dated *Morse*), the district court came to this quick conclusion:

> In the present case, Plaintiff's speech was not at a school assembly, as in *Fraser*, and was not in a school-sponsored newspaper, as in *Kuhlmeier*. It was not produced in connection with any class or school project. Although the intended audience was undoubtedly connected to Kentlake High School, the speech was entirely outside of the school's supervision or control.[42]

The district court did not offer any additional reason why it determined that the speech was beyond school control. *Emmett* has been cited in five subsequent cases,[43] but only one echoed *Emmett's* findings that the expression was not student speech.[44]

Emmett isn't the only case that has separated a student's cyberspeech from the school environment. In *Nixon v. Hardin*,[45] a female student's angry tweets regarding a former friend drew a suspension from her school. The girl meant them as jokes; the school heard them as threats. The federal district court saw something else:

Here, the speech had no connection to HCMS whatever other than the fact that both the speaker and the target of the speech studied there. The speech was not made at school, directed at the school, or involved the use of school time or equipment. No disruption of school activities or impact on the school environment has been shown. Thus, it is the finding of the Court that the Defendants have fallen short of establishing that summary judgment should be granted in their favor.[46]

In both *Emmett* and *Nixon*, the courts could have applied an access or nexus approach, but chose to refrain. *Emmett* was decided in 2000, which made it one of the early online speech cases, but *Nixon* was in 2013. The *Nixon* court acknowledged *Doninger, Kowalski, S.J.W.* and *Wyner* in its analysis, but deemed them irrelevant given that the tweets were off-campus and apparently not disruptive.

The challenge of inconsistency: We have three approaches to dealing with cyberspeech, but our challenge still remains. How do we know which the courts will apply in any given situation? The fact remains that we don't know—and nothing highlights this challenge more than a pair of cases out of the Third Circuit involving fake profiles of principals. In *J.S. v. Blue Mountain School District*,[47] a three-judge panel of the Third Circuit applied *Tinker* and upheld the punishment of a student who had created a mock MySpace profile of her principal on her home computer. In *Layshock v. Hermitage School District*,[48] a different three-judge panel of the Third Circuit applied *Tinker* and overturned the punishment of a student for creating a mock MySpace profile of his principal. Both parodies were somewhat crude and vulgar and both were created on home computers during non-school hours.

The two cases were reheard *en banc* by the full Third Circuit, and while the court found in favor of both students, they did so applying different approaches. In *J.S. v. Blue Mountain School District*,[49] the court evaluated the off-campus question in favor of the student by noting: "unlike the students in *Doninger, Lowery,* and *LaVine*, J.S. did not even intend for the speech to reach the school—in fact, she took specific steps to make the profile 'private' so that only her friends could access it. The fact that her friends happen to be Blue Mountain Middle School students is not surprising, and does not mean that J.S.'s speech targeted the school."[50] In *Layshock v. Hermitage School District*,[51] on the other hand, the court found in favor of the student because "[t]he School District's attempt to forge a nexus between the School and Justin's profile by relying upon his 'entering' the District's website to

7. Facebook and Twitter and Texting, Oh My! Cyberspeech

'take' the District's photo of Trosch is unpersuasive at best. The argument equates Justin's act of signing onto a web site with the kind of trespass he would have committed had he broken into the principal's office or a teacher's desk; and we reject it."[52]

Neither of the cases directly referenced each other, so it's unclear why one case took a hybrid access/nexus approach while the other specifically looked at nexus when addressing the off-campus question. Therein lies our problem: if one court looking at two factually similar cases and applying identical precedents chooses not to use the same approach to evaluate a necessary legal question—how can we reasonably expect schools to know how to approach this question proactively? Supreme Court guidance would be helpful here, but the Court rejected certiorari when both school districts appealed.[53]

Ignoring the off-campus question: Of course, some courts have found a way around the off-campus question: ignore it and settle the case on other issues. When a group of high school female students posted racy (though legal) photos of themselves at a slumber party on Facebook and were suspended from their volleyball team, an Indiana federal district court stated that the off-campus question was irrelevant because their school couldn't make the *Tinker*-standard disruption argument anyway.[54] In Washington, several students were suspended for posting a video to YouTube that featured classmates making crude or sexual gestures toward a teacher when she could not see them, as well as shots of the teacher bending over with raunchy commentary and music.[55] The federal district court decided that regardless if the video was protected as expression, the act of making it, especially the lewd actions without the teacher's knowledge or consent, was not.[56]

Moving Forward

Online speech cases are a clear example of the lag between technology and law. MySpace peaked as a social media site in December 2008,[57] but the courts were still hashing out MySpace lawsuits in 2013. The variety of approaches that various district and circuit courts have taken only further complicates the question: how far can a school reach into the digital world when students speak online?

If we take a step back and look at some of the overarching themes

Students' Right to Speak

to the court analysis of student cyberspeech, we see the following big questions:

- Was the speech created, distributed or viewed on school grounds?
- Was the speech created *because* of the school? In other words, would the student have created it if he or she were not a student?
- Did the speech intend to connect to the school?
- Did the speech cause a *Tinker*-level disruption?

This analysis does feel like it's missing, or at the very least, *assuming* a first step—is the speaker a student and is this student speech? By defining the speech by its possible audience or its intent to irritate, we lose the essential connection of speech to the student and school that places the speech under school authority. After all, such an approach could conceivably support a school's attempt to discipline speech by a non-student (though admittedly, it would be hard to imagine what that discipline might look like—suspension or expulsion doesn't mean much to someone who isn't an enrolled student.)

Remember that the Court in *Reno v. ACLU* declined to treat Internet speech differently than offline speech—the same First Amendment applies. We should be cautious, then, when looking at online student speech that we aren't regulating differently under the sole justification of protecting an audience. While the government authority in *Reno* was as "sovereign" and in student speech cases it is as "educator," the main idea of rejecting online speech regulation or punishment on the basis of one potential audience, to the loss of others, should still be recognized as important.[58]

Cases have also placed student online speech under school jurisdiction when the speech leads to other actions or disruptions at the school, regardless if it was accessed at the school. Schools can and should deal with disruptive actions during the school day or disruptive student speech, but they should be wary of trying to police speech around the clock and across cyberspace. Consider this concurrence from the *en banc* decision of *J.S. v. Blue Mountain*:

> Applying *Tinker* to off-campus speech would create a precedent with ominous implications. Doing so would empower schools to regulate students' expressive activity no matter where it takes place, when it occurs, or what subject matter it

7. Facebook and Twitter and Texting, Oh My! Cyberspeech

involves—so long as it causes a substantial disruption at school. *Tinker*, for example, authorizes schools to suppress political speech—speech "at the core of what the First Amendment is designed to protect"—if it substantially disrupts school activities. Suppose a high school student, while at home after school hours, were to write a blog entry defending gay marriage. Suppose further that several of the student's classmates got wind of the entry, took issue with it, and caused a significant disturbance at school. While the school could clearly punish the students who acted disruptively, if *Tinker* were held to apply to off-campus speech, the school could also punish the student whose blog entry brought about the disruption. That cannot be, nor is it, the law.[59]

As you think about cyberspeech from a policy perspective, ensure that it is both right for you as educators and administrators, as well as right for your students, to create a clear and consistent approach to student speech.

8

Starting Your Own Conversation About Student Speech

So now what?

It's a fair question. Understanding the many dimensions of student speech in public schools is one thing; figuring out what to do with that knowledge is quite another. A common sense application is to use it to develop a proactive student speech policy that allows students and teachers a clear sense of where and when they are empowered to act. The first step is starting the conversation.

Emerson's *System of Freedom of Expression*[1] suggests a discussion related to free speech protection or regulation should address several key elements:

- A fundamental connection between the speech in question and the purpose behind the First Amendment
- Clarity in the term "expression"
- Factors that support the speech when balanced against other compelling governmental or societal interests
- Functional definitions of terms that are critical to understanding the discussion
- Clarity in the term "abridgement," to recognize the full range of actions that may restrict speech
- Alignment with other forms of First Amendment doctrine to maintain consistency in identical situations.[2]

Through our explorations so far, we can see that these elements are equally important to the development of public school student

8. Starting Your Own Conversation About Student Speech

speech policy. When we look at student speech policy as a whole, we should have a good sense of why, as Dworkin wrote regarding academic freedom, such speech has a value "so we can judge how important it is and when it should yield to other, competing values."[3] When we start our discussions, then, we should look at the following elements:

1. Definitions of the key terms
2. A list of key values served by student free speech
3. A standard of review
4. Guidance on application

Definitions of Key Terms

Expression: It may seem self-explanatory, but a good starting point for definitions is the concept of "expression." Where the real definition is needed is when we're dealing with something other than text or the spoken word. According to the Supreme Court in *Spence v. Washington*,[4] conduct can be deemed expression if "an intent to convey a particularized message [is] present, and in the surrounding circumstances the likelihood [is] great that the message would be understood by those who viewed it."[5] The conduct must be "inherently expressive," which is to say that it can be understood as expressive on its own and not by some explanatory speech that accompanies it.[6]

An example of conduct-expression analysis is seen in *Chalifoux v. New Caney Independent School District*.[7] This case dealt with students disciplined for wearing rosaries to school contrary to school policy, created after a police liaison had learned an area gang adopted the rosary as a membership symbol. Restricting the rosaries was seen as a safety regulation to reduce the presence of gang symbols in school.[8] The students argued that the ban was an unconstitutional restriction of expression; the school claimed it was a restriction on conduct.

The federal district court began by asking if "the symbol intends to convey a particularized message and there is a 'great likelihood' that the message will be understood by those observing it."[9] While both the students and school agreed the intent in wearing the rosary was to convey a message of personal faith, the school said observers were likely to misinterpret the message. The court disagreed, stating:

Students' Right to Speak

Defendants read Plaintiffs' religious message too narrowly. Even assuming that some persons are not familiar with the rosary, undoubtedly they are familiar with the crucifix attached to the center of the rosary, which is recognized universally as a symbol of Christianity. Accordingly, there is a great likelihood that those persons unable to associate Plaintiffs' rosaries with Catholicism nevertheless, will understand that Plaintiffs are Christians. Moreover, the evidence at trial showed that wearing a rosary as a necklace is not so abnormal that persons familiar with the rosary would be unlikely to understand Plaintiffs' religious message. Therefore, the Court finds that the symbolic speech at issue in this case is a form of religious expression protected under the First Amendment.[10]

Declaring the conduct was protected expression led the court to deem wearing the rosary akin to "pure speech." The court applied *Tinker* and found no indication of disruption.[11]

The line between expression and action, Emerson noted, is often unclear, especially because "all expression has some physical element."[12] Yet by paying close attention to the expressive quality and clarity of an action, the likelihood of its intended message being understood, and the impact of regulation on that expressive nature of the conduct specifically, we can reliably separate expression from action.

Student: The definition of "student" that we've suggested here is "someone who is exploring theories, beliefs or institutions through an intentional and disciplined relationship with a school that is based in such exploration." Maybe that's more than you need—perhaps you'll decide to simply base a definition off of enrollment status. The purpose behind this definition, however, is to determine when a person is a student and *when that person isn't*. If you don't define "student," then consider defining the parameters of studenthood. Where does it start and stop in a day, a week or a year?

Student speech, therefore, is speech not only spoken by a student, but that also impacts his or her studenthood through its connection to the exploration, the intentionality, or the relationship with the school. This kind of definition may also seem obvious, but it creates space for both students and teachers to understand when student speech policy is in play.

These definitions help us shift our focus away from physical location of speech and instead toward speakers and audiences—the *people* of speech—which will help tackle the problems of cyberspeech as well. Ultimately, that's why student speech is a concern; it isn't the location of the speech, but rather the opportunities for students to speak and the impact

8. Starting Your Own Conversation About Student Speech

of their speech on others. The more we can make the policy about people, the more responsive it will be to social and technological change and in the end, we increase the likelihood of a more consistent approach.

Publications: Defining the character of student publications is a key element to a strong student speech policy. As discussed in Chapter 6, a 3-P approach (platform, practice, professional) can head off a lot of problems before they start as well as lend consistency to how issues are addressed, should they occur, but those terms still need strong definition so that everyone involved knows what they mean.

Fundamental Assumptions or Values Supporting Student Free Speech

One of the biggest ideas behind the *Tinker* decision is that speech is protected by default, and schools need to justify why it should be restricted. That can create an adversarial mindset of schools vs. students. It doesn't have to—as you discuss student speech policy, reflect on the positive aspects of free speech within an academic environment. Through exploration of law, sociology, history and philosophy, we can say that free speech for public school students has the following benefits:

Education's role in democracy	Socialization into communities
Speech and expression by public school students needs First Amendment protection because it helps students achieve a significant goal of modern education: to cultivate the drive and ability to engage in the rights and responsibilities of citizens in an American democracy.	Speech and expression by public school students needs First Amendment protection to allow students to experience the different levels of appropriate public discourse necessary for socialization into community.
The right of self-realization	**Effective, participatory education**
Speech and expression by public school students needs First Amendment protection because it helps students on their journey toward self-realization while they are actively pursuing self-knowledge.	Speech and expression by public school students needs First Amendment protection so students can fulfill their role in a participatory and orderly system of education. When student speech "dissents," it needs more protection, but when student speech "blocks" education, the school has a responsibility to act.

Students' Right to Speak

The discussion of the "why" behind student free speech is important for teachers and students alike, because it allows both groups to ground their actions in purpose. It allows us to get away from content-based or viewpoint-based arguments about speech—"you can't say that because I don't like it"—and instead asks us to explore how an expressive act actually benefits the student, the learning environment or the community. In doing so, we engage rights and responsibilities of free speech.

There is a lot of misunderstanding of the concept of "free speech," and that misunderstanding is by no means limited to minors. When radio personality Laura Schlessinger faced flak from listeners and advertisers after she used a derogatory racial term toward a caller of color, she announced she was leaving her syndicated talk show because:

> I want to regain my First Amendment rights. I want to be able to say what's on my mind and in my heart and what I think is helpful and useful without somebody getting angry, some special-interest group deciding this is the time to silence a voice of dissent and attack affiliates, attack sponsors. I'm sort of done with that.[13]

Former Miss California Carrie Prejean told the world she believed she did not get the Miss USA crown because she stated during the competition that she did not believe same-sex couples should be allowed to marry. In a press conference after the pageant, she announced:

> On April 19th, on that stage, I exercised my freedom of speech and I was punished for doing so. This should not happen in America. It undermines the Constitutional rights for which my grandfather fought for.[14]

Both of these women are, quite simply, wrong. The First Amendment protects individuals from government abridgement of speech, not from the private sector. And nowhere in the guarantee of free expression is there protection from legitimate consequences. When examples like these and others fly unchecked, however, they create a false interpretation of freedom of speech that suggests "I can say what I want and no one can do anything about it." Engaging with the "why" behind free speech encourages more thoughtful consideration of the right and the purpose it serves.

Maybe there's some eye-rolling at the previous statement—let's be clear, there's no expectation that articulating a "why" behind student free speech is going to suddenly transform a group of students into

8. Starting Your Own Conversation About Student Speech

highly introspective orators and debaters. When a problem does arise, however, a strong student speech policy that articulates the "why" aspect of free speech will give student and school common ground and common language to work through the conflict—keeping it in house and out of court.

A Clear and Functional Standard of Review

Schools already know the need for clear due process procedures. Crack open any school district policy or student code of conduct and you will find a list of disciplinary possibilities, when they'll apply, how they can be administered, how they can be appealed, and where the buck stops. That level of clarity is valuable, as it puts all relevant parties on the same page.

When crafting a student speech policy, consider bringing in a similar level of detail to create clarity and consistency. Not only is clear detail an asset to students, but to the teachers on the front lines as well. Public school teachers find themselves confronted with a need to learn, understand and apply a wide-ranging area of law, but are often given little opportunity for in-depth formal training. A 1996 survey of 731 colleges and universities nationwide showed that only 8 percent of institutions offered an undergraduate education law course, and a 2006 national survey of teachers revealed the majority had never taken a course in school law.[15] Moreover, only one state (Nevada) required teachers to complete a course in education law as a condition of licensure.[16] Other states declared an expectation that education law is a component of the undergraduate curriculum for teachers, but not necessarily as a separate class. While many teachers have the opportunity to take a course specifically addressing education law as a part of graduate studies, doing so is not a requirement for licensure.

The lack of education law training is not meant to criticize the work of teachers at any level. Teachers, Gajda points out, "are trained to become competent professionals in a multitude of domains (e.g., methods of instruction, technology, special education, [and] ethical dispositions)."[17] Expecting a level of familiarity with the law that equals that of legal professionals or the courts is unreasonable at best and at

Students' Right to Speak

worst disrespectful of the intense responsibilities of modern public schoolteachers. But the complexity of an approach to student speech law that lacks consistency puts teachers and administrators in a difficult situation, where they are as uncertain of their own rights as they are of their students.'

As Justice Thomas pointed out in *Morse*,[18] "I am afraid that our jurisprudence now says that students have a right to speak in schools except when they don't."[19] That guidance is no guidance for public schools seeking a clear direction as they tackle issues of student speech. Just as the obscenity standard could not survive as "I know it when I see it,"[20] so too does student speech need a more concrete, consistent approach.

When courts address First Amendment issues of speech, they generally ask the following questions:

1. Is this speech in an unprotected category, like obscenity?
2. Is this speech in a less protected category, like commercial speech?
3. Is the government in this situation acting as something other than sovereign (like educator, employer or landlord)?

If the court can answer "yes" to any of those questions, then it can apply a series of precedents that guide how to balance speech rights and competing rights. If all answers are "no," then the speech is assumed to have the fullest First Amendment protection possible, and the government must prove that its regulation is narrowly tailored to advance a compelling state interest. By definition, the regulation cannot be underinclusive, or it will not advance the interest, and it cannot be overinclusive, or it will not be considered narrowly tailored.

An example of this analysis, called strict scrutiny, in action can be seen in *Video Software Dealers Association v. Schwarzenegger*,[21] in which the video game industry challenged a California statute restricting sales and rentals of violent video games to minors and requiring such games to bear state-approved warning stickers:

> [T]he State has not produced substantial evidence that supports the Legislature's conclusion that violent video games cause psychological or neurological harm to minors. Even if it did, the Act is not narrowly tailored to prevent that harm and there remain less-restrictive means of forwarding the State's purported interests, such as the improved ESRB rating system, enhanced educational campaigns, and parental controls.[22]

8. Starting Your Own Conversation About Student Speech

A student speech policy can develop a similar approach to determine if speech is open to discipline by the school. There are clearly forms of speech that are not protected by the First Amendment. *Fraser*,[23] *Hazelwood*,[24] and *Morse*[25] created some "less protected" categories of student speech: speech that is "vulgar and offensive,"[26] "school-sponsored"[27] or "promoting illegal drug use"[28] respectively. Everything else is addressed through the educational strict scrutiny of *Tinker*, where the "material or substantial interference"[29] is the compelling interest, and the requirement that the school either be certain or reasonably certain such an interference is likely[30] is the narrow tailoring.

If we're thinking about a standard of review in student speech policy, we might structure it around the following questions:

Ask	Because
1. Is this type of speech unprotected in general?	If the speech is obscene, defamatory or threatening, it lacks protection. These areas of speech law have some pretty specific definitions.
2. What kind of speech are we dealing with? Student speech? Student press? Something else?	Taking this step ensures that you're working with speech that's clearly under your authority.
3. Does the speech clearly advocate illegal drug use?	The *Morse* precedent says "a principal may, consistent with the First Amendment, restrict student speech at a school event, when that speech is reasonably viewed as promoting illegal drug use."
4. Is the speech school-sponsored, in a nonpublic forum and/or bear the school's imprimatur?	The *Hazelwood* precedent tells us that speech can be regulated for a legitimate pedagogical purpose.
5. Is the speech clearly lewd or vulgar and lack social/political meaning?	The *Fraser* precedent says "The First Amendment does not prevent the school officials from determining that to permit a vulgar and lewd speech ... would undermine the school's basic educational mission."
6. Does this speech lack educational value and pose a disruptive risk?	This question combines the value inherent in free speech for students with the *Tinker* standard to balance student rights with the needs of the educational environment.

How a finished policy will look on paper will differ from district to district, state to state. A model policy here will actually not be helpful—

Students' Right to Speak

speech policies must reflect the specific needs of their communities and be couched in the voice of their learning environments. A perfect policy for a rural district in the Midwest may be a poor fit for an urban setting on the West Coast. The basics of strong policy, however, can be addressed with the information discussed thus far. A good policy includes a rationale/reason, statement of purpose, guide on implementation, suggestions on evaluation, and definitions of key terms.[31] We've touched on all of those:

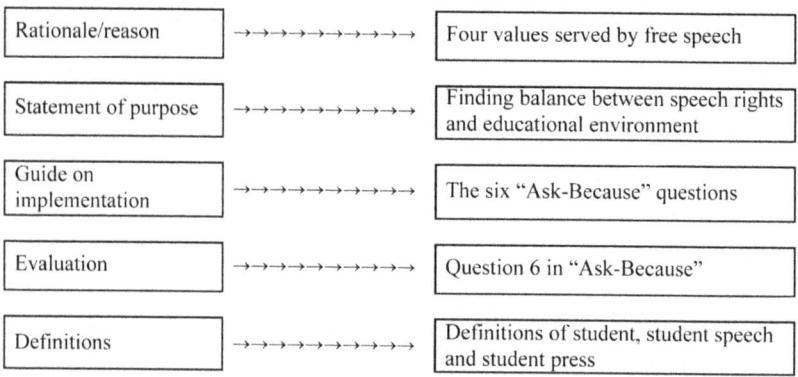

These ideas can help you think about how you might structure and discuss a solid student speech policy can bring a level of detail and thoroughness to the work that will help it create a place for free speech to thrive and ensuring an efficient educational environment.

There is value in student speech policies, especially in their impact on the day-to-day work of the school. The impact of such policy can feed into a school's or district's goal to prepare its students for the rights and responsibilities of a democracy by giving them the space to explore free speech under the guidance of trained professionals dedicated to their cognitive and social growth.

Strong student speech policy can also help avoid the uncertainty of the courts. The prevailing ad hoc approach to student speech cases in state and federal courts has led to a confusing range of precedents that offers little guidance and leads to conflicting outcomes in similar situations, even within the same jurisdiction. Students become frustrated and uncertain about their democratic rights, schools spend time and money (both in short supply) working through the legal process,

8. Starting Your Own Conversation About Student Speech

individual teachers or administrators experience their own self-doubt and concern for their careers and courts struggle to reconcile the situations before them with the limited precedential guidance given by the Supreme Court. Even the courts recognize that their decisions often make the overall picture cloudier rather than clearer:

> A reasonable school official facing this question for the first time would find no "pre-existing" body of law from which he could draw *clear guidance and certain conclusions*. Rather, a reasonable school official would encounter a body of case law sending inconsistent signals as to how far school authority to regulate student speech reaches beyond the confines of campus.[32]

There are many who would argue that student speech is not worthy of First Amendment protection due to the immaturity of the speakers and the need for school authority, and many who would argue that students will not use the right to free speech responsibly. By preventing students from experiencing those rights and responsibilities first-hand, however, schools create a self-fulfilling prophecy that has far-reaching effects.[33] Students who are conditioned to be compliant and told they are not free to express their opinions or share their perspectives are simply not going to do so, creating a mindset that may carry into adulthood and discourage them from participating in their political or civic lives.[34] Consider Putnam's work in *Bowling Alone*[35] and his documented drop in civic engagement in younger generations. While the causes of this drop are many (Putnam singles out television), we don't strengthen efforts to improve civic engagement by daily placing students in a controlled environment where they are told their opinions are not welcome and lack merit.

Students need to be "trained in democratic processes."[36] The "what" and "why" of free speech, like other constitutional responsibilities, must be nurtured so students are confident not only that they can use it, but that they *should* use it. As the Second Circuit noted in *James v. Board of Education*[37]:

> It would be foolhardy to shield our children from political debate and issues until the eve of their first venture into the voting booth. Schools must play a central role in preparing their students to think and analyze and to recognize the demagogue. Under the circumstances present here, there was a greater danger that the school, by power of example, would appear to the students to be sanctioning the very "pall of orthodoxy," condemned in *Keyishian*, which chokes freedom of dissent.[38]

Students' Right to Speak

It's clear that schools and communities are aware of the civic drop-off discussed by Putnam and are working to address it through civic engagement initiatives at both the K–12 and college/university level. High schools have introduced community service requirements for graduation, and colleges have created elaborate engagement programs that offer credit opportunities while improving local or wider communities. Such opportunities for involvement have been shown to help people "affiliate, commit, and to feel responsible to groups larger than themselves."[39] A stronger protection of free speech for students walks hand-in-hand with civic engagement efforts, for learning how to share opinions about our civic lives, even (and especially) conflicting opinions, is an essential aspect of democracy.[40]

If civic engagement must be taught, so too must the most basic precepts of free expression. Without specific instruction, Backus notes, "students are incapable of using their freedom of speech effectively, let alone understanding the rationale and purpose of protected speech and the need for self-constraint and civility."[41] Teaching through experience and allowing students to make mistakes and learn from them can help instill First Amendment values that feed into greater civic and political engagement. Proactive student speech policies create the space to allow these techniques to occur and flourish.

Youth and inexperience have long been the rationale for restricting freedom, out of concern for the individual or the community. If you agree with a minimum age to drink, drive, vote, serve in the military, marry or enter into legal contracts, you likely do so either overtly or subconsciously with protection in mind, to keep people safe from themselves or each other. Yet "youth" and "immaturity" are not synonyms. In a dissent to *Ginsberg v. New York*, Justice Douglas wrote, "If the problem of state and federal regulation of 'obscenity' is in the field of substantive due process, I see no reason to limit the legislatures to protecting children alone. The 'juvenile delinquents' I have known are mostly over 50 years of age."[42]

More importantly, and more relevant to this discussion, when people assume the role of "student," they do not automatically assume the same status as "children." Students of all ages share a common goal of learning, and are subject to the common authority of government-as-educator as opposed to government-as-sovereign. They share a common need for the freedom to test ideas in the marketplace of ideas that

8. Starting Your Own Conversation About Student Speech

is their learning environment, and to express opinions that help them learn to navigate the social mores that will guide their nonstudent lives.

Freedom of speech for students in public schools is not about taking authority away from schools or tying the hands of teachers and administrators as they engage in one of society's highest callings—the education of the next generation. One law text written for public school teachers closed by stating, "One objective of this book has been to alleviate educators' fears that the scales of justice have been tipped against them."[43] It is a sad state of affairs if teachers feel the law is working against rather than for them. The purpose here, with creating a strong student speech policy, is to offer teachers and administrators a tool by which to better assess the constitutional protections of student speech, avoid legal challenges, preserve their curricular speech and enhance the learning opportunities of their students.

Free speech carries with it tremendous power. Free speech has raised countries and brought tyrants low. It has been wielded by heroes and villains, by saviors and despots. It is wonderful and it is frightening. But it is also necessary, so necessary that we must allow our students to learn and experience it so that they may use it well and wisely. To restrict it is to hold students back from attaining the civic and political awareness they will need in a system of self-government. To offer free speech to students is a risk, but a worthy one:

> But our Constitution says we must take this risk; and our history says that it is this sort of hazardous freedom—this kind of openness—that is the basis of our national strength and of the independence and vigor of Americans who grow up and live in this relatively permissive, often disputatious, society.[44]

Chapter Notes

Introduction

1. To be honest, I don't know if it was balmy. But the circumstances suggest it would be.
2. Lander v. Seaver, 32 Vt. 114 (Vt. 1859).
3. *Id.* at 120.
4. 393 U.S. 503, 506 (1969).
5. 551 U.S. 393, 410 (2007) (Thomas, J. concurring).
6. *See* Lawrence Alexander & Paul Horton, *The Impossibility of a Free Speech Principle*, 78 NW. U. L. REV 1321 (1983–84).
7. *See* J.S. v. Blue Mountain School District, 650 F.3d 915 (3d Cir. 2011) (en banc) and Layshock v. Hermitage School District, 650 F.3d 205 (3d Cir. 2011) (en banc). These cases both dealt with students suspended for creating mock profiles of their principals on MySpace. The cases were heard by separate three-judge panels from the Third Circuit. Layshock won, J.S. did not. The two cases were heard by the Third Circuit *en banc*, which held for the students. The U.S. Supreme Court declined certiorari.
8. Martin Redish & Kevin Finnerty. *What did you learn in school today? Free speech, values inculcation and the democratic-educational paradox.* 88 CORNELL L. REV 62, 66 (2002).
9. "Schools" in this text generally means "public schools," unless otherwise specified. Private schools are not government actors and therefore are not fully subject to the First Amendment.
10. *See* Betsy Levin, *Educating Youth for Citizenship: The Conflict between Authority and Individual Rights in the Public School*, 95 YALE L.J. 1647, 1649 (1985).
11. ANNE DUPRE, SPEAKING UP: THE UNINTENDED COSTS OF FREE SPEECH IN PUBLIC SCHOOLS 2 (Harvard University Press 2009).
12. Richard Roe, *Valuing Student Speech: The Work of the Schools as Conceptual Development*, 79 CAL. L. REV 1269, 1330 (1991).
13. JACK NELSON, CAPTIVE VOICES 133 (Schocken Books 1974).
14. MF Hertz & C. David-Ferdon, *Electronic Media and Youth Violence: A CDC Issue Brief for Educators and Caregivers* (Centers for Disease Control, 2008). The CDC defines "electronic aggression" as "any type of harassment or bullying (teasing, telling lies, making fun of someone, making rude or mean comments, spreading rumors, or making threatening or aggressive comments) that occurs through email, a chat room, instant messaging, a website (including blogs), or text messaging." Hertz at 3.
15. Redish *supra* note 8.
16. Josh Davis & Josh Rosenberg, *The Immanent Structure of Free Speech Doctrine: Bong Hits, Jesus, and the Role of Public Schools in Controlling Student Speech*, Electronic copy available at: http://ssrn.com/abstract=1206314 (2008) at *74.
17. Eisner v. Stamford Board of Education, 440 F.2d 803, 807 (2d Cir. 1971).
18. 381 U.S. 479 (1965).
19. Robert Bork, *Neutral Principles and Some First Amendment Problems*, 47 IND. L.J. 1, 9 (1971–72).
20. Richard Garnett, *Can There Really be "Free Speech" in Public Schools?*, 12 LEWIS & CLARK L. REV. 45, 58 (2008).
21. For more discussion of this concept, see Garner Weng, *Type No Evil: The Proper Latitude of Public Education Institutions*

in *Restricting Expressions of Their Students on the Internet*, 20 HASTINGS COMM. & ENT. L. J. 751, 801 (1997–98).

22. LaVine v. Blaine School District, 279 F.3d 719, 726 (9th Cir. 2002) (Reinhardt, Judge dissenting).

23. Full examination of Tinker v. Des Moines is coming. Keep reading.

24. Douglas Laycock, *High-Value Speech and the Basic Educational Mission of a Public School: Some Preliminary Thoughts*, 12 LEWIS & CLARK L. REV. 111, 113 (2008).

25. Diane Ravitch, *Education and Democracy* in MAKING GOOD CITIZENS: EDUCATION AND CIVIL SOCIETY 15, 16 (Diane Ravitch & Joseph Viteritti, eds., 2001).

26. CHARLES BEARD, THE UNIQUE FUNCTION OF EDUCATION IN AMERICAN DEMOCRACY 17 (National Education Association 1937).

27. Bruce Boston & Barbara Gomez, *Every Student a Citizen: Creating the Democratic Self* 3 (Education Commission of the States 2000).

28. National Center for Education Statistics, *The Nation's Report Card: Civics 2010* 8, 18, 35 (U.S. Department of Education 2011).

29. Beard *supra* note 26 at 46.

30. *See* GERALD GRANT, THE WORLD WE CREATED AT HAMILTON HIGH (Harvard University Press 1988).

31. *See* MICHELLE FINE, FRAMING DROPOUTS: NOTES OF THE POLITICS OF AN URBAN HIGH SCHOOL (State University of New York Press 1991).

32. *See* Pickering v. Board of Education, 391 U.S. 563 (1968) and Connick v. Myers, 461 U.S. 138 (1983).

33. *See* John Garvey, *Children and the First Amendment*, 57 TEX L. REV. 321 (1979).

34. Garnett *supra* note 20.

35. *See* ROBERT PUTNAM, BOWLING ALONE (Simon & Schuster 2000).

Chapter 1

1. National Center for Education Statistics, *Fast Facts: Back to School Statistics*, INSTITUTE OF EDUCATION SCIENCES, http://nces.ed.gov/fastfacts/display.asp?id=372 (last visited May 24, 2015). The data did not specify how many students in either group were 18, but NCES data did show that of the 68% of all people aged 18–19 attending public schools, only 19% were still in a secondary school while the remaining 49% of attendees were in college or university.

2. Paul Baier, *The Constitutionality of Minimum Age Requirements for Public Office: Reading Joseph Story on Constitution Day*, 60 LA. L. REV 481, 491 (2000). Baier recounts the story of a person from Missouri who attempted to have his age assessed from date of conception, as the Missouri General Assembly had declared life begins at conception. The Eighth Circuit rejected this argument, as conception dates are hazy while birth dates are concrete. Stiles v. Blunt, 912 F.2d 260, 269 (8th Cir. 1990).

3. Oliver Wendell Holmes, Jr., *Law in Science and Science in Law*, 12 HARV. L. REV. 443, 457 (1899).

4. Elizabeth Scott, *The Legal Construction of Childhood*, 13 (December 2000) available at http://papers.ssrn.com/paper.taf?abstract_id=244666.

5. *See* Anne Dailey, *Children's Constitutional Rights*, 95 MINN. L. REV. 2099 (2011).

6. The states' motivation was also financial—the Voting Rights Act Amendments of 1970 required states to allow 18-year-olds to vote in federal elections, but could not mandate the same age requirement for state elections. However, if states wanted to maintain a 21-year-old state voting age, they would have to conduct separate elections, using separate ballots. Such an effort would have been both expensive and a logistical nightmare. *See* Oregon v. Mitchell, 400 U.S. 112 (1970).

7. JOHN S. MILL, ON LIBERTY 11 (W.W. Norton & Company 1975) (1859).

8. *Id.*

9. Forty-five states prohibit minors from getting tattoos. Thirty-eight of those states also prohibit body piercing on minors without parental permission. National Conference of State Legislatures, *Tattoos and Body Piercings for Minors*, http://www.ncsl.org/issues-research/health/tattooing-and-body-piercing.aspx (last visited June 24, 2015).

10. *See* Judith McMullen, *Underage Drinking: Does Current Policy Make Sense?* 10 LEWIS & CLARK L. REV. 333 (2006).

11. *Id.* at 360.

Chapter Notes—1

12. *An Overview of Minors' Consent Law*, STATE POLICIES IN BRIEF (Guttmacher Institute, Jul. 2015).
13. 428 U.S. 52 (1976). Two physicians brought suit in this case against a Missouri statute that, among other things, required written consent from a parent or guardian before allowing for an abortion of an unmarried woman under age 18. The Court determined the State could not constitutionally impose a blanket parental consent requirement as a condition for an unmarried minor's abortion. *Planned Parenthood* 428 U.S. at 72–75.
14. 443 U.S. 622 (1979). The case examined a Massachusetts statute that required parental consent for a minor's abortion, though denial of consent could be overridden by a court if the minor showed "good cause." The Court determined the law created a "parental veto" and unconstitutionally withheld the right of a mature and competent minor to make decisions over her own body.
15. Privileges are opportunities to engage in activities, and can be withheld or canceled without extensive due process. Rights have more legal protection if the government attempts to withhold them.
16. In many states, driving is a graduated privilege, with restricted rights between ages 16 and 18 and full privileges after 18. McMullen *supra* note 10 at 360.
17. 390 U.S. 629 (1968).
18. *Id.* at 643.
19. *Id.* at 642–43.
20. Insert your own joke here.
21. U.S. CONST. amend. XXVI. Congress had amended the Voting Rights Act in 1970 to allow 18-year-olds to vote, but the Supreme Court declared in *Oregon v. Mitchell* that the amendment could only apply to federal elections, not state and local (see *supra* note 6). To avoid a significant amount of electoral confusion about who could vote where/when, the states quickly moved to ratify the 26th Amendment in 1971.
22. Wynell Schamel, *The 26th Amendment and Youth Voting Rights*, 60 SOCIAL EDUC. 374, 374 (1996).
23. *Id.*
24. U.S. CONST. article I, § 2.
25. U.S. CONST. article I, § 3.
26. U.S. CONST., article II, § 1.
27. Baier, *supra* note 2 at 486.
28. 387 U.S. 1 (1967).
29. Roper v. Simmons, 543 U.S. 551 (2005).
30. Graham v. Florida, 130 S. Ct. 2011 (2010).
31. National Minimum Drinking Age Act, 23 U.S.C. § 158 (1984).
32. KERN ALEXANDER AND M. DAVID ALEXANDER, AMERICAN PUBLIC SCHOOL LAW, 6TH EDITION 258 (Thomson West 2005).
33. 4 Whart. 9 (Pa 1838). This Supreme Court of Pennsylvania case upheld the removal of a child from her parents, who were deemed unfit, and her placement in a state-run facility.
34. Scott *supra* note 4 at 6 fn10.
35. 321 U.S. 158 (1944).
36. *Id.* at 166–67 (internal citations omitted).
37. KEVIN SAUNDERS, SAVING OUR CHILDREN FROM THE FIRST AMENDMENT 122 (New York University Press 2003).
38. Ginsburg v. New York, 390 U.S. 629 (1968). The Supreme Court, however, was careful to point out that parents could still purchase such material for their children. Blocking the direct sale to minors was deemed in both the child's and society's best interest.
39. FCC v. Pacifica Foundation, 438 U.S. 726 (1978). The Court again pointed out parents had the ability to purchase objectionable material for their children, but for the good of all, indecent material could be directed to time slots when children were less likely to be in the audience. In both *Pacifica* and *Ginsburg*, *parens patriae* was not explicitly invoked, but the actions taken are consistent with that doctrine.
40. Reno v. ACLU, 521 U.S. 844 (1997). The statute also failed on vagueness and overbreadth.
41. Dailey *supra* note 5 at 2105.
42. *See* Pierce v. Society of Sisters, 268 U.S. 510 (1925).
43. *See* Mozert v. Hawkins County Public Schools, 827 F.2d 1058 (6th Cir. 1987), in which parents contested the reading curriculum, stating it encouraged anti–Christian sentiment, or Fields v. Palmdale School District, 447 F.3d 1187 (9th Cir. 2006), in which parents sought to have a survey on sexual attitudes suppressed.
44. *See* Griswold v. Driscoll, 616 F.3d 53 (1st Cir. 2010). Parents contested the use of a textbook that they claimed unfairly represented Turkish culture and history.

Chapter Notes—1

45. *See* Board of Education v. Pico, 457 U.S. 853 (1982). This very confusing plurality decision appeared to come to some consensus that materials could not be removed from a library solely because parents disagreed with the viewpoints presented.
46. *Fields* 447 F.3d at 1190.
47. 262 U.S. 390 (1923).
48. *Id.* at 403.
49. 406 U.S. 205 (1972).
50. *Id.* at 221–222.
51. Jacob Tabor, *Students' First Amendment Rights in the Age of the Internet: Off-Campus Cyberspeech and School Regulation*, 50 Boston Coll. L. Rev 561, 573 (2009).
52. Randall Bowden, *Evolution of Responsibility: From In Loco Parentis to Ad Meliora Vertamur*, 127 Educ. 480, 480 (2007).
53. 294 F.2d 150 (5th Cir. 1961).
54. *Id.* at 157–58.
55. 469 U.S. 325 (1985).
56. Trachtman v. Anker, 563 F.2d 512, 516 (2d Cir. 1977).
57. Betsy Levin, *Educating Youth for Citizenship: The Conflict between Authority and Individual Rights in the Public School*, 95 Yale L.J. 1647, 1678 (1985).
58. 478 U.S. 675 (1986).
59. *Id.* at 681.
60. 551 U.S. 393 (2007).
61. *Id.* at 408.
62. LaVine v. Blaine School District, 257 F.3d 981, 987 (9th Cir. 2001).
63. Nan Stein, *Bullying or Sexual Harassment? The Missing Discourse of Rights in an Era of Zero Tolerance*, 45 Ariz. L. Rev. 783, 792 (2003).
64. S.G. v. Sayreville, 333 F.3d 417 (3d Cir. 2003). The suspension was upheld.
65. Stein *supra* note 63 at 792. This situation was settled out of court.
66. *LaVine* 257 F.3d at 981. The Ninth Circuit affirmed the emergency expulsion, but granted the parents' request to have negative documentation removed from their son's academic file after he passed psychological screenings.
67. Jones v. Arkansas, 347 Ark. 409 (Ark. 2002). The Supreme Court of Arkansas upheld the school's actions.
68. Cuff v. Valley Central School District, 677 F.3d 109 (2d Cir. 2012).
69. Davis v. Monroe County Board of Education, 526 U.S. 629 (1999).
70. Title 20 U.S.C. §§1681–1688, prohibiting discrimination within public schools based on gender.
71. *Davis* 526 U.S. at 653–54.
72. "Dear Colleague" Letter from Russlyn Ali, Assistant Secretary for Civil Rights, U.S. Department of Education Office for Civil Rights (Oct. 26, 2010).
73. Charles Beard, The Unique Function of Education in American Democracy 17–20 (National Education Association 1937).
74. Charles Beard, Mary Beard & William Beard, The Beards' New Basic History of the United States 75 (Doubleday & Co. 1968).
75. *Id.* at 76.
76. *Id.* at 211.
77. John Eastman, *When Did Education Become a Civil Right? An Assessment of State Constitutional Provisions for Education 1776–1900*, 42 Am. Journ. Legal Hist 1, 22 (1998).
78. Diane Ravitch, *Education and Democracy* in Making Good Citizens: Education and Civil Society, 15, 18–20 (Diane Ravitch & Joseph Viteritti, eds, Yale University Press 2001).
79. *Id.* at 24.
80. Arthur Powell, Eleanor Farrar & David Cohen, The Shopping Mall High School: Winners and Losers in the Educational Marketplace 267–275 (Houghton Mifflin Company 1985).
81. Richard Arum, Judging School Discipline: The Crisis of Moral Authority 51–60 (Harvard University Press 2003).
82. Wilson v. Board of Education of the City of Chicago, 137 Ill. App. 187, 194 (Ill. App. Ct. 1907). Wilson was contesting a district-wide rule banning members of "secret societies" from participating in school activities.
83. State ex rel Dresser v. District Board of School District No. 1, 135 Wis. 619, 624 (Wis. 1908).
84. Pugsley v. Sellmeyer, 158 Ark. 247, 252 (Ark. 1923).
85. School District of Abington Township v. Schempp, 374 U.S. 203, 279 (1963) (emphasis added). *See also* Trachtman v. Anker, 563 F.2d 512, 519 (2d Cir. 1977): "[I]t is not the function of the courts to reevaluate the wisdom of the actions of state officials charged with protecting the health and welfare of public school students."

86. 529 U.S. 217, 232 (2000). In this case, a student contested the use of segregated student fees to fund activities with which he did not agree, aligning the practice with compelled speech.
87. 432 F.3d 606, 611 (5th Cir. 2005).
88. Nuxoll v. Indian Prairie School District #204, 523 F.3d 668, 671 (7th Cir. 2008).
89. Walz v. Egg Harbor Township Board of Education, 342 F.3d 271 (3d Cir. 2003) or Morgan v. Swanson, 659 F.3d 359 (5th Cir. 2011).
90. Scott v. School Board of Alachua County, 324 F.3d 1246 (11th Cir. 2003) or Hardwick v. Heyward, 711 F.3d 426 (4th Cir. 2013).
91. Bruce Hafen, *Developing Student Expression Through Institutional Authority: Public Schools as Mediating Structures*, 48 Ohio St. L. J. 663, 664 (1987).
92. James Ryan, *The Supreme Court and Public Schools*, 86 Va. L. Rev. 1335, 1340 (2000).
93. "[C]onstitutional rights do not mature and come into being magically only when one attains the state-defined age of majority. Minors, as well as adults, are protected by the Constitution and possess constitutional rights." *Planned Parenthood of Central Missouri v. Danforth*, 428 U.S. 52, 74 (1976).

Chapter 2

1. School District of Abington Township v. Schempp, 374 U.S. 203, 230 (1963) (Brennan, J. concurring) (emphasis added).
2. *See* Ingraham v. Wright, 430 U.S. 651 (1977). The decision clarified, however, that corporal punishment could be banned by state law.
3. This topic will be discussed at length in the next chapter.
4. For greater discussion on this split, see James Ryan, *The Supreme Court and Public Schools*, 86 Va. L. Rev. 1335 (2000).
5. *Id.* at 1338.
6. *Id.* at 1340.
7. U.S. Const. amend. I.
8. United States v. Seeger, 380 U.S. 163, 176 (1965).
9. Wisconsin v. Yoder, 406 U.S. 205 (1972): "The very concept of ordered liberty precludes allowing every person to make his own standards on matters of conduct in which society as a whole has important interests." *Yoder* 406 U.S. at 215–16.
10. *See* Everson v. Board of Education, 330 U.S. 1, 8–16 (1947). Jefferson's quote came from a letter written to the Danbury Baptist Association, *see* Reynolds v. United States, 98 U.S. 145, 164 (1879).
11. 330 U.S. 1 (1947). This case struck down a New Jersey program that reimbursed busing costs to families who sent their children to parochial school.
12. *Id.* at 15–16 (emphasis in original).
13. *See, e.g.* Employment Services v. Smith, 494 U.S. 872 (1990) (Free Exercise does not protect use of peyote in religious ceremonies contrary to state law) or Church of Lukumi Babulu Aye v. City of Hialeah, 508 U.S. 520 (1993) (Santeria church does not have constitutional right to engage in animal sacrifice as a religious ceremony).
14. 374 U.S. 398 (1963).
15. *Id.* at 402 (internal citations omitted).
16. 333 U.S. 203 (1948).
17. *Id.* at 210.
18. Pierce v. Society of Sisters, 268 U.S. 510 (1925).
19. 827 F.2d 1058 (6th Cir. 1987).
20. *Id.* at 1064.
21. *Id.* at 1070.
22. 370 U.S. 421 (1962).
23. *Id.* at 425.
24. 374 U.S. 203 (1963).
25. *Id.* at 226.
26. 472 U.S. 38 (1985).
27. *Id.* at 70–71 (O'Connor, J. concurring).
28. *Id.* at 60.
29. *Id.*
30. 505 U.S. 577 (1992).
31. *Id.* at 589.
32. *Id.* at 593.
33. 454 U.S. 263 (1981).
34. *Id.* at 274 n14.
35. 515 U.S. 819, 839 (1995).
36. 496 U.S. 226 (1990).
37. 20 U.S.C. § 4071.
38. *Mergens* 496 U.S. at 250.
39. Slotterback v. Interboro School District, 766 F. Supp. 280 (E.D. Pa. 1991), Peck v. Upshur County Board of Education, 155 F.3d 274 (4th Cir. 1998) and Leal v. Everett, 2015 U.S. Dist. LEXIS 20167 (W.D. Wash. 2015).
40. Chalifoux v. New Caney Independ-

Chapter Notes—3

ent School District, 976 F. Supp. 659 (S.D. Tex. 1997).
41. *See* Peck v. Upshur, 155 F.3d 274 (4th Cir. 1998).
42. 347 U.S. 483 (1954).
43. 163 U.S. 537 (1896).
44. *Brown* 347 U.S. at 493.
45. *Id.* at 494.
46. 518 U.S. 515 (1996).
47. *Id.* at 545–546.
48. Title IX of the Education Amendments of 1972, 86 Stat. 373, as amended, 20 U. S. C. § 1681(a): "No person in the United States shall, on the basis of sex, be excluded from participation in, be denied the benefits of, or be subjected to discrimination under any education program or activity receiving Federal financial assistance."
49. The Supreme Court held in *Cannon v. University of Chicago* (441 U.S. 677, 1979), that Title IX is also enforceable through an implied private right of action, and in *Franklin v. Gwinnett County Public Schools* (503 U.S. 60, 1992), that plaintiffs may pursue monetary damages.
50. Gebser v. Lago Vista Independent School District, 524 U.S. 274 (1998).
51. Davis v. Monroe County Board of Education, 526 U.S. 629 (1999).
52. U.S. CONST. amend. IV.
53. U.S. CONST. amend. XIV.
54. 469 U.S. 325 (1985).
55. *Id.* at 333.
56. Id. at 341–42. (internal citations omitted).
57. For greater discussion of this concept, see J.M. Sanchez, *Expelling the Fourth Amendment from American Schools: Students' Rights Six Years After T.L.O.*, 21 J.L. & EDUC. 381 (1992).
58. *See* Klump v. Nazareth Area School District, 425 F. Supp. 2d 622 (E.D. Pa. 2006) or J.W. v. Desoto County School District, No 09–00155 (N.D. Miss. 2010).
59. 129 S. Ct. 2633 (2009).
60. *Id.* at 2642.
61. Vernonia School District v. Acton, 515 U.S. 646 (1995).
62. Board of Education v. Earls, 536 U.S. 822 (2002).
63. *Vernonia* 515 U.S. at 665.
64. 419 U.S. 565 (1975).
65. *Id.* at 574.
66. *Id.* at 582. The Court noted that schools could choose to allow for these procedures if they wished.
67. *Id.* at 581.
68. *Id.* at 580.
69. 435 U.S. 78 (1978). This case dealt with a student dropped from medical school for failing to make adequate academic progress. She claimed her removal from the program without the benefit of due process was unconstitutional, but the Supreme Court distinguished a removal for disciplinary reasons from a removal for failing to meet pre-stated academic guidelines.
70. Ingraham v. Wright, 430 U.S. 651 (1977).

Chapter 3

1. Christine Ammer, *Out of the mouths of babes*, THE AMERICAN HERITAGE DICTIONARY OF IDIOMS (2003). http://idioms.thefreedictionary.com/Out+of+the+mouths+of+babes (last visited May 26, 2015).
2. 32 Vt. 114 (Vt. 1859).
3. *Id.* at 114.
4. *Id.* at 122. The court declined to give teachers the full discretionary powers granted other public employees, as those would extend beyond the classroom, but put teachers in the role of "master" within their academic environments, thus giving them the right to take reasonable actions to maintain their classrooms.
5. *Id.* at 120.
6. *Id.* at 123.
7. 135 Wis. 619 (Wis. 1908).
8. *Id.* at 624–25.
9. *Id.* at 627.
10. *Id.*
11. *Id.* at 628.
12. 27 Cal. App. 51 (Cal. Ct. App. 1915).
13. Id. at 52–53.
14. Id. at 55.
15. *Id.* at 56.
16. 268 U.S. 652 (1925).
17. DAVID HUDSON, JR., LET THE STUDENTS SPEAK! A HISTORY OF THE FIGHT FOR FREE EXPRESSION IN AMERICAN SCHOOLS, 21 (Beacon Press 2011).
18. "You shall not make for yourself an image in the form of anything in heaven above or on the earth beneath or in the waters below. *You shall not bow down to them or worship them*; for I, the LORD your God, am a jealous God, punishing the children for the sin of the parents to the third and

Chapter Notes—3

fourth generation of those who hate me, but showing love to a thousand generations of those who love me and keep my commandments." Exodus 20: 4–6 (New International Version Bible) (emphasis added).
19. *Minersville v. Gobitis*, 310 U.S. 586 (1940).
20. 319 U.S. 624 (1943).
21. *Id.* at 632.
22. 249 U.S. 47, 52 (1919).
23. *Barnette* 319 U.S. at 640.
24. *Id.* at 642.
25. *Id.* at 644 (Black, J. concurring).
26. *Declaration of the Rights of the Child* 1959 U.N.Y.B 198–99.
27. RICHARD ARUM, JUDGING SCHOOL DISCIPLINE: THE CRISIS OF MORAL AUTHORITY, 51–54 (Harvard University Press 2003).
28. 363 F.2d 744 (5th Cir. 1966).
29. 363 F.2d 749 (5th Cir. 1966).
30. *Burnside* 363 F.2d at 748.
31. *Blackwell* 363 F.2d at 751.
32. Considering the suspensions began in February, this was a sizeable punishment. *Blackwell* 363 F.2d at 752.
33. *Burnside* 363 F.2d at 749.
34. *Blackwell* 363 F.2d at 751.
35. *Id.* at 754.
36. *Id.*
37. Kristi Bowman, *The Civil Rights Roots of Tinker's Disruption Tests*, 58 AM. U. L. REV. 1129, 1148 (2009).
38. James Ryan, *The Supreme Court and Public Schools*, 86 Va. L. Rev. 1335, 1359 (2000).
39. Hudson *supra* note 17 at 59.
40. The policy specifically cited armbands, and did not apply to other wearable symbols.
41. An interesting side note to this story is that the Tinkers' younger siblings, who were in elementary school, also wore armbands but were not suspended. Instead the elementary school chose to use the armbands as a teachable moment about speech and protest. Hudson *supra* note 17 at 60.
42. *Tinker v. Des Moines Independent Community School District*, 258 F. Supp. 971 (S.D. Iowa 1966).
43. Hudson *supra* note 17 at 61.
44. 383 F.2d 988 (8th Cir. 1967).
45. Recording of Oral Argument at 31:04, Tinker v. Des Moines Independent School District, 393 U.S. 503 (1969) (No. 21) *available at* http://www.oyez.org/ cases/1960–1969/1968/1968_21 #argument (last visited June 27, 2015).
46. Tinker v. Des Moines Independent School District, 393 U.S. 503 (1969).
47. *Id.* at 506.
48. *Id.* at 508.
49. *Id.* at 513.
50. *Id.* at 509.
51. *Id.* at 511.
52. *Id.* at 517 (Black, J. dissenting).
53. *Id.* at 526.
54. 337 U.S. 1 (1949).
55. For more discussion of this aspect of *Tinker, see* John Taylor, *Tinker and Viewpoint Discrimination*, 77 UMKC L. Rev. 569, 590 (2009).
56. 299 F. Supp. 102 (S.D. N.Y. 1969).
57. 307 F. Supp. 517 (C.D. Cal. 1969).
58. *Zucker* 299 F. Supp at 105.
59. *Baker* 307 F. Supp at 527.
60. *Id.*
61. 440 F.2d 803 (2d Cir. 1971).
62. 607 F.2d 1043 (2d Cir. 1979).
63. The Fourth Circuit addressed a similar situation in Baughman v. Freienmuth (478 F.2d 1345, 4th Cir. 1973) when it deemed that a prior review requirement needed to contain precise criteria so that a student would understand what was and was not permissible in order to survive constitutional analysis.
64. *Eisner* 440 F.2d at 807–808.
65. *Thomas* 607 F.2d at 1046.
66. *Id.* at 1051.
67. *Id.*
68. Melton v. Young, 465 F.2d 1332 (6th Cir. 1972).
69. *Id.* at 1334.
70. Augustus v. School Board of Escambia County, 507 F.2d 152 (5th Cir. 1975).
71. *Id.* at 156.
72. 477 F.2d 171 (9th Cir. 1973).
73. *Id.* at 174.
74. *Id.* at 175.
75. *Id.* at 176. Ultimately, the student's suspension was partially upheld—the court determined his signs were protected speech, but his role in orchestrating the walkout was not.
76. 577 F. Supp. 1560 (D. Me. 1984).
77. *Id.* at 1561. The quote was taken from the January 24, 1983, issue of *Time* magazine.
78. *Id.* at 1570.
79. *Id.* at 1573–74.
80. *Id.* at 1574.
81. 478 U.S. 675 (1986).

Chapter Notes—3

82. *Id.* at 687 (Brennan, J, concurring).
83. Fraser v. Bethel School District, 755 F.2d 1356 (9th Cir. 1985).
84. *Id.* at 1363.
85. *Fraser* 478 U.S. at 680–81.
86. 441 U.S. 68 (1979). This case dealt with a citizenship requirement for public school teachers in the state of New York. The Court upheld its constitutionality.
87. *Fraser* 478 U.S. at 681.
88. *Id.*
89. *Id.* at 681–82.
90. *Id.* at 685.
91. *Id.* at 692 (Stevens, J, dissenting) (internal citations omitted).
92. Harper v. Edgewood Board of Education, 655 F. Supp. 1353 (S.D. Ohio 1987).
93. *Id.* at 1355.
94. *Id.* at 1356, quoting Jackson v. Dorrier, 424 F.2d 213 (6th Cir. 1970).
95. 484 U.S. 260 (1988).
96. Kuhlmeier v. Hazelwood, 607 F. Supp. 1450 (E.D. Mo. 1985).
97. Hazelwood School District v. Kuhlmeier, 795 F.2d 1368 (8th Cir. 1986).
98. *Hazelwood* 484 U.S. at 266.
99. *Id.*
100. Hague v. CIO, 307 U.S. 496 (1939).
101. These are referred to as "limited" or "designated" public forums. *See* Perry Education Association v. Perry Local Educators' Association, 460 U.S. 37 (1983).
102. ISKCON v. Lee, 505 U.S. 672 (1992).
103. *Hazelwood* 484 U.S. at 268–70.
104. *Id.* at 269.
105. *Id.* at 272–73.
106. *Id.* at 270–71.
107. *Id.* at 272–73.
108. *Id.* at 283–89 (Brennan, J. dissenting).
109. *Id.* at 291.
110. Chandler v. McMinnville School District, 978 F.2d 524, 529 (9th Cir. 1992). In this case, a pair of students wore a variety of buttons on their clothing using the word "scab" in a negative way, to protest the replacement teachers hired in place of the school's regular instructors on strike for contract issues. Both students were suspended for refusing to remove their buttons. The court found that the buttons themselves did not rise to the level of disruptive speech.
111. Boroff v. Van Wert City Board of Education, 220 F.3d 465 (6th Cir. 2000).
112. *Id.* at 470.
113. Dean v. Utica Community Schools, 345 F. Supp. 2d 799 (E.D. Mich. 2004).
114. *Id.* at 805, citing Kincaid v. Gibson, 236 F.3d 342, 354 (6th Cir. 2002) (en banc).
115. *Id.* at 804.
116. Slotterback v. Interboro School District, 766 F. Supp. 280 (E.D. Pa. 1991). The majority of the analysis focused on whether the regulation was motivated by the religious content of the speech, but also weighed whether a hallway, where educational activity is not central, could be considered a limited public forum.
117. Muller v. Jefferson Lighthouse School, 98 F.3d 1530 (7th Cir. 1996). As with Slotterback, the majority of the decision focused on Establishment/Free Exercise elements of the case, but did determine that hallways were a place for more personal communication.
118. Searcey v. Harris, 888 F.2d 1314 (11th Cir. 1989).
119. SG v. Sayerville Board of Education, 333 F.3d 417 (3d Cir. 2003).
120. *Id.* at 421.
121. 976 F. Supp. 659 (S.D. Tex. 1997).
122. Baxter v. Vigo County School Corporation, 26 F.3d 728 (7th Cir. 1994).
123. 370 F.3d 1252 (11th Cir. 2004).
124. *Id.* at 1271. Holloman had at one point raised his fist in silent protest when told he was required to recite the pledge or face punishment, which the dissent argued was a significant disruption. The rest of the case focused on the teacher's use of the Bible in the classroom.
125. 445 F.3d 1166 (9th Cir. 2006).
126. *Id.* at 1176.
127. *Id.* at 1185.
128. LaVine v. Blaine School District, 257 F.3d 981 (9th Cir. 2001).
129. *Id.* at 991–92.
130. LaVine v. Blaine School District, 279 F.3d 719, 724 (9th Cir. 2002) (Kleinfeld, Judge, dissenting).
131. Porter v. Ascension Parish School Board, 393 F.3d 608, 612 (5th Cir. 2004).
132. *Id.*
133. *Id.* at 615.
134. *Id.* at 618. The administrators, however, were granted qualified immunity from personal liability in this case because the line between on-campus and off-campus speech was so murky, it would be difficult for a reasonable person to determine if he or she had crossed it.

Chapter Notes—3

135. *See* J.S. v. Bethlehem, 569 Pa. 638 (Pa. 2002).
136. *See* Layshock v. Hermitage School District, 496 F. Supp. 2d 587 (W.D. Pa. 2007).
137. *See* Killion v. Franklin Regional School District, 136 F. Supp. 2d 446 (W.D. Pa. 2001).
138. 551 U.S. 393 (2007).
139. *Id.* at 399.
140. Frederick v. Morse, 439 F.3d 1114 (9th Cir. 2006).
141. Morse v. Frederick, 551 U.S. 393, 400–01 (2007).
142. *Id.* at 403.
143. *Id.* at 409.
144. *Id.* at 402. There was debate over whether the statement actually promoted drug use—Frederick claimed it was a nonsense phrase he had seen on a snowboard and had created the banner solely to get attention from the attending media.
145. *Id.* at 418 (Thomas, J, concurring).
146. *Id.* at 422 (Alito, J, concurring).
147. *See* Ponce v. Socorro Independent School District, 508 F.3d 765 (5th Cir. 2007).
148. *Morse* 551 U.S. at 444 (Stevens, J, dissenting).
149. 395 U.S. 444 (1969).
150. *Id.* at 447.
151. Keep a Breast Foundation, http://www.keep-a-breast.org/programs/i-love-boobies/ (last visited May 28, 2015).
152. *Id.*
153. 2012 U.S. Dist. LEXIS 187689 (W.D. Wis, 2012).
154. *Id.* at 22. Judge Barbara Crabb noted that she might not personally have made the same decision in the same situation, but the core question was if the interpretation of "boobies" as vulgar was reasonable.
155. B.H. v. Easton Area School District, 725 F.3d 293 (3d Cir. 2013).
156. *Morse* 551 U.S. at 422 (Alito, J. concurring).
157. *Easton* 725 F.3d at 310, discussing Marks v. United States, 430 U.S. 188, 193 (1977) ("[when] no single rationale explaining the result enjoys the assent of five Justices, the holding of the Court may be viewed as that position taken by those Members who concurred in the judgments on the narrowest grounds").
158. *Id.* at 315.
159. *Id.* at 320.
160. J.A. v. Fort Wayne Community Schools, 2013 U.S. Dist. LEXIS 117667 (N.D. Ind., 2013) at *11 (internal citations omitted).
161. *Id.* at *20.
162. 523 F.3d 668 (7th Cir. 2008).
163. *Id.* at 676.
164. Dariano v. Morgan Hill, 767 F.3d 764 (9th Cir. 2014).
165. Hardwick v. Heyward, 711 F.3d 426 (4th Cir. 2013).
166. Cuff v. Valley Central School District, 677 F.3d 109 (2d Cir. 2012).
167. *Id.* at 114.
168. *Easton* 725 F.3d at 338 (Greenaway, Judge dissenting).
169. McCauley v. University of the Virgin Islands, 618 F.3d 232, 246 (3d Cir. 2010).
170. 272 F. Supp. 947 (D. S.C. 1967).
171. *Id.* at 950–51.
172. 194 F. Supp. 2d 1011 (C.D. Cal. 2002).
173. *Id.* at 1027.
174. 620 F.2d 516 (5th Cir. 1980).
175. *Id.* at 522.
176. 74 F. Supp. 2d 940 (C.D. Cal. 1999).
177. *Id.* at 949–52.
178. Hosty v. Carter, 412 F.3d 731 (7th Cir. 2005) (en banc). The court found the newspaper to be a limited-purpose public forum that could not be censored by the university strictly on the basis of content or viewpoint.
179. Burnham v. Ianni, 119 F.3d 668 (8th Cir. 1997).
180. *Id.* at 676.
181. 408 U.S. 169 (1972).
182. *Id.* at 180.
183. *Id.* at 185–190.
184. *Id.* at 192–93.
185. *Id.* at 180–81.
186. *See* Sweezy v. New Hampshire, 354 U.S. 234 (1957) or Keyishian v. Board of Regents, 385 U.S. 589 (1967).
187. *Healy* 408 U.S. at 184.
188. *Id.*
189. 454 U.S. 263 (1981).
190. Chess v. Widmar, 480 F. Supp. 907 (W.D. Missouri 1979).
191. Chess v. Widmar, 635 F.2d 1310 (8th Cir. 1980).
192. *Id.* at 267–68.
193. *Id.* at 280 (Stevens, J, concurring).
194. 867 F.2d 1344 (11th Cir. 1989).
195. *Id.* at 1347.
196. 424 U.S. 1 (1976). Although I don't

think anyone really needed the Supreme Court to tell us this.

197. *See* Abood v. Detroit Board of Education, 431 U.S. 209 (1977).

198. 515 U.S. 819 (1995).

199. "WAP had acquired CIO status soon after it was organized. This is an important consideration in this case, for had it been a 'religious organization,' WAP would not have been accorded CIO status. As defined by the Guidelines, a 'religious organization' is 'an organization whose purpose is to practice a devotion to an acknowledged ultimate reality or deity.' App. to Pet. for Cert. 66a. At no stage in this controversy has the University contended that WAP is such an organization." *Rosenberger* 515 U.S. at 826.

200. Activities that would not be covered included charitable contributions, religious activity or electioneering. *Id.* at 824–25.

201. Rosenberger v. Rector and Visitors of University of Virginia, 795 F. Supp. 175 (W.D. Va. 1992).

202. Rosenberger v. Rector and Visitors of University of Virginia, 18 F.3d 269 (4th Cir. 1994).

203. *Rosenberger* 515 U.S. at 834.

204. The Student Activities Fund was also examined under forum analysis and found to be a limited public forum "more in a metaphysical than a spatial or geographic sense." *Id.* at 830. As such, regulations could not result in viewpoint discrimination.

205. *Id.* at 836.

206. *Id.* at 845.

207. 529 U.S. 217 (2000).

208. Southworth v. Grebe, 1996 U.S. Dist. LEXIS 20980 (W.D. Wis. 1996).

209. Southworth v. Grebe, 151 F.3d 717 (7th Cir. 1998).

210. *See* Abood v. Detroit Bd. of Ed., 431 U.S. 209 (1977), in which a group of nonunion teachers challenged the requirement that they pay a fee to the union, as all teachers benefited from its bargaining efforts, because the union also used contributions to pay for political lobbying. The Supreme Court found for the teachers and required that the union separate nonunion fees from union dues to ensure the former were not spent on activities unrelated to teacher representation with the district. *Also* Keller v. State Bar of Cal., 496 U.S. 1 (1990), which upheld a state requirement that all lawyers join the bar association and contribute toward activities that were "germane" to their profession.

211. *Southworth* 529 U.S. at 232.

212. Part of the decision dealt with a rarely used funding mechanism that involved a student referendum. This particular process was remanded to the lower courts for further investigation, as it risked neutrality by substituting the majority's views for the minority's. *Id.* at 234–35.

213. Doe v. University of Michigan, 721 F. Supp 852, 856 (E.D. Mich. 1989).

214. UWM Post, Inc. v. Board of Regents of the University of Wisconsin, 774 F. Supp. 1163 (E.D. Wis. 1991).

215. *Doe* 721 F. Supp at 868.

216. *UWM Post* 774 F. Supp. at 1181.

217. 537 F.3d 301 (3d Cir. 2008).

218. Temple University is one of Pennsylvania's four state-related universities (the others are Penn State University, the University of Pittsburgh and Lincoln University).

219. *DeJohn* 537 F.3d at 305.

220. *Id.* at 319–20. In the middle of the appeal, Temple revised its sexual harassment policy to better align with constitutional requirements, but the Third Circuit determined the case could continue to ensure the university did not revert to its old policy once the case had concluded.

221. Salehpour v. University of Tennessee, 159 F.3d 199 (6th Cir. 1998).

222. *Id.* at 208.

223. Brown v. Li, 308 F.3d 939 (9th Cir. 2002).

224. *Id.* at 953–54.

225. 800 N.W.2d 811 (Minn. Ct. App. 2011).

226. *Id.* at 818.

227. *Id.* at 821, internal citations omitted.

228. Tatro v. University of Minnesota, 816 N.W.2d 509 (Minn. 2012).

229. *Id.* at 520.

230. *Id.* at 521. The university was able to meet this standard.

231. Lyle Olson, Roger Van Ommeren and Marshel Rossow, *A Paradigm for State High School Press Laws* 3 (presented at the annual meeting of the Association for Education in Journalism and Mass Communication, Scholastic Journalism Division, Kansas City, MO, August 1993).

232. Don Pember and Clay Calvert, Mass Media Law 8 (17th ed. McGraw Hill 2011).

233. See Erica Salkin, *The Speech, Not the Speaker: Protecting Public School Student Expression*, 11 COMM. L. REV. 1 (2011).
234. Arkansas Student Publications Act, ARK. STAT. ANN. §§6–18–1201–1204 (1995).
235. Colorado Student Free Expression Law, COLO. REV. STAT. § 22–1–120 (1990).
236. Illinois College Campus Press Act, 110 ILCS 13 (2007).
237. Iowa Student Free Expression Law, IOWA CODE § 280.22 (1989).
238. Kansas Student Publications Act, KAN. STAT. ANN. §§ 72.1504–72.1506 (1992).
239. Student Journalists—Free Expression, N.D. CENT. CODE §§ 15–10 and 15.1–06 (2015).
240. Oregon Student Free Expression Law (Public College and Universities), ORE. REV. STAT. § 351.649 (2007), Oregon Student Free Expression Law (Public Secondary Schools), ORE. REV. STAT. § 336.477 (2007).
241. Corder v. Lewis Palmer School District, 566 F.3d 1219, 1235–36 (10th Cir. 2009).
242. Washington Administrative Code: Student Rights, WAC 392–40–215 (1977).
243. Pennsylvania Administrative Code: Student Rights and Responsibilities, 22 PA. CODE § 12.9 (2005).
244. *Id.* at (c).
245. Massachusetts Student Free Expression Law, MASS. GEN. LAWS ANN. ch. 71, § 82 (1988).
246. *Id.*
247. California Community College Free Expression Law, CALIF. EDUC. CODE § 7612 (1977). This law protects "the use of bulletin boards, the distribution of printed materials or petitions, and the wearing of buttons, badges, or other insignia" so long as it is not libelous, obscene or incites illegal or disorderly activity.
248. California Student Free Expression Law, CAL. EDUC. CODE § 48907 (1977). The law states "Pupils of the public schools, including charter schools, shall have the right to exercise freedom of speech and of the press including, but not limited to, the use of bulletin boards, the distribution of printed materials or petitions, the wearing of buttons, badges, and other insignia, and the right of expression in official publications, whether or not the publications or other means of expression are supported financially by the school or by use of school facilities."

249. California Leonard Law, CALIF. EDUC. CODE § 66301 (2006). This law prohibits "subjecting a student to disciplinary sanction solely on the basis of conduct that is speech or other communication that, when engaged in outside a campus of those institutions, is protected from governmental restriction by the First Amendment to the United States Constitution or Section 2 of Article I of the California Constitution."
250. California Leonard Law, CALIF. EDUC. CODE § 48950 (1992). This law prohibits "subjecting any high school pupil to disciplinary sanctions solely on the basis of conduct that is speech or other communication that, when engaged in outside of the campus, is protected from governmental restriction by the First Amendment to the United States Constitution or Section 2 of Article 1 of the California Constitution."
251. California Leonard Law, CALIF. EDUC. CODE § 94367 (1992). This law prohibits private colleges from "subjecting any student to disciplinary sanctions solely on the basis of conduct that is speech or other communication that, when engaged in outside the campus or facility of a private postsecondary institution, is protected from governmental restriction by the First Amendment to the United States Constitution or Section 2 of Article 1 of the California Constitution."
252. L.D. Olson. L. D., R. Van Ommeren, R., & M. Rossow, *High School Press Freedom Legislation: A Survey of Key Promoters* 9 (presented at the annual meeting of the Association for Education in Journalism and Mass Communication, Scholastic Journalism Division, August 1995).
253. JACK NELSON, CAPTIVE VOICES 117 (Schocken Books 1974).

Chapter 4

1. My son, Nicolas, told me this joke. Look, his first professional citation! Proud mama moment.
2. Charter schools have a degree of separation from regular public schools, the extent of which varies from state to state, but because their creation is enabled through state mandate, they are still considered government institutions and sub-

Chapter Notes—4

ject to the provisions of state and federal constitutions. *See* Brammer-Hoelter v. Twin Peaks Charter Academy, 602 F.3d 1175 (10th Cir. 2010) (stating a charter school administrator's demand that teachers sign a contract stating they would not discuss school matters during non-school hours or gather during their leisure time was an unconstitutional prior restraint of speech and association).

3. Robert Post, *Between Governance and Management: The History and Theory of the Public Forum*, 34 UCLA L. REV. 1713, 1766 (1987).

4. Tinker v. Des Moines Independent Community School District, 393 U.S. 503, 508 (1969).

5. "Student." MERRIAM-WEBSTER DICTIONARY, http://www.merriam-webster.com/dictionary/student (last visited June 28, 2015).

6. 20 U.S.C. § 1232g.

7. 20 U.S.C. §1232g(a)(6). "Attendance" is defined as "in person or by paper correspondence, videoconference, satellite, Internet, or other electronic information and telecommunications technologies for students who are not physically present in the classroom." (34 CFR Part 99.3).

8. M. David Merrill, Leston Drake, Mark J. Lacy, Jean Pratt & the ID2 Research Group, *Reclaiming Instructional Design*, 36 EDUC. TECH. 5, 6 (1996).

9. D.H. Jonassen, J. Hernandez-Serrano, & I. Choi, *Integrating constructivism and learning technologies*. In J. M. Spector & T.M. Anderson (Eds.), INTEGRATION AND HOLISTIC PERSPECTIVES ON LEARNING, INSTRUCTION, AND TECHNOLOGY. 104 (Kluwer Academic 2000).

10. *Id.* at 105.

11. AMY GUTMANN, DEMOCRATIC EDUCATION, 175 (Princeton University Press 1999).

12. Gutmann's definition of a "scholar," however, could also easily encompass the teachers at educational institutions as well, so we cannot rely on her definition as the sole basis for describing a "student."

13. Richard Garnett, *Can There Really Be Free Speech in Public Schools?*, 12 LEWIS & CLARK L. REV. 45, 51–52 (2008).

14. Benjamin Heidlage, *A Relational Approach to Schools' Regulation of Youth Online Speech*, 84 NYU L. REV. 572, 594 (2009).

15. The distinction of "based in that ex-ploration" separates students from faculty at the college/university level, as faculty members are also continuously learning through their own research or other knowledge acquisition. I think it is fair to say that faculty members' primary relationships with their educational institutions, however, are employment based, which removes them from my definition of student.

16. 391 U.S. 563 (1968).

17. *Id.* at 571–72. There were some falsehoods in the letter, which the Court determined would be fair game for a libel lawsuit if the school district could prove actual malice.

18. 429 U.S. 167 (1976).

19. *Id.* at 175.

20. 429 U.S. 274 (1977).

21. 461 U.S. 138 (1983).

22. *Id.* at 147.

23. 547 U.S. 410 (2006).

24. *Id.* at 421.

25. "The problem in any case is to arrive at a balance between the interests of the teacher, as a citizen, in commenting upon matters of public concern and the interest of the State, as an employer, in promoting the efficiency of the public services it performs through its employees." *Pickering* 391 U.S. at 568; "[T]he Court has repeatedly emphasized the need for affirming the comprehensive authority of the States and of school officials, consistent with fundamental constitutional safeguards, to prescribe and control conduct in the schools. Our problem lies in the area where students in the exercise of First Amendment rights collide with the rules of the school authorities" *Tinker* 393 U.S. at 507 (internal citations omitted).

26. *See* John Trebilcock, *Off Campus: School Board Control Over Teacher Conduct*. 35 TULSA L. J. 445 (2000).

27. 27 Cal. App. 51 (Cal. App. Ct. 1915).

28. Trisha LeBoeuf, *Dorm Mold Story Leads to Adviser's Termination, Student Journalists Allege*, STUDENT PRESS LAW CENTER, June 3, 2015, http://www.splc.org/article/2015/06/dorm-mold-story-leads-to-advisers-termination-student-journalists-allege (last visited June 28, 2015).

29. 618 F.3d 232 (3d Cir. 2010).

30. *Id.* at 242 (internal citations omitted).

31. *Id.* at 242–243.

32. 668 F.2d 214 (3d Cir. 1981). In this case, three high school students alleged

their freedom of expression was violated when the school superintendent canceled their spring play based on the concerns of some parents regarding a handful of sexually explicit scenes. The court found for the school.

33. *Id.* at 219–220 (Rosenn, Judge, concurring).

34. 333 F.3d 417 (3d Cir. 2003). This case dealt with the suspension of a kindergarten student for pretending to shoot a friend on the playground during a game of cops and robbers. The school had recently passed a zero-tolerance policy regarding violence, which included any statement or action that suggested firearms. The court found for the school.

35. *Id.* at 423.

36. 408 U.S. 169 (1972).

37. *Id.* at 201 (Rehnquist, J, concurring).

38. 537 F.3d 301 (3d Cir. 2008).

39. Alabama Student Party v. Student Government Association of the University of Alabama, 867 F.2d 1344 (11th Cir. 1989). The University claimed the student government program was a "learning laboratory," allowing the court to assess the program as an aspect of curriculum.

40. Axson-Flynn v. Johnson, 356 F.3d 1277 (10th Cir. 2004).

41. *Id.* at 1284 (internal citations omitted).

42. Kincaid v. Gibson, 236 F.3d 342, 346 (6th Cir. 2001).

43. *Id.* at 348.

44. 412 F.3d 731 (7th Cir. 2005) (en banc).

45. *Id.* at 734.

46. *Id.* at 738.

47. *Id.* at 738.

48. *See* Morgan v. Swanson, 659 F.3d 359 (5th Cir. 2011).

49. *See* K.A. v. Pocono Mountain School District, 710 F.3d 99 (3d Cir. 2013) or Gilio v. School Board, 905 F. Supp. 2d 1262 (M.D. Fla. 2012).

50. *See* Cuff v. Valley Central School District, 677 F.3d 109 (2d Cir. 2012).

51. K.A. 710 F.3d at 109.

52. *Morgan* 659 F.3d at 386.

53. Sarah-Jayne Blakemore & Suparna Choudhury, *Development of the Adolescent Brain: Implications for Executive Function and Social Cognition*, 47 JOURN. CHILD PSYCHOL. & PSYCHIATRY 296, 296 (2006).

54. *Id.*

55. *Id.* at 301.

56. *Id.* at 300.

57. Deanna Kuhn, *Do Cognitive Changes Accompany Developments in the Adolescent Brain?* 1 PERSP. ON PSYCHOL. SCI. 59, 65 (2006).

58. JOHN DEWEY, DEMOCRACY AND EDUCATION: AN INTRODUCTION TO THE PHILOSOPHY OF EDUCATION, 63 (Macmillan Company 1916).

59. ARTHUR POWELL, ELEANOR FARRAR & DAVID COHEN, THE SHOPPING MALL HIGH SCHOOL: WINNERS AND LOSERS IN THE EDUCATIONAL MARKETPLACE, 276 (Houghton Mifflin Company 1985).

60. BARBARA SCHNEIDER & DAVID STEVENSON, THE AMBITIOUS GENERATION: AMERICA'S TEENAGERS, MOTIVATED BUT DIRECTIONLESS, 21 (Yale University Press 1999).

61. GERALD GRANT, THE WORLD WE CREATED AT HAMILTON HIGH, 31 (Harvard University Press 1988).

62. *See* Lewis Friedland and Shauna Morimoto, *The Changing Lifeworld of Young People: Risk, Resume-Padding and Civic Engagement*, CIRCLE Working Paper 40 (Sept. 2005).

63. Schneider & Stevenson *supra* note 60 at 74. This percentage was remarkably consistent across gender, racial and ethnic lines.

64. Anthony Carnevale, Stephen Rose and Ban Cheah, *The College Payoff: Education, Occupations, Lifetime Earnings* 1 (Georgetown University Center on Education and the Workforce, 2011).

65. *Id.*

66. CHARLES BEARD, THE UNIQUE FUNCTION OF EDUCATION IN AMERICAN DEMOCRACY, 97 (National Education Association and the Department of Superintendence 1937).

67. Kenneth Clark, *"Vestibule Adolescence" and Other Threats to Children and Youth* 163–165 (1959), included in CHILDREN AND YOUTH IN AMERICA: A DOCUMENTARY HISTORY (Robert Bremner, ed., Harvard University Press 1974).

68. Susan Jekielek & Brett Brown, *The Transition to Adulthood: Characteristics of Young Adults Ages 18 to 24 in America* 1 (Child Trends/The Annie E. Casey Foundation, 2005).

69. *Id.* at 8.

70. JJ Arnett, *Learning to Stand Alone: The Contemporary American Transition to Adulthood in Cultural and Historical Context*, 41 HUM. DEV. 295, 296 (1998).

Chapter Notes—5

71. JJ Arnett, *Emerging Adulthood: A Theory of Development from the Late Teens through the Twenties*, 55 Am. Psychol. 469, 469 (2000).
72. *Id.* at 477.
73. Gary Fine, Gifted Tongues: High School Debate and Adolescent Culture, 17 (Princeton University Press 2001).
74. Murray Milner Jr., Freaks, Geeks and Cool Kids: American Teenagers, Schools and the Culture of Consumption, 166 (Routledge 2004).
75. *See* Lew Zipin, *Dark Funds of Knowledge, Deep Funds of Pedagogy: Exploring Boundaries Between Lifeworlds and Schools*, 30 Discourse 317 (2009). Zipin defines a "school-world" as "infused with institutional features that enforce hierarchy within their borders and police how life-based cultural embodiments enter into school relations." (at 326).
76. Morse v. Frederick, 551 U.S. 393, 411–12 (2007) (Thomas, J., concurring).
77. James Coleman, The Adolescent Society: The Social Life of the Teenager and Its Impact on Education, 3–10 (The Free Press of Glencoe 1963).
78. Philip Cusick, Inside High School: A Student's World, 12 (Holt, Rinehart and Winston, Inc. 1973).
79. Powell, Farrar & Cohen, *supra* note 59 at 290–300.
80. *Id.*
81. *Id.* at 8–9.
82. *Id.* at 118, 172.
83. Elinor Burkett, Another Planet: A Year in the Life of a Suburban High School, 312 (HarperCollins 2001).
84. 668 F.2d 214 (3d Cir. 1981).
85. *Id.* at 219–220 (Rosenn, Judge concurring) (emphasis added).
86. Amy Gutmann, *What is the Value of Free Speech for Students?*, 29 Ariz. St. L.J. 519, 532 (1997).
87. Richard Roe, *Valuing Student Speech: The Work of the Schools as Conceptual Development*, 79 Cal. L. Rev. 1269, 1297 (1991).
88. *Id.* at 1299.
89. Granted, there is concern about social promotion that advances students to the next grade to simply keep them with their age groups, but the intent of the grade system is to retain students who do not meet minimum requirements.
90. Roe *supra* note 87 at 1327.
91. *See* Settle v. Dickson County School Board, 53 F.3d 152 (6th Cir, 1995) for an example of this idea in action.

Chapter 5

1. John S. Mill, On Liberty 11 (WW Norton and Company 1975) (1859).
2. Thomas Scanlon, *A Theory of Freedom of Expression*, 1 Phil. & Pub. Aff. 204 (1972). Richard Fallon defined autonomy as well, calling the ability "to deliberate with critical insight and self-awareness and to choose from abundant options." Richard Fallon, Jr. *Two Senses of Autonomy*, 46 Stan. L. Rev. 875, 877 (1994).
3. David Richards, *Free Speech and Obscenity Law: Toward a Moral Theory of the First Amendment*, 123 U. Pa. L. Rev. 45, 83 (1974–75).
4. 390 U.S. 629 (1968).
5. 393 U.S. 503 (1969).
6. *Ginsburg* 390 U.S. at 649–50 (Stewart, J, concurring).
7. John Garvey, *Children and the First Amendment*, 57 Tex. L. Rev. 321, 323 (1979).
8. Craig Calhoun, *Introduction* in Habermas And The Public Sphere (Craig Calhoun, ed., MIT Press 1993).
9. Richard Roe, *Valuing Student Speech: The Work of the Schools as Conceptual Development*, 79 Cal. L. Rev. 1269, 1277 (1991) (emphasis added).
10. Anne Dailey, *Children's Constitutional Rights*, 95 Minn. L. Rev. 2099, 2145 (2011).
11. Amy Gutmann. Democratic Education, 122 (Princeton University Press 1999).
12. Thomas I. Emerson, The System of Freedom of Expression, 6 (Random House, 1970).
13. *See* C. Edwin Baker, *Scope of the First Amendment Freedom of Speech*, 25 UCLA L. Rev. 964 (1978).
14. Robert Trager and Joseph Russomanno, *Free Speech for Public School Students: A "Basic Educational Mission"* 22 (presented at the annual meeting of the Association for Education in Journalism and Mass Communication, Kansas City, Mo., August 1993).
15. Alexander Meiklejohn, Political Freedom 75 (Harper & Brothers 1960) (1948).
16. *Id.* at 26.

17. WALTER BERNS, THE FIRST AMENDMENT AND THE FUTURE OF AMERICAN DEMOCRACY 169 (Regnery Gateway 1985).
18. CASS SUNSTEIN, REPUBLIC.COM 11 (Princeton University Press 2011) (2002).
19. KEVIN SAUNDERS, SAVING OUR CHILDREN FROM THE FIRST AMENDMENT 21 (New York University Press 2003).
20. Amy Gutmann, *What is the Value of Free Speech for Students?* 29 ARIZ. ST. L.J. 519, 528 (1997).
21. Lee v. Weisman, 505 U.S. 577, 590 (1992).
22. *See* Robert Post, *Between Governance and Management: The History and Theory of the Public Forum*, 34 UCLA L. REV. 1713 (1987).
23. J. Peter Byrne, *Academic Freedom: A Special Concern of the First Amendment*, 99 YALE L.J. 251, 336 (1985).
24. ISAIAH BERLIN, FOUR ESSAYS ON LIBERTY 21 (Oxford University Press 1969).
25. Roe *supra* note 9 at 1322.
26. Martin Redish and Kevin Finnerty, *What Did You Learn in School Today? Free Speech, Values Inculcation and the Democratic-Educational Paradox*, 88 CORNELL L. REV. 62, 70 (2002).
27. ROBERT WHEELER LANE, BEYOND THE SCHOOLHOUSE GATE: FREE SPEECH AND THE INCULCATION OF VALUES 59 (Temple University Press 1995).
28. C. Edwin Baker, *The Media that Citizens Need*, 147 U. PA. L. REV. 317, 319–20 (1999). Baker went on to write that a hybrid of these approaches was the most realistic way to conceptualize modern democracy.
29. Laura Stein, *Speech Without Rights: The Status of Public Sphere on the Internet*, 11 COMM. REV. 1, 4 (2008).
30. Sunstein *supra* note 18 at 142.
31. CHARLES A. BEARD, MARY R. BEARD AND WILLIAM BEARD, THE BEARDS' NEW BASIC HISTORY OF THE UNITED STATES 75 (Doubleday & Co. 1968).
32. *Id.* at 155.
33. Meiklejohn *supra* note 15 at 89.
34. 347 U.S. 483 (1954).
35. *Id.* at 493.
36. 374 U.S. 203 (1963).
37. *Id.* at 230 (Brennan, J. concurring).
38. 441 U.S. 68 (1979).
39. *Id.* at 79.
40. Wieman v. Updegraff, 344 U.S. 183, 196 (1952) (Frankfurter, J., concurring). This case overturned an Oklahoma statute requiring state employees to take a loyalty oath as a condition of employment.
41. Patricia Avery and Annette Simmons, *Civic Life as Conveyed in United States Civics and History Textbooks*, 15 INTL. J SOC. EDUC. 105, 114 (2001).
42. SIDNEY VERBA, KAY SCHLOZMAN & HENRY BRODY, VOICE AND EQUALITY: CIVIC VOLUNTARISM IN AMERICAN POLITICS 3 (Harvard University Press 1995).
43. DAVID HUDSON JR., LET THE STUDENTS SPEAK! A HISTORY OF THE FIGHT FOR FREE EXPRESSION IN AMERICAN SCHOOLS 67 (Beacon Press 2011).
44. Betsy Levin, *Educating Youth for Citizenship: The Conflict Between Authority and Individual Rights in the Public School*, 95 YALE L. J. 1647, 1654 (1985).
45. *See* Zucker v. Panitz, 299 F. Supp. 102 (S.D. N.Y. 1969) or Trachtman v. Anker, 563 F.2d 512 (2d Cir. 1977). In *Zucker*, the district court found the experience argument convincing, but it *Trachtman*, the Second Circuit did not.
46. Alexander Meiklejohn, *The First Amendment is an Absolute*, 1961 SUP. CT. REV. 245 (1961).
47. Gutmann *supra* note 11 at xiii.
48. 250 U.S. 616 (1919).
49. *Id.* at 630 (Holmes, J. dissenting).
50. Robert Post, *Meiklejohn's Mistake: Individual Autonomy and the Reform of Public Discourse*, 64 U. COLO. L. REV. 1109, 1112–13 (1993).
51. Eisner v. Stamford Board of Education, 440 F.2d 803, 807 (2d Cir. 1971).
52. Seyfried v. Walton, 668 F.2d 214, 219 (3d Cir 1981) (Rosenn, Judge, concurring).
53. B.H. v. Easton Area School District, 725 F.3d 293, 324 (3d Cir. 2013).
54. Stanton v. Brunswick School Department, 577 F. Supp. 1560, 1575 (D. Me. 1984) (emphasis in original). This case dealt with the high school senior who wished to include a description of execution by electrocution as her yearbook senior quote.
55. JONATHAN RAUCH, KINDLY INQUISITORS: THE NEW ATTACKS ON FREE THOUGHT 114 (University of Chicago Press 1994).
56. *See* The Flat Earth Society, http://www.theflatearthsociety.org/cms/ (last visited June 1, 2015).
57. *See* Bruce Hafen, *Developing Student Expression through Institutional Authority: Public Schools as Mediating Structures*, 48 OHIO ST. L. J. 663, 704 (1987) or John Tay-

lor, *Tinker and Viewpoint Discrimination*, 77 UMKC L. REV. 569, 626 (2009).

58. Malcolm Stewart, *The Public Schools, and the Inculcation of Community Values*, 18 J. LAW & EDUC. 23, 52 (1989).

59. Muller v. Jefferson Lighthouse School, 98 F.3d 1530, 1538 (7th Cir. 1996).

60. Nuxoll v. Indian Prairie School District #204, 523 F.3d 668, 671 (7th Cir. 2008). A concurrence by Circuit Judge Rovner affirmed the court's decision to overturn a disciplinary action based on a student's refusal to remove an anti-gay t-shirt, but disagreed with the assertion that students had nothing to offer the marketplace of ideas.

61. Norman Thomas, *Can Our Schools Face Facts?* 9 PROG. EDUC 338, 340 (1932).

62. DIANA HESS, CONTROVERSY IN THE CLASSROOM: THE DEMOCRATIC POWER OF DISCUSSION 71 (Routledge 2009).

63. STEVEN SHIFFRIN, DISSENT, INJUSTICE AND THE MEANINGS OF AMERICA 114 (Princeton University Press 1999).

64. JOHN DEWEY, DEMOCRACY AND EDUCATION, AN INTRODUCTION TO THE PHILOSOPHY OF EDUCATION 109 (Macmillan Company 1916).

65. John O'Connor, *Civic Engagement in Higher Education*, CHANGE: THE MAGAZINE OF HIGHER LEARNING, Sept./Oct. 2006, at 52–58.

66. Francesca Polletta and James Jasper, *Collecting Identity and Social Movements* 27 ANN. REV. OF SOC. 283, 285 (2001).

67. Hadley Arkes, *Civility and the Restriction of Speech: Rediscovering the Defamation of Groups*, 1974 SUP. CT. REV. 281, 282 (1974).

68. HADLEY ARKES, THE PHILOSOPHER IN THE CITY: THE MORAL DIMENSIONS OF URBAN POLITICS 11–12 (Princeton University Press 1981).

69. See Robert Post, *Meiklejohn's Mistake: Individual Autonomy and the Reform of Public Discourse*, 64 U. COLO. L. REV. 1109 (1993).

70. 315 U.S. 568 (1942).
71. *Id.* at 572.
72. 337 U.S. 1 (1949).
73. *Id.* at 4.
74. 403 U.S. 15 (1971).
75. *Id.* at 26.

76. CHARLES BEARD, THE UNIQUE FUNCTION OF EDUCATION IN AMERICAN DEMOCRACY 46 (National Education Association 1937).

77. *See* ROBERT HESS AND JUDITH TORNEY, THE DEVELOPMENT OF POLITICAL ATTITUDES IN CHILDREN (Doubleday & Co. 1968).

78. Douglas Laycock, *High-value Speech and the Basic Educational Mission of a Public School: Some Preliminary Thoughts*, 12 LEWIS & CLARK 111, 121 (2008).

79. *See* Lane *supra* note 27 and Harper v. Edgewood Board of Education, 655 F. Supp. 1353 (S.D. Ohio 1987).

80. SG v. Sayreville Board of Education, 333 F.3d 417, 423 (3d Cir. 2003). The court deferred to the school's determination that such behavior supported violence and needed to be discouraged.

81. 445 F.3d 1166, 1185 (9th Cir. 2006). Despite a claim that such a stance was akin to viewpoint discrimination, the Ninth Circuit declared that per *Tinker*, viewpoints that were in and of themselves materially disruptive could be restricted without triggering a free speech violation.

82. 478 U.S. 675 (1986).
83. *Id.* at 681.
84. *Id.* at 683.

85. Stanton v. Brunswick School Department, 577 F. Supp. 1560, 1574 (D. Me. 1984).

86. *Bethel* 478 U.S. at 692 (Stevens, J. dissenting).

87. K.J. v. Sauk Prairie School District, 2012 U.S. Dist. LEXIS 187689 (W.D. Wis, 2012) at *23.

88. 725 F.3d 293 (3d Cir. 2013).

89. *See* J.S. v. Blue Mountain, 650 F.3d 915 (3d Cir. 2011) (en banc). "J.S. embarrassed, belittled, and possibly defamed McGonigle. If J.S. were not disciplined, it would demonstrate to the student body that this form of speech is acceptable behavior—whether on or off campus." *Id.* at 945 (Fisher, Circuit Judge, dissenting).

90. Boroff v. Van Wert City Board of Education, 220 F.3d 465 (6th Cir. 2000).

91. R.O. v. Ithaca City School District, 645 F.3d 533 (2d Cir. 2011).

92. D.C. v. Valley Central School District, 2013 U.S. Dist. LEXIS 74177 (S.D. N.Y. 2013).

93. Mary Sue Backus, *OMG! Missing the Teachable Moment and Undermining the Future of the First Amendment*, 60 CASE W. RES. L. REV. 153, 195 (2009).

94. Redish & Finnerty *supra* note 26 at 84–92.

95. Murad Hussain, *Freedom of Speech and Adolescent Public School Students*, 47

Journ. Am. Acad. Child & Adoles. Psychiatry. 614, 617 (2009).
96. Beard et. al. *supra* note 31 at 340–42.
97. Mill *supra* note 1 at 55.
98. Richards *supra* note 3 at 62.
99. *See* Scanlon *supra* note 2.
100. Gutmann *supra* note 11 at 53.
101. Beard *supra* note 76 at 71.
102. Louis Joughin, ed. *1967 Joint Statement on Rights and Freedoms of Students*, Academic Freedom and Tenure: A Handbook of the American Association of University Professors, 66–74 (University of Wisconsin Press 1969). The statement begins, "Academic institutions exist for the transmission of knowledge, the pursuit of truth, the development of students, and the general wellbeing of society. Free inquiry and free expression are indispensible to the attainment of these goals."
103. American Civil Liberties Union, *Academic Freedom in the Secondary Schools*, 9–20 (ACLU 1968). Under the section "Freedom of Expression and Communication," the ACLU writes, "The right of every student to have access to varied points of view, to confront and study controversial issues, to be treated without prejudice or penalty for what he reads or writes, and to have facilities for learning available in the school library and the classroom may not be derogated or denied."
104. Bruce Hafen, *Developing Student Expression through Institutional Authority: Public Schools as Mediating Structures*, 48 Ohio St. L. J. 663, 696 (1987).
105. Lynn Schofield Clark and Rachel Monserrate, *High School Journalism and the Making of Young Citizens*, 12 Journ. 417, 430 (2011).
106. "Dear Colleague" Letter from Russlyn Ali, Assistant Secretary for Civil Rights, U.S. Department of Education Office for Civil Rights (Oct. 26, 2010).
107. *Tinker* 393 U.S. at 513.
108. Sypniewski v. Warren Hills Regional Board of Education, 307 F.3d 243, 264 (3d Cir. 2002).
109. Harper v. Poway, 455 F.3d 1052, 1053 (9th Cir. 2006) (en banc) (Reinhardt, Judge, concurring).
110. Brannon Denning and Molly Taylor, *Morse v. Frederick and the Regulation of Cyberspace*, 35 Hastings Const. L.Q. 835, 884 (2007).
111. 347 Ark. 409 (Ark. 2002).
112. For example, in a libel lawsuit, the same criteria would be used to determine public/private person status, along with the same corresponding level of fault.
113. William Shakespeare, Hamlet, act 1, sc. 3. Spoken by Polonius to his son, Laertes; despite the advice, the rest of the play does not go well for either character.
114. Even if it's so clean. ("It's certainly uncontaminated by cheese.") "The Cheese Shop" *Monty Python's Flying Circus*, third season, first shown 11/30/1972.
115. *Tinker* 393 U.S. at 509.
116. *Tinker* 393 U.S. at 511.
117. James Ryan, *The Supreme Court and Public Schools*, 86 Va. L. Rev. 1335, 1424 (2000).
118. Roe *supra* note 9 at 1288–89 (1991).
119. *See* Emily Waldman, *A Post-Morse Framework for Students' Potentially Hurtful Speech (Religious and Otherwise)*, 37 J.L. & Educ. 463 (2008).
120. *Nuxoll* 523 F.3d at 674.
121. The incitement standard is so difficult for precisely this rationale.
122. 408 U.S. 169 (1972).
123. 53 F.3d 152 (6th Cir. 1995).
124. The teacher testified that she wanted to ensure students did not select topics with which they were too familiar, as that would be less of a challenge to research and present. Because the student was a devout Christian, the teacher was concerned that the student's strong familiarity with the facts of Christ's life would make the assignment easier for her than it was for other students and less academically rigorous for the student. *Id.* at 154.
125. 477 F.2d 171 (9th Cir. 1973).
126. Arthur Powell, Eleanor Farrar & David Cohen, The Shopping Mall High School: Winners and Losers in the Educational Marketplace 2 (Houghton Mifflin Company 1985).
127. Redish and Finnerty, *supra* note 26 at 65.
128. Thomas v. Board of Education, Granville Central School District, 607 F.2d 1043, 1049 (2d Cir. 1979).
129. Michelle Fine, Framing Dropouts: Notes on the Politics of an Urban Public High School 32–34 (University of New York Press 1991).
130. Wooster v. Sunderland, 27 Cal. App. 51, 55 (Cal. App. Ct. 1915).

Chapter Notes—6

131. *See* Pickering v. Board of Education, 391 U.S. 563 (1968).
132. Mill *supra* note 1 at 10–11.
133. ABE FORTAS, CONCERNING DISSENT AND CIVIL DISOBEDIENCE 29 (Signet Books 1968).
134. U.S. Department of Education, National Center for Education Statistics. *Indicators of School Crime and Safety: 2013*, INSTITUTE OF EDUCATION SCIENCES https://nces.ed.gov/programs/crimeindicators/crimeindicators2013/key.asp (last visited July 4, 2015). In 1999, 7.6% of students ages 12–18 reported criminal victimization at school during the previous six months. In 2011, that number was 3.9%.
135. *Id.*
136. Broussard v. Waldron School District, 2012 U.S. Dist. LEXIS 125046 (W.D. Ark, 2012) at *18.

Chapter 6

1. Katherine Schaeffer, *Photos of Condom-Wrapped Banana, Hookah Prompt Prior Review Debate at Michigan High School*, STUDENT PRESS LAW CENTER, Mar. 16, 2015, http://www.splc.org/article/2015/03/photo-of-condom-wrapped-banana-prompts-prior-review-debate-at-michigan-high-school (last visited June 5, 2015).
2. Near v. Minnestoa, 283 U.S. 697, 716 (1931).
3. *See*, for example, New York Times v. U.S., 403 U.S. 713 (1971), in which the Supreme Court struck down an attempt by the Nixon administration to censor the New York Times and the Washington Post from printing portions of the Pentagon Papers.
4. 427 U.S. 539 (1976).
5. *Id.* at 567.
6. U.S. CONST. AMEND I.
7. Potter Stewart, *Or of the Press*, 26 HASTINGS L.J. 631, 634 (1974–75).
8. *Id.*
9. LEE BOLLINGER, IMAGES OF A FREE PRESS 20 (University of Chicago Press 1991).
10. *Id.* at 28–31.
11. C. Edwin Baker, *The Media that Citizens Need*, 147 U. PA. L. REV. 317, 360 (1999).
12. Ashley Lutz, *These 6 Corporations Control 90% of the Media in America*, BUSINESS INSIDER (June 14, 2012) http://www.businessinsider.com/these-6-corporations-control-90-of-the-media-in-america-2012-6#ixzz3cJl4TJJ0 (last visited June 6, 2015).
13. Baker *supra* note 11 at 372.
14. Dane S. Claussen. *High School Student Newspapers in U.S. Youth Culture: From Gossip to Politics to Social Issues; From Vocational Education to PR tool, to Forum for Expression and Back Again* 2 (Presented to the Scholastic Journalism Division, AEJMC Convention, New Orleans Aug 4–7 1999).
15. *Id.* at 6–13.
16. *Id.* at 15.
17. DEATH BY CHEESEBURGER: HIGH SCHOOL JOURNALISM IN THE 1990S AND BEYOND 4 (Carol Knopes, ed., The Freedom Forum 1994).
18. Mary Benedict, David H. Weaver and J. Herbert Altschull. *High School Students and the Newspaper: Educating Media Consumers*, 53 JOURN. QUARTERLY 280, 286 (1976).
19. *Id.* at 284.
20. Jack Dvorak and Changhee Choi, *High School Journalism, Academic Performance Correlate*, 30 NEWSPAPER RES. J. 75, 77 (2009).
21. *Id.* at 79–83.
22. *Id.* at 87.
23. Lynn Schofield Clark and Rachel Monserrate, *High School Journalism and the Making of Young Citizens*, 12 JOURN. 417 (2011).
24. *Id.* at 427.
25. Hazelwood School District v. Kuhlmeier, 484 U.S. 260 (1988).
26. *Id.* at 273.
27. *Id.* at 272.
28. *Id.* at 271.
29. 236 F.3d 342 (6th Cir. 2001).
30. *Id.* at. 348 (internal citations removed).
31. *Hazelwood* 484 U.S. at 269.
32. 198 Cal. App. 3d 47 (Cal. Ct. App. 1988)
33. *Id.* at 54.
34. Lange v. Diercks, No. 1–587/11–0191. (Iowa Ct. App. 2011) at *12.
35. Burch v. Barker, 861 F.2d 1149, 1152 (9th Cir. 1988).
36. *See* Boucher v. School Board of the School District of Greenfield, 134 F.3d 821 (7th Cir. 1998).
37. *See* Pangle v. Bend-Lapine School

District, 169 Ore. App. 376 (Court of Appeals of Oregon 2000).
38. 725 F. Supp. 687, 689 (E.D. N.Y. 1989). This case was brought by a newspaper adviser who was fired after allowing his students to run an editorial critical of the then-proposed holiday honoring Dr. Martin Luther King.
39. *Id.* at 690.
40. Paye v. Gibraltar School District, 1991 U.S. Dist. LEXIS 16480 (E.D. Mich. 1991). This case dealt with a literary magazine that drew complaints due to the language of some student contributions.
41. 236 F.3d 342 (6th Cir. 2001).
42. 246 F. Supp. 2d 820 (N.D. Ohio 2003).
43. 345 F. Supp. 2d 799 (E.D. Mich. 2004).
44. *Id.* at 807.
45. *Id.*
46. *Id.* at 808.
47. *Kincaid* 236 F.3d at 351 (internal citations omitted).
48. *Draudt* 246 F. Supp. 2d at 829.
49. R.O. v. Ithaca City School District, 645 F.3d 533 (2d Cir. 2011).
50. 137 N.J. 585 (N.J. 1994).
51. *Id.* at 593.
52. *Id.*
53. http://www.splc.org.
54. Katherine Schaeffer, *Athletic Director's Resignation Prompts Censorship of Calif. High School Newspaper, Adviser Says,* STUDENT PRESS LAW CENTER, Mar. 24, 2105, http://www.splc.org/article/2015/03/athletic-director-resignation-prompts-censorship-of-calif-high-school-newspaper-adviser-says (last visited June 9, 2015).
55. Mariana Viera, *Va. High School Censors Story About Marijuana 'Dabbing',*" STUDENT PRESS LAW CENTER, Mar. 24, 2015, http://www.splc.org/article/2015/03/va-high-school-censors-story-about-marijuana-dabbing (last visited June 9, 2015).
56. See *supra* note 1.
57. Society of Professional Journalists Mission statement, https://www.spj.org/spjinfo.asp (last visited June 10, 2015): "The Society of Professional Journalists is dedicated to the perpetuation of a free press as the cornerstone of our nation and our liberty. To ensure that the concept of self-government outlined by the United States Constitution remains a reality into future centuries, the American people must be well-informed in order to make decisions regarding their lives and their local and national communities. It is the role of journalists to provide this information in an accurate, comprehensive, timely, and understandable manner."
58. *Hazelwood* 484 U.S. at 271 (internal citations omitted).
59. J.S. MILL, ON LIBERTY 10–11 (W.W. Norton and Company 1859) (1975).
60. 345 F. Supp. 2d 799, 803 (E.D. Mich. 2004). Key concerns were the use of pseudonyms and sourcing from USA Today. District administrators supported the prior restraint because they did not feel it was appropriate for a student to cover the lawsuit.
61. *Id.* at 811 fn 5.
62. 418 U.S. 241, 258 (1974).
63. 131 F.3d 241 (1st Cir. 1997).
64. *Id.* at 253.
65. Tinker v. Des Moines Independent Community School District, 393 U.S. 503, 508–09 (1969).

Chapter 7

1. Pew Research Center, *Social Networking Fact Sheet,* http://www.pewinternet.org/fact-sheets/ (last visited June 15, 2015).
2. *Id.*
3. Brandon Gaille, *Interesting Facts about Blogs,* WPVIRTUOSO, Nov. 20, 2013, http://www.wpvirtuoso.com/how-many-blogs-are-on-the-internet/ (last visited June 15, 2015).
4. *How Much Email Do We Use Daily?,* SOURCEDIGIT, Feb. 19, 2014, http://sourcedigit.com/4233-much-email-use-daily-182-9-billion-emails-sentreceived-per-day-worldwide/ (last visited June 15, 2015).
5. State ex rel Dresser v. District Board of School District No. 1, 135 Wis. 619, 627 (Wis. 1908).
6. O'Rourke v. Walker, 102 Conn. 130 (Conn. 1925).
7. *Id.* at 135–36.
8. Fenton v. Stear, 423 F. Supp. 767, 772 (W.D. Penn. 1976).
9. Klein v. Smith, 635 F. Supp. 1440, 1441 (D. Me. 1986).
10. 607 F.2d 1043 (2d Cir. 1979).
11. *Id.* at 1045.

Chapter Notes—7

12. *Id.* at 1051.
13. Killion v. Franklin Regional School District, 136 F. Supp. 2d 446 (W.D. Pa. 2001).
14. Porter v. Ascension Parish School Board, 393 F.3d 608 (5th Cir. 2004).
15. *Id.* at 615.
16. Tom McBride and Ron Nief, *2018 List*, THE MINDSET LIST, 2014, https://www.beloit.edu/mindset/ (last visited July 4, 2015).
17. MARSHALL MCLUHAN, UNDERSTANDING MEDIA: THE EXTENSIONS OF MAN (McGraw-Hill 1964).
18. Spoiler: There are none.
19. *See* Reno v. ACLU, 521 U.S. 844 (1997).
20. *Id.* at 882.
21. For example, a Chicago suburban school district required all students participating in extracurricular activities to sign pledge agreeing that evidence of illegal or inappropriate behavior posted to the Internet could be grounds for disciplinary action. Mary Sue Backus, *OMG! Missing the Teachable Moment and Undermining the Future of the First Amendment*, 60 CASE W. RES. 153, 181 (2009).
22. *See* Frank LoMonte, *That Didn't Take Long—Unrepentant Free-Speech Violator Chicago State Resumes Its Censoring Ways*, STUDENT PRESS LAW CENTER, Apr. 6, 2012, http://www.splc.org/wordpress/?p=3480 (last visited July 4, 2015). According to the blog posting, CSU "circulated a campus-wide gag order that threatens discipline against any employee who says anything about the university, even on social media, without vetting it through the CSU public-relations office."
23. State ex rel Dresser v. District Board of School District No. 1, 135 Wis. 619 (Wis. 1908).
24. Fenton v. Stear, 423 F. Supp. 767 (W.D. Penn. 1976).
25. J.C. ex rel. R.C. v. Beverly Hills Unified School, 711 F. Supp. 2d 1094, 1107 (C.D. Cal. 2010). This case dealt with the suspension of a student for posting a short video to YouTube of an off-campus conversation she had with friends discussing their mutual dislike of another student at the school. The video upset the named student, who brought it to the attention of the school.
26. 807 A.2d 847 (Pa. 2002).
27. *Id.* at 865.
28. 647 F.3d 754 (8th Cir. 2011).
29. *Id.* at 766.
30. S.J.W. v. Lee's Summit R-7 School District, 696 F.3d 771, 773 (8th Cir. 2012).
31. *Id.* at 778. The court noted that school was able to establish a significant amount of disturbance among teachers and students when the site was made public, which satisfied the *Tinker* standard in the eyes of the court.
32. 652 F.3d 565 (4th Cir. 2011).
33. *Id.* at 573.
34. 894 F. Supp. 2d 1128 (D. Minn 2012).
35. *Id.* at 1133–34.
36. 642 F.3d 334 (2d Cir. 2011).
37. *Id.* at 348.
38. 728 F.3d 1062 (9th Cir. 2013).
39. *Id.* at 1069.
40. 92 F. Supp.2d 1088 (W.D. Wash. 2000).
41. *Id.* at 1089.
42. *Id.* at 1090.
43. Killion v. Franklin Regional School District, 136 F. Supp. 2d 446 (W.D. Penn. 2001); Coy v. Board of Education of Canton City, 205 F. Supp. 2d 791 (N.D. Ohio 2002); J.C. ex rel. R.C. v. Beverly Hills Unified School, 711 F. Supp. 2d 1094 (C.D. Calif. 2010); J.S. v. Bethlehem Area School District, 757 A.2d 412 (Pa. Commw. Ct. 2000) AND 807 A.2d 847 (Pa. 2002); and Porter v. Ascension Parish School Board, 393 F.3d 608 (5th Cir. 2004).
44. Porter v. Ascension Parish School Board, 393 F.3d 608 (5th Cir. 2004).
45. 988 F. Supp. 2d 826 (W.D. Tenn. 2013).
46. *Id.* at 839.
47. 593 F.3d 286 (3d Cir. 2010) (vacated, overturned by JS v. Blue Mountain School District, 650 F.3d 915, 3d Cir. 2011, en banc).
48. 593 F.3d 249 (3d Cir. 2010) (vacated, overturned by Layshock v. Hermitage School District, 650 F.3d 205, 3d Cir. 2011, en banc).
49. J.S. v. Blue Mountain, 650 F.3d 915 (3d Cir. 2011) (en banc),
50. *Id.* at 931.
51. Layshock v Hermitage School District, 650 F.3d 205 (3d Cir. 2011) (en banc).
52. *Id.* at 214–15.
53. Blue Mt. Sch. Dist. v. J. S., 2012 U.S. LEXIS 726 (U.S., Jan. 17, 2012).
54. T.V. v. Smith-Green, No. 1:09-CV-290-PPS (N.D. Ind. Aug. 10, 2011).
55. Requa v. Kent School District, 492 F. Supp. 2d 1272 (W.D. Wash. 2007).

56. *Id.* at 1280.
57. Timothy Stenovec, *Myspace History: A Timeline of the Social Network's Biggest Moments*, THE HUFFINGTON POST, June 29, 2011, http://www.huffingtonpost.com/2011/06/29/myspace-history-timeline_n_887059.html (last visited June 19, 2015).
58. *See* Reno v. ACLU, 521 U.S. 844 (1997) and Ashcroft v. ACLU, 535 U.S. 564 (2002).
59. J.S. v. Blue Mountain, 650 F.3d 915, 939 (3d Cir. 2011) (en banc) (Smith, Circuit Judge, concurring).

Chapter 8

1. THOMAS I. EMERSON, THE SYSTEM OF FREE EXPRESSION (Vintage Books 1970).
2. *Id.* at 17–20.
3. RONALD DWORKIN, FREEDOM'S LAW: THE MORAL REASONINGS OF THE AMERICAN CONSTITUTION, 245 (Harvard University Press 1996).
4. 418 U.S. 405 (1974). This case dealt with the conviction of a Washington man for displaying an American flag upside, contrary to state statute, to protest the U.S. involvement in Cambodia and the actions of the National Guard at Kent State. The Court determined the man's actions were expression and protected under the First Amendment.
5. *Id.* at 410–11.
6. Rumsfeld v. FAIR, 547 U.S. 47, 66 (2006).
7. 976 F. Supp. 659 (S.D. Tex. 1997).
8. *Id.* at 666.
9. *Id.* at 665, internal citation removed.
10. *Id.*
11. *Id.* at 667. The ban was also struck down for vagueness.
12. Emerson *supra* note 1 at 18.
13. Paul Farhi, *"Dr. Laura" to end radio show over racial controversy*, THE WASHINGTON POST, Aug. 8, 2010, accessed through Newspaper Source Plus, WPT053818968610.
14. News Corpse, *Carrie Prejean Dishonors the First Amendment*, May 12, 2009, http://www.newscorpse.com/ncWP/?p=1266 (last visited June 21, 2015).
15. Rebecca Gajda, *States' Expectations for Teachers' Knowledge About School Law*, ACTION IN TEACHER EDUCATION, Summer 2008, at 16.
16. *Id.* at 21.
17. *Id.* at 16.
18. Morse v. Frederick, 551 U.S. 393 (2007).
19. *Id.* at 418 (Thomas, J. concurring).
20. Jacobellis v. Ohio, 378 U.S. 184, 197 (1964) (Stewart, J. concurring).
21. 556 F.3d 950 (9th Cir. 2009). The case was appealed to the Supreme Court, which affirmed the Ninth Circuit Court's decision. Brown v. Entertainment Media Association, 131 S. Ct. 2729 (2011).
22. *Id.* at 967.
23. Bethel School District v. Fraser, 478 U.S. 675 (1986).
24. Hazelwood v. Kuhlmeier, 484 U.S. 260 (1988).
25. Morse v. Frederick, 551 U.S. 393 (2007).
26. *Fraser* 478 U.S. at 685.
27. *Hazelwood* 484 U.S. at 273.
28. *Morse* 551 U.S. at 403.
29. Tinker v. Des Moines Independent Community School District, 393 U.S. 503, 510–11 (1969).
30. *Id.* at 509.
31. *See* "Policy Writing Framework," http://www.eduweb.vic.gov.au/edulibrary/public/schacc/tmpltpolicywriting.pdf (last visited July 19, 2015).
32. Porter v. Ascension Parish School Board, 393 F.3d 608, 620 (5th Cir. 2004) (emphasis added). The student in this case had drawn the picture at home two years previously. His younger brother had borrowed the sketch pad that held the drawing and brought it to school for his own use, found the drawing by his brother and showed it to another student, who brought it to the attention of a school official.
33. AMY GUTMANN, DEMOCRATIC EDUCATION 92–3 (Princeton University Press 1999).
34. ROBERT HESS AND JUDITH TORNEY, THE DEVELOPMENT OF POLITICAL ATTITUDES IN CHILDREN, 70 (Doubleday & Co. 1968).
35. *See* ROBERT PUTNAM, BOWLING ALONE (Simon & Schuster 2000).
36. STEVEN SHIFFRIN, DISSENT, INJUSTICE AND THE MEANINGS OF AMERICA 114 (Princeton University Press 1999).
37. 461 F.2d 566 (2d Cir. 1972). This case actually dealt with the dismissal of a high school teacher for wearing a black armband to school to protest the Vietnam War, but the rationale for the dismissal was such symbolic speech was inappropriate for the student audience.

38. *Id.* at 574.
39. Lonnie Sherrod, Constance Flanagan and James Youniss, *Dimensions of Citizenship and Opportunities for Youth Development: The What, Why, When, Where and Who of Citizenship Development* 6 APP. DEVELOP. SCI. 264, 265 (2002).
40. DIANA HESS, CONTROVERSY IN THE CLASSROOM: THE DEMOCRATIC POWER OF DISCUSSION 162 (Routledge 2009).
41. Mary Sue Backus, *OMG! Missing the Teachable Moment and Undermining the Future of the First Amendment—TISNF!* 60 CASE W. RES. L. REV. 153, 199–200 (2009).
42. 390 U.S. 629, 654–55 (Douglas, J. dissenting).
43. STEPHEN THOMAS, NELDA CAMBRON-MCCABE & MARTHA MCCARTHY, PUBLIC SCHOOL LAW: TEACHERS' AND STUDENTS' RIGHTS 504 (Pearson/Allyn & Bacon 2009).
44. *Tinker* 393 U.S. at 508–09.

Works Cited

Alexander, Kern & Alexander, M. David, *American Public School Law*, 6th Edition (Thomson West 2005).
Alexander, Lawrence & Horton, Paul, *The Impossibility of a Free Speech Principle*, 78 Nw. U. L. Rev 1321 (1983–84).
Ali, Russlyn, "Dear Colleague" Letter from Assistant Secretary for Civil Rights, U.S. Department of Education Office for Civil Rights (Oct. 26, 2010).
American Civil Liberties Union, *Academic Freedom in the Secondary Schools* (ACLU, 1968).
Ammer, Christine, *Out of the Mouths of Babes*, The American Heritage Dictionary of Idioms (2003), http://idioms.thefreedictionary.com/Out+of+the+mouths+of+babes.
Arkansas Student Publications Act, Ark. Stat. Ann. §§ 6–18–1201–1204 (1995).
Arkes, Hadley, *Civility and the Restriction of Speech: Rediscovering the Defamation of Groups*, 1974 Sup. Ct. Rev. 281 (1974).
Arkes, Hadley, *The Philosopher in the City: The Moral Dimensions of Urban Politics* (Princeton University Press 1981).
Arnett, JJ, *Emerging Adulthood: A Theory of Development from the Late Teens through the Twenties*, 55 Am. Psychol. 469 (2000).
Arnett, JJ, *Learning to Stand Alone: The Contemporary American Transition to Adulthood in Cultural and Historical Context*, 41 Hum. Dev. 295 (1998).
Arum, Richard, *Judging School Discipline: The Crisis of Moral Authority* (Harvard University Press 2003).
Avery, Patricia & Simmons, Annette, *Civic Life as Conveyed in United States Civics and History Textbooks*, 15 Intl. J Soc. Educ. 105 (2001).
Backus, Mary Sue, *OMG! Missing the Teachable Moment and Undermining the Future of the First Amendment*, 60 Case W. Res. L. Rev. 153 (2009).
Baier, Paul, *The Constitutionality of Minimum Age Requirements for Public Office: Reading Joseph Story on Constitution Day*, 60 La. L. Rev 481 (2000).
Baker, C. Edwin, *Human Liberty and Freedom of Speech* (Oxford University Press 1989).
Baker, C. Edwin, *The Media that Citizens Need*, 147 U. Pa. L. Rev. 317 (1999).
Baker, C. Edwin, *Scope of the First Amendment Freedom of Speech*, 25 UCLA L. Rev. 964 (1978).
Beard, Charles, *The Unique Function of Education in American Democracy* (National Education Association 1937).
Beard, Charles, Beard, Mary & Beard, William Beard, *The Beards' New Basic History of the United States* (Doubleday & Co. 1968).
Benedict, Mary, Weaver, David H. and Altschull, J. Herbert, *High School Students and the Newspaper: Educating Media Consumers*, 53 Journ. Quarterly 280, 286 (1976).

Works Cited

Berlin, Isaiah, *Four Essays on Liberty* (Oxford University Press 1969).
Berns, Walter, *The First Amendment and the Future of American Democracy* (Regnery Gateway 1985).
Blakemore, Sarah-Jayne & Choudhury, Suparna, *Development of the Adolescent Brain: Implications for Executive Function and Social Cognition*, 47 Journ Child Psychol. & Psychiatry 296 (2006).
Bollinger, Lee, *Images of a Free Press* (University of Chicago Press 1991).
Bork, Robert, *Neutral Principles and Some First Amendment Problems*, 47 Ind. L.J. 1 (1971–72).
Boston, Bruce & Gomez, Barbara, *Every Student a Citizen: Creating the Democratic Self* (Education Commission of the States 2000).
Bowden, Randall, *Evolution of Responsibility: From In Loco Parentis to Ad Meliora Vertamur*, 127 Educ. 480, 480 (2007).
Bowman, Kristi, *The Civil Rights Roots of Tinker's Disruption Tests*, 58 Am. U. L. Rev. 1129 (2009).
Burkett, Elinor, *Another Planet: A Year in the Life of a Suburban High School* (Harper-Collins 2001).
Byrne, J. Peter, *Academic Freedom: A Special Concern of the First Amendment*, 99 Yale L.J. 251 (1989).
Calhoun, Craig, *Introduction* in *Habermas and the Public Sphere* (Craig Calhoun, ed., MIT Press 1993).
California Community College Free Expression Law, Calif. Educ. Code § 7612 (1977).
California Leonard Law, Calif. Educ. Code § 48950 (1992).
California Leonard Law, Calif. Educ. Code § 66301 (2006).
California Leonard Law, Calif. Educ. Code § 94367 (1992).
California Student Free Expression Law, Cal. Educ. Code § 48907 (1977).
Carnevale, Anthony Carnevale, Rose, Stephen & Cheah, Ban, *The College Payoff: Education, Occupations, Lifetime Earnings* (Georgetown University Center on Education and the Workforce 2011).
Clark, Kenneth, *"Vestibule Adolescence" and Other Threats to Children and Youth* 163–165 (1959), included in *Children and Youth in America: A Documentary History* (Robert Bremner, ed., Harvard University Press, 1974).
Clark, Lynn Schofield & Monserrate, Rachel, *High School Journalism and the Making of Young Citizens*, 12 Journ. 417 (2011).
Claussen, Dane S., *High School Student Newspapers in U.S. Youth Culture: From Gossip to Politics to Social Issues; From Vocational Education to PR tool, to Forum for Expression and Back Again* 2 (Presented to the Scholastic Journalism Division, AEJMC Convention, New Orleans Aug 4–7 1999).
Coleman, James, *The Adolescent Society: The Social Life of the Teenager and Its Impact on Education* (The Free Press of Glencoe 1963).
Colorado Student Free Expression Law, Colo. Rev. Stat. § 22-1-120 (1990).
Cusick, Philip, *Inside High School: A Student's World* (Holt, Rinehart and Winston, Inc. 1973).
Dailey, Anne, *Children's Constitutional Rights*, 95 Minn. L. Rev. 2099 (2011).
Davis, Josh & Rosenberg, Josh, *The Immanent Structure of Free Speech Doctrine: Bong Hits, Jesus, and the Role of Public Schools in Controlling Student Speech*, Electronic copy available at: http://ssrn.com/abstract=1206314 (2008).
Denning, Brannon Denning & Taylor, Molly, *Morse v. Frederick and the Regulation of Cyberspace*, 35 Hastings Const. L.Q. 835 (2007).
Dewey, John, *Democracy and Education, An Introduction to the Philosophy of Education* (Macmillan Company 1916).

Works Cited

Dupre, Anne, *Speaking Up: The Unintended Costs of Free Speech in Public Schools* (Harvard University Press 2009).
Dvorak, Jack and Choi, Changhee, *High School Journalism, Academic Performance Correlate*, 30 Newspaper Res. J. 75 (2009).
Dworkin, Ronald, *Freedom's Law: The Moral Reasonings of the American Constitution* (Harvard University Press 1996).
Eastman, John, *When Did Education Become a Civil Right? An Assessment of State Constitutional Provisions for Education 1776–1900*, 42 Am. Journ. Legal Hist 1 (1998).
Emerson, Thomas I., *The System of Freedom of Expression* (Random House 1970).
Equal Access Act, 20 U.S.C. § 4071.
Fallon, Richard, Jr. *Two Senses of Autonomy*, 46 Stan. L. Rev. 875 (1994).
Family Educational Rights and Privacy Act (FERPA), 20 U.S.C. § 1232g.
Farhi, Paul, *"Dr. Laura" to End Radio Show over Radio Controversy*, The Washington Post, C05 (August 18, 2010).
Fine, Gary, *Gifted Tongues: High School Debate and Adolescent Culture* (Princeton University Press 2001).
Fine, Michelle, *Framing Dropouts: Notes of the Politics of an Urban High School* (State University of New York Press 1991).
Fortas, Abe, *Concerning Dissent and Civil Disobedience* (Signet Books 1968).
The Flat Earth Society, http://www.theflatearthsociety.org/cms/.
Friedland, Lewis & Morimoto, Shauna, *The Changing Lifeworld of Young People: Risk, Resume-Padding and Civic Engagement*, CIRCLE Working Paper 40 (Sept. 2005).
Gaille, Brandon, *Interesting Facts About Blogs*, WPVirtuoso (Nov. 20, 2013) http://www.wpvirtuoso.com/how-many-blogs-are-on-the-internet/.
Gajda, Rebecca, *States' Expectations for Teachers' Knowledge About School Law*, Action in Teacher Education (Summer 2008).
Garnett, Richard, *Can There Really Be "Free Speech" in Public Schools?*, 12 Lewis & Clark L.Rev. 45 (2008).
Garvey, John, *Children and the First Amendment*, 57 Tex L. Rev. 321 (1979).
Grant, Gerald, *The World We Created at Hamilton High* (Harvard University Press 1988).
Gutmann, Amy, *Democratic Education* (Princeton University Press 1999).
Gutmann, Amy, *What Is the Value of Free Speech for Students?*, 29 Ariz. St. L.J. 519 (1997).
Guttmacher Institute, *An Overview of Minors' Consent Law*, State Policies in Brief (Mar. 2012).
Hafen, Bruce, *Developing Student Expression Through Institutional Authority: Public Schools as Mediating Structures*, 48 Ohio St. L. J. 663 (1987).
Heidlage, Benjamin, *A Relational Approach to Schools' Regulation of Youth Online Speech*, 84 NYU L. Rev. 572 (2009).
Hertz, MF & David-Ferdon, C., *Electronic Media and Youth Violence: A CDC Issue Brief for Educators and Caregivers* (Centers for Disease Control 2008).
Hess, Diana, *Controversy in the Classroom: The Democratic Power of Discussion* (Routledge 2009).
Hess, Robert & Torney, Judith, *The Development of Political Attitudes in Children* (Doubleday & Co. 1968).
Holmes, Jr., Oliver Wendell, *Law in Science and Science in Law*, 12 Harv. L.Rev. 443 (1899).
Hudson, David, Jr. *Let the Students Speak! A History of the Fight for Free Expression in American Schools* (Beacon Press 2011).
Hussain, Murad, *Freedom of Speech and Adolescent Public School Students*, 47 Journ. Am. Acad. Child & Adoles. Psychol. 614 (2009).

Works Cited

Illinois College Campus Press Act, 110 ILCS 13 (2007).
Iowa Student Free Expression Law, Iowa Code § 280.22 (1989).
Jekielek, Susan & Brown, Brett, *The Transition to Adulthood: Characteristics of Young Adults Ages 18 to 24 in America* (Child Trends/The Annie E. Casey Foundation 2005).
Jonassen, D.H., Hernandez-Serrano, J. and Choi, I., *Integrating Constructivism and Learning Technologies.* In J. M. Spector & T.M. Anderson (Eds.), *Integration and Holistic Perspectives on Learning, Instruction, and Technology* (Kluwer Academic 2000).
Joughin, Louis (ed.), *1967 Joint Statement on Rights and Freedoms of Students*, Academic Freedom and Tenure: A Handbook of the American Association of University Professors (University of Wisconsin Press 1969).
Journalism Education Association Scholastic Press Rights, http://jeasprc.org/.
Kansas Student Publications Act, Kan. Stat. Ann. §§ 72.1504–72.1506 (1992).
Keep a Breast Foundation, http://www.keep-a-breast.org/.
Knopes, Carol (ed.), *Death by Cheeseburger: High School Journalism in the 1990s and Beyond* (The Freedom Forum 1994).
Kuhn, Deanna, *Do Cognitive Changes Accompany Developments in the Adolescent Brain?* 1 Persp. on Psychol. Sci 59 (2006).
Lane, Robert Wheeler, *Beyond the Schoolhouse Gate: Free Speech and the Inculcation of Values* (Temple University Press 1995).
Laycock, Douglas, *High-Value Speech and the Basic Educational Mission of a Public School: Some Preliminary Thoughts*, 12 Lewis & Clark L. Rev. 111 (2008).
LeBoeuf, Trisha, *Dorm Mold Story Leads to Adviser's Termination, Student Journalists Allege*, Student Press Law Center, June 3, 2015, http://www.splc.org/article/2015/06/dorm-mold-story-leads-to-advisers-termination-student-journalists-allege.
Levin, Betsy, *Educating Youth for Citizenship: The Conflict between Authority and Individual Rights in the Public School*, 95 Yale L.J. 1647 (1985).
LoMonte, Frank, *That Didn't Take Long—Unrepentant Free-Speech Violator Chicago State Resumes Its Censoring Ways*, Student Press Law Center (April 6, 2012) http://www.splc.org/wordpress/?p=3480
Lutz, Ashley, *These 6 Corporations Control 90% of the Media in America*, Business Insider (June 14, 2012) http://www.businessinsider.com/these-6-corporations-control-90-of-the-media-in-america-2012-6#ixzz3cJl4TJJ0.
Massachusetts Student Free Expression Law, Mass. Gen. Laws Ann. ch. 71, § 82 (1988).
McBride, Tom and Nief, Ron, *2018 List*, The Mindset List, 2014, https://www.beloit.edu/mindset/.
McLuhan, Marshall, *Understanding Media: The Extensions of Man* (McGraw-Hill 1964).
McMullen, Judith, *Underage Drinking: Does Current Policy Make Sense?* 10 Lewis & Clark L. Rev. 333 (2006).
Meiklejohn, Alexander, *The First Amendment Is an Absolute*, 1961 Sup. Ct. Rev. 245 (1961).
Meiklejohn, Alexander, *Political Freedom* (Harper & Brothers 1960) (1948).
Merriam-Webster Dictionary, http://www.merriam-webster.com.
Merrill, M. David, Drake, Leston, Lacy, Mark J., Pratt, Jean and the ID2 Research Group, *Reclaiming Instructional Design*, 36 Educ. Tech. 5 (1996).
Mill, John S., *On Liberty* (W.W. Norton & Company 1975) (1859).
Milner, Jr., Murray, *Freaks, Geeks and Cool Kids: American Teenagers, Schools and the Culture of Consumption* (Routledge 2004).
Monty Python's Flying Circus, "The Cheese Shop" third season, first shown 11/30/1972.

Works Cited

National Center for Education Statistics, *Fast Facts: Back to School Statistics*, http://nces.ed.gov/fastfacts/display.asp?id=372.
National Center for Education Statistics, *The Nation's Report Card: Civics 2010* (U.S. Department of Education 2011).
National Conference of State Legislatures, *Tattoos and Body Piercings for Minors*, http://www.ncsl.org/issues-research/health/tattooing-and-body-piercing.aspx.
National Minimum Drinking Age Act, 23 U.S.C. § 158 (1984).
National Scholastic Press Association, http://studentpress.journ.umn.edu/nspa/.
Nelson, Jack, *Captive Voices* (Schocken Books 1974).
New International Version Bible.
News Corpse, *Carrie Prejean Dishonors the First Amendment* (May 12, 2009) http://www.newscorpse.com/ncWP/?p=1266.
North Dakota Student Journalists—Free Expression, N.D. Cent. Code §§ 15–10 and 15.1–06 (2015).
O'Connor, John, *Civic Engagement in Higher Education*, Change: The Magazine of Higher Learning, Sept./Oct .2006.
Olson, Lyle Olson, Van Ommeren, Roger & Rossow, Marshel, *High School Press Freedom Legislation: A Survey of Key Promoters* (presented at the annual meeting of the Association for Education in Journalism and Mass Communication, Scholastic Journalism Division, August 1995).
Olson, Lyle Olson, Van Ommeren, Roger & Rossow, Marshel, *A Paradigm for State High School Press Laws* (presented at the annual meeting of the Association for Education in Journalism and Mass Communication, Scholastic Journalism Division, Kansas City, MO, August 1993).
Oregon Student Free Expression Law (Public College and Universities), Ore. Rev. Stat. § 351.649 (2007),
Oregon Student Free Expression Law (Public Secondary Schools), Ore. Rev. Stat. § 336.477 (2007).
Oyez.org, Recording of Oral Argument, Tinker v. Des Moines Independent School District, 393 U.S. 503 (1969) (No. 21) *available at* http://www.oyez.org/cases/1960–1969/1968/1968_21 #argument.
Pember, Don & Calvert, Clay, *Mass Media Law* (17th ed. McGraw-Hill 2011).
Pennsylvania Administrative Code: Student Rights and Responsibilities, 22 Pa. Code § 12.9 (2005).
Pew Research Center, *Social Networking Fact Sheet*, http://www.pewinternet.org/fact-sheets/.
Polletta, Francesca & Jasper, James, *Collecting Identity and Social Movements* 27 Ann. Rev. of Soc. 283 (2001).
Post, Robert, *Between Governance and Management: The History and Theory of the Public Forum*, 34 UCLA L. Rev 1713 (1987).
Post, Robert, *Meiklejohn's Mistake: Individual Autonomy and the Reform of Public Discourse*, 64 U. Colo. L. Rev. 1109 (1993).
Powell, Arthur, Farrar, Eleanor & Cohen, David, *The Shopping Mall High School: Winners and Losers in the Educational Marketplace* (Houghton Mifflin Company 1985).
Putnam, Robert, *Bowling Alone* (Simon & Schuster 2000).
Rauch, Jonathan, *Kindly Inquisitors: The New Attacks on Free Thought* (University of Chicago Press 1994).
Ravitch, Diane, *Education and Democracy* in *Making Good Citizens: Education and Civil Society* (Diane Ravitch & Joseph Viteritti, eds., 2001).
Redish, Martin & Finnerty, Kevin, *What Did You Learn IN School Today? Free Speech, Values Inculcation and the Democratic-Educational Paradox*. 88 Cornell L. Rev 62, 66 (2002).

Works Cited

Richards, David, *Free Speech and Obscenity Law: Toward a Moral Theory of the First Amendment*, 123 U. Pa. L. Rev. 45 (1974–75).
Roe, Richard, *Valuing Student Speech: The Work of the Schools as Conceptual Development*, 79 Cal. L. Rev 1269 (1991).
Ryan, James, *The Supreme Court and Public Schools*, 86 Va. L. Rev. 1335 (2000).
Salkin, Erica, *The Speech, Not the Speaker: Protecting Public School Student Expression*, 11 Comm. L. Rev. 1 (2011).
Sanchez, J.M., *Expelling the Fourth Amendment from American Schools: Students' Rights Six Years After T.L.O.*, 21 J.L. & Educ. 381 (1992).
Saunders, Kevin, *Saving Our Children from the First Amendment* (New York University Press 2003).
Scanlon, Thomas, *A Theory of Freedom of Expression*, 1 Phil. & Pub. Aff. 204 (1972).
Schaeffer, Katherine, *Athletic Director's Resignation Prompts Censorship of Calif. High School Newspaper Adviser Says*, Student Press Law Center (Mar. 24, 2105) http://www.splc.org/article/2015/03/athletic-director-resignation-prompts-censorship-of-calif-high-school-newspaper-adviser-says.
Schaeffer, Katherine, *Photos of Condom-Wrapped Banana, Hookah Prompt Prior Review Debate at Michigan High School*, Student Press Law Center (Mar. 16, 2015) http://www.splc.org/article/2015/03/photo-of-condom-wrapped-banana-prompts-prior-review-debate-at-michigan-high-school.
Schamel, Wynell, *The 26th Amendment and Youth Voting Rights*, 60 Social Educ. 374 (1996).
Schneider, Barbara & Stevenson, David, *The Ambitious Generation: America's Teenagers, Motivated but Directionless* (Yale University Press 1999).
Scott, Elizabeth, *The Legal Construction of Childhood* (December 2000) *available at* http://papers.ssrn.com/paper.taf?abstract_id=244666.
Shakespeare, William, *Hamlet*.
Sherrod, Lonnie, Flanagan, Constance & Youniss, James, *Dimensions of Citizenship and Opportunities for Youth Development: The What, Why, When, Where and Who of Citizenship Development* 6 App. Develop. Sci. 264 (2002).
Shiffrin, Steven, *Dissent, Injustice and the Meanings of America* (Princeton University Press 1999).
Society of Professional Journalists, https://www.spj.org.
SourceDigit, *How Much Email Do We Use Daily?* (Feb. 19, 2014) http://sourcedigit.com/4233-much-email-use-daily-182-9-billion-emails-sentreceived-per-day-worldwide/.
Stein, Laura, *Speech Without Rights: The Status of Public Sphere on the Internet*, 11 Comm. Rev. 1 (2008).
Stein, Nan, *Bullying or Sexual Harassment? The Missing Discourse of Rights in an Era of Zero Tolerance*, 45 Ariz. L. Rev. 783 (2003).
Stenovec, Timothy, *Myspace History: A Timeline of the Social Network's Biggest Moments*, The Huffington Post (June 29, 2011) http://www.huffingtonpost.com/2011/06/29/myspace-history-timeline_n_887059.html.
Stewart, Malcolm, *The Public Schools, and the Inculcation of Community Values*, 18 J. Law & Educ. 23 (1989).
Stewart, Potter, *Or of the Press*, 26 Hastings L.J. 631 (1974–75).
Student Press Law Center, http://www.splc.org.
Sunstein, Cass, republicwww (Princeton University Press 2011) (2002).
Tabor, Jacob, *Students' First Amendment Rights in the Age of the Internet: Off-Campus Cyberspeech and School Regulation*, 50 Boston Coll. L. Rev 561 (2009).
Taylor, John, *Tinker and Viewpoint Discrimination*, 77 UMKC L. Rev. 569 (2009).
Thomas, Norman, *Can Our Schools Face Facts?* 9 Prog. Educ 338 (1932).

Works Cited

Thomas, Stephen, Cambron-McCabe, Nelda & McCarthy, Martha, *Public School Law: Teachers' and Students' Rights* (6th ed., Pearson/Allyn & Bacon 2009).

Title IX of the Education Amendments of 1972, 86 Stat. 373, as amended, 20 U. S. C. § 1681(a).

Trager, Robert & Russomanno, Joseph, *Free Speech for Public School Students: A "Basic Educational Mission,"* 22 (presented at the annual meeting of the Association for Education in Journalism and Mass Communication, Kansas City, Mo., August 1993).

Trebilcock, John, *Off Campus: School Board Control Over Teacher Conduct*, 35 Tulsa L. J. 445 (2000).

United Nations, *Declaration of the Rights of the Child*, 1959 U.N.Y.B 198–99.

United States Constitution.

United States Department of Education, National Center for Education Statistics. *Indicators of School Crime and Safety: 2013*, Institute of Education Sciences https://nces.ed.gov/programs/crimeindicators/crimeindicators2013/key.asp

Verba, Sidney, Schlozman, Kay & Brody, Henry, *Voice and Equality: Civic Voluntarism in American Politics* (Harvard University Press 1995).

Viera, Mariana, *Va. High School Censors Story about Marijuana "Dabbing,"* Student Press Law Center (Mar. 24, 2015) http://www.splc.org/article/2015/03/va-high-school-censors-story-about-marijuana-dabbing.

Waldman, Emily, *A Post-Morse Framework for Students' Potentially Hurtful Speech (Religious and Otherwise)*, 37 J.L. & Educ. 463 (2008).

Washington Administrative Code: Student Rights, WAC 392–40–215 (1977).

Weng, Garner, *Type No Evil: The Proper Latitude of Public Education Institutions in Restricting Expressions of Their Students on the Internet*, 20 Hastings Comm. & Ent. L. J. 751 (1998).

Zipin, Lew, *Dark Funds of Knowledge, Deep Funds of Pedagogy: Exploring Boundaries Between Lifeworlds and Schools*, 30 Discourse: Studies in the Cultural Politics of Education 317 (2009).

Cases Cited

Abood v. Detroit Bd. of Ed., 431 US 209 (1977).
Abrams v. United States, 250 U.S. 616 (1919).
Alabama Student Party v. Student Government Association of the University of Alabama, 867 F.2d 1344 (11th Cir. 1989).
Ambach v. Norwick, 441 U.S. 68 (1979).
Ashcroft v. ACLU, 535 U.S. 564 (2002).
Augustus v. School Board of Escambia County, 507 F.2d 152 (5th Cir. 1975).
Axson-Flynn v. Johnson, 356 F.3d 1277 (10th Cir. 2004).
B.H. v. Easton Area School District, 725 F.3d 293 (3d Cir. 2013).
Baker v. Downey City Board of Education, 307 F. Supp. 517 (C.D. Cal. 1969).
Baughman v. Freienmuth, 478 F.2d 1345 (4th Cir. 1973).
Baxter v. Vigo County School Corporation, 26 F.3d 728 (7th Cir. 1994).
Bellotti v. Baird, 443 U.S. 622 (1979).
Bethel School District v. Fraser, 478 U.S. 675 (1986).
Blackwell v. Issaquena County Board of Education, 363 F.2d 749 (5th Cir. 1966).
Blue Mt. Sch. Dist. v. J. S., 2012 U.S. LEXIS 726 (U.S., Jan. 17, 2012).
Board of Curators of the University of Missouri v. Horowitz, 435 U.S. 78 (1978).
Board of Education v. Earls, 536 U.S. 822 (2002).
Board of Education v. Pico, 457 U.S. 853 (1982).
Board of Education of the Westside Community Schools v. Mergens, 496 U.S. 226 (1990).
Board of Regents v. Southworth, 529 U.S. 217 (2000).
Boroff v. Van Wert City Board of Education, 220 F.3d 465 (6th Cir. 2000).
Boucher v. School Board of the School District of Greenfield, 134 F.3d 821 (7th Cir. 1998).
Brammer-Hoelter v. Twin Peaks Charter Academy, 602 F.3d 1175 (10th Cir. 2010).
Brandenburg v. Ohio, 395 U.S. 444 (1969).
Broussard v. Waldron School District, 2012 U.S. Dist. LEXIS 125046 (W.D. Ark, 2012).
Brown v. Board of Topeka, 347 U.S. 483 (1954).
Brown v. Entertainment Media Association, 131 S. Ct. 2729 (2011).
Brown v. Li, 308 F.3d 939 (9th Cir. 2002).
Buckley v. Valeo, 424 U.S. 1 (1976).
Burbridge v. Sampson, 74 F. Supp. 2d 940 (C.D. Cal. 1999).
Burch v. Barker, 861 F.2d 1149 (9th Cir. 1988).
Burnham v. Ianni, 119 F.3d 668 (8th Cir. 1997).
Burnside v. Byars, 363 F.2d 744 (5th Cir. 1966).
Cannon v. University of Chicago, 441 U.S. 677 (1979).
Chalifoux v. New Caney Independent School District, 976 F. Supp. 659 (S.D. Tex. 1997).

Cases Cited

Chandler v. McMinnville School District, 978 F.2d 524, 529 (9th Cir. 1992).
Chaplinsky v. New Hampshire, 315 U.S. 568 (1942).
Chess v. Widmar, 480 F. Supp. 907 (W.D. Missouri 1979).
Chess v. Widmar, 635 F.2d 1310 (8th Cir. 1980).
Chiras v. Miller, 432 F.3d 606 (5th Cir. 2005).
Church of Lukumi Babulu Aye v. City of Hialeah, 508 U.S. 520 (1993).
City of Madison Joint School District No. 8 v. WERC, 429 U.S. 167 (1976).
Cohen v. California, 403 U.S. 15 (1971).
Connick v. Myers, 461 U.S. 138 (1983).
Corder v. Lewis Palmer School District, 566 F.3d 1219 (10th Cir. 2009).
Coy v. Board of Education of the North Canton City Schools, 205 F. Supp.2d 791 (N.D. Ohio 2002).
Cuff v. Valley Central School District, 677 F.3d 109 (2d Cir. 2012).
D.C. v. Valley Central School District, 2013 U.S. Dist. LEXIS 74177 (S.D. N.Y. 2013).
D.J.M. v. Hannibal Pub. Sch. Dist. #60, 647 F.3d 754 (8th Cir. 2011).
Dariano v. Morgan Hill, 767 F.3d 764 (9th Cir. 2014).
Davis v. Monroe County Board of Education, 526 U.S. 629 (1999).
Dean v. Utica Community Schools, 345 F. Supp 2d 799 (E.D. Mich. 2004).
DeJohn v. Temple University, 537 F.3d 301 (3d Cir. 2008).
Desilets v. Clearview Regional Board of Education, 137 N.J. 585 (N.J. 1994).
Dixon v. Alabama State Board of Education, 294 F.2d 150 (5th Cir. 1961).
Doe v. University of Michigan, 721 F. Supp 852 (E.D. Mich 1989).
Doninger v. Niehoff, 642 F.3d 334 (2d Cir. 2011).
Draudt v. Wooster City School District Board of Education, 246 F. Supp. 2d 820 (N.D. Ohio 2003).
Eisner v. Stamford Board of Education, 440 F.2d 803 (2d Cir. 1971).
Emmett v. Kent School District No. 415, 92 F. Supp. 2d 1088 (W.D. Wa. 2000).
Employment Services v. Smith, 494 U.S. 872 (1990).
Engel v. Vitale, 370 U.S. 421 (1962).
Everson v. Board of Education, 330 U.S. 1 (1947).
Ex Parte Crouse, 4 Whart. 9 (Pa. 1838).
FCC v. Pacifica Foundation 438 U.S. 726 (1978).
Fenton v. Stear, 423 F. Supp. 767 (W.D. Penn. 1976).
Fields v. Palmdale School District, 447 F.3d 1187 (9th Cir. 2006).
Franklin v. Gwinnett County Public Schools, 503 U.S. 60 (1992).
Fraser v. Bethel School District, 755 F.2d 1356 (9th Cir. 1985).
Frederick v. Morse, 439 F.3d 1114 (9th Cir. 2006).
Garcetti v. Ceballos, 547 U.S. 410 (2006).
Gebser v. Lago Vista Independent School Dist., 524 U.S. 274 (1998).
Gilio v. School Board, 905 F. Supp. 2d 1262 (M.D. Fla. 2012).
Ginsburg v. New York, 390 U.S. 629 (1968).
Gitlow v. New York, 268 U.S. 652 (1925).
Goss v. Lopez, 419 U.S. 565 (1975).
Graham v. Florida, 130 S. Ct. 2011 (2010).
Griswold v. Connecticut, 381 U.S. 479 (1965).
Griswold v. Driscoll, 616 F.3d 53 (1st Cir. 2010).
Hague v. CIO, 307 U.S. 496 (1939).
Hammond v. South Carolina State College, 272 F. Supp. 947 (D. S.C. 1967).
Hardwick v. Heyward, 711 F.3d 426 (4th Cir. 2013).
Harper v. Edgewood Board of Education, 655 F. Supp. 1353 (S.D. Ohio 1987).
Harper v. Poway, 445 F.3d 1166 (9th Cir. 2006).
Harper v. Poway, 455 F.3d 1052 (9th Cir. 2006) (en banc).

Cases Cited

Hazelwood School District v. Kuhlmeier, 484 U.S. 260 (1988).
Hazelwood School District v. Kuhlmeier, 795 F.2d 1368 (8th Cir. 1986).
Healy v. James, 408 U.S. 169 (1972).
Holloman v. Harland, 370 F.3d 1252 (11th Cir. 2004).
Hosty v. Carter, 412 F.3d 731 (7th Cir. 2005) (en banc).
Illinois ex rel. McCollum v. Board of Education of School District 71, 333 U.S. 203 (1948).
In re Gault, 387 U.S. 1 (1967).
Ingraham v. Wright, 430 U.S. 651 (1977).
ISKCON v. Lee, 505 U.S. 672 (1992).
J.A. v. Fort Wayne Community Schools, 2013 U.S. Dist. LEXIS 117667 (N.D. Ind., 2013).
J.C. ex rel. R.C. v. Beverly Hills Unified School, 711 F. Supp. 2d 1094 (C.D. Cal. 2010).
J.S. v. Bethlehem Area School District, 807 A.2d 847 (Pa. 2002).
J.S. v. Bethlehem Area School District, 757 A.2d 412 (Pa. Commw. Ct. 2000).
J.S. v. Bethlehem Area School District, 569 Pa. 638 (Pa. 2002).
J.S. v. Blue Mountain School District, 593 F.3d 286 (3d Cir. 2010).
J.S. v. Blue Mountain School District, 650 F.3d 915 (3d Cir. 2011) (en banc).
J.W. v. Desoto County School District, No 09–00155 (N.D. Miss. 2010).
Jacobellis v. Ohio, 378 U.S. 184 (1964).
James v. Board of Education, 461 F.2d 566 (2d Cir. 1972).
Jones v. Arkansas, 347 Ark. 409 (Ark. 2002).
K.A. v. Pocono Mountain School District, 710 F.3d 99 (3d Cir. 2013).
K.J. v. Sauk Prairie School District, 2012 U.S. Dist. LEXIS 187689 (W.D. Wis, 2012).
Karp v. Becken, 477 F.2d 171 (9th Cir. 1973).
Keller v. State Bar of Cal., 496 U.S. 1 (1990).
Keyishian v. Board of Regents, 385 U.S. 589 (1967).
Khademi v. South Orange Community College District, 194 F. Supp. 2d 1011 (C.D. Cal. 2002).
Killion v. Franklin Regional School District, 136 F. Supp. 2d 446 (W.D. Pa. 2001).
Kincaid v. Gibson, 236 F.3d 342 (6th Cir. 2001).
Klein v. Smith, 635 F. Supp. 1440 (D. Me. 1986).
Klump v. Nazareth Area School District, 425 F. Supp. 2d 622 (E.D. Penn 2006).
Kowalski v. Berkeley County Schools, 652 F.3d 565 (4th Cir. 2011).
Kuhlmeier v. Hazelwood, 607 F. Supp. 1450 (E.D. Mo. 1985).
Lander v. Seaver, 32 Vt. 114 (Vt. 1859).
Lange v. Diercks, No. 1–587/11–0191. (Iowa Ct. App. 2011).
LaVine v. Blaine School District, 257 F.3d 981 (9th Cir. 2001).
LaVine v. Blaine School District, 279 F.3d 719 (9th Cir. 2002) (en banc).
Layshock v. Hermitage School District, 650 F.3d 205 (3d Cir. 2011) (en banc).
Layshock v. Hermitage School District, 496 F. Supp. 2d 587 (W.D. Pa. 2007).
Layshock v. Hermitage School District, 593 F.3d 249 (3d Cir. 2010).
Lee v. Weisman, 505 U.S. 577 (1992).
Leeb v. DeLong, 198 Cal. App. 3d 47 (Cal. Ct. App. 1988).
McCauley v. University of the Virgin Islands, 618 F.3d 232 (3d Cir. 2010).
Melton v. Young, 465 F.2d 1332 (6th Cir. 1972).
Meyer v. Nebraska, 262 U.S. 390 (1923).
Miami Herald Publishing Company v. Tornillo, 418 U.S. 241 (1974).
Minersville v. Gobitis, 310 U.S. 586 (1940).
Morgan v. Swanson, 659 F.3d 359 (5th Cir. 2011).
Morse v. Frederick, 551 U.S. 393 (2007).
Mt. Healthy v. Doyle, 429 U.S. 274 (1977).

Cases Cited

Mozert v. Hawkins County Public Schools, 827 F.2d 1058 (6th Cir. 1987).
Muller v. Jefferson Lighthouse School, 98 F.3d 1530 (7th Cir. 1996).
Near v. Minnesota, 283 U.S. 697 (1931).
Nebraska Press Association v. Stuart, 427 U.S. 539 (1976).
New Jersey v. T.L.O., 469 U.S. 325 (1985).
New York Times v. U.S., 403 U.S. 713 (1971).
Nixon v. Hardin County Board of Education, 988 F. Supp. 2d 826 (W.D. Tenn. 2013).
Nuxoll v. Indian Prairie School District #204, 523 F.3d 668 (7th Cir. 2008).
Oregon v. Mitchell, 400 U.S. 112 (1970).
O'Rourke v. Walker, 102 Conn. 130 (Conn. 1925).
Pangle v. Bend-Lapine School District, 169 Ore. App. 376 (Court of Appeals of Oregon 2000).
Paye v. Gibraltar School District, 1991 U.S. Dist. LEXIS 16480 (E.D. Mich. 1991).
Peck v. Upshur County Board of Education, 155 F.3d 274 (4th Cir. 1998).
Perry Education Association v. Perry Local Educators' Association, 460 U.S. 37 (1983).
Pickering v. Board of Education, 391 U.S. 563 (1968).
Pierce v. Society of Sisters, 268 U.S. 510 (1925).
Planned Parenthood of Central Missouri v. Danforth, 428 U.S. 52 (1976).
Plessy v. Ferguson, 163 U.S. 537 (1896).
Ponce v. Socorro Independent School District, 508 F.3d 765 (5th Cir. 2007).
Porter v. Ascension Parish School Board, 393 F.3d 608 (5th Cir. 2004).
Prince v. Massachusetts, 321 U.S. 158 (1944).
Pugsley v. Sellmeyer, 158 Ark. 247 (Ark.1923).
R.O. v. Ithaca City School District, 645 F.3d 533 (2d Cir. 2011).
R.S. v. Minnewaska Area School District, 894 F. Supp. 2d 1128 (D. Minn 2012).
Reno v. ACLU, 521 U.S. 844 (1997).
Requa v. Kent School District, 492 F. Supp. 2d 1272 (W.D. Wash. 2007).
Reynolds v. United States, 98 U.S. 145 (1879).
Romano v. Harrington, 725 F. Supp. 687 (E.D. N.Y. 1989).
Roper v. Simmons, 543 U.S. 551 (2005).
Rosenberger v. Rector and Visitors of University of Virginia, 18 F.3d 269 (4th Cir. 1994).
Rosenberger v. Rector and Visitors of University of Virginia, 795 F. Supp. 175 (W.D. Va. 1992).
Rosenberger v. Rector, 515 U.S. 819 (1995).
Rumsfeld v. FAIR, 547 U.S. 47 (2006).
S.G. v. Sayreville, 333 F.3d 417 (3d Cir. 2003).
S.J.W. v. Lee's Summit R-7 School District, 696 F.3d 771 (8th Cir. 2012).
Safford v. Redding, 129 S. Ct. 2633 (2009).
Salehpour v. University of Tennessee, 159 F.3d 199 (6th Cir. 1998).
Schenck v. United States, 249 U.S. 47 (1919).
School District of Abington Township v. Schempp, 374 U.S. 203 (1963).
Scott v. School Board of Alachua County, 324 F.3d 1246 (11th Cir. 2003).
Searcey v. Harris, 888 F.2d 1314 (11th Cir. 1989).
Settle v. Dickson County School Board, 53 F.3d 152 (6th Cir. 1995).
Seyfried v. Walton, 668 F.2d 214, 218 (3d Cir. 1981).
Shamloo v. Mississippi State Board of Trustees, 620 F.2d 516 (5th Cir. 1980).
Slotterback v. Interboro School District, 766 F. Supp. 280 (E.D. Pa. 1991).
Southworth v. Grebe, 151 F.3d 717 (7th Cir. 1998).
Southworth v. Grebe, 1996 U.S. Dist. LEXIS 20980 (W.D. Wis. 1996).
Spence v. Washington, 418 U.S. 405 (1974).
Stanton v. Brunswick School Department, 577 F. Supp. 1560 (D. Me. 1984).

Cases Cited

State ex rel Dresser v. District Board of School District No. 1, 135 Wis. 619 (Wis. 1908).
Stiles v. Blunt, 912 F.2d 260 (8th Cir. 1990).
Sweezy v. New Hampshire, 354 U.S. 234 (1957).
Sypniewski v. Warren Hills Regional Board of Education, 307 F.3d 243 (3d Cir. 2002).
T.V. v. Smith-Green, No. 1:09-CV-290-PPS (N.D. Ind. Aug. 10, 2011).
Tatro v. University of Minnesota, 800 N.W.2d 811 (Minn. Ct. App. 2011).
Tatro v. University of Minnesota, 816 N.W.2d 509 (Minn. 2012).
Terminiello v. Chicago, 337 U.S. 1 (1949).
Thomas v. Board of Education, Granville Central School District, 607 F.2d 1043 (2d Cir. 1979).
Tinker v. Des Moines Independent Community School District, 258 F. Supp. 971 (S.D. Iowa 1966).
Tinker v. Des Moines Independent Community School District, 383 F.2d 988 (8th Cir. 1967).
Tinker v. Des Moines Independent Community School District, 393 U.S. 503 (1969).
Trachtman v. Anker, 563 F.2d 512 (2d Cir. 1977).
United States v. Seeger, 380 U.S. 163 (1965).
United States v. Virginia, 518 U.S. 515 (1996).
UWM Post, Inc. v. Board of Regents of the University of Wisconsin, 774 F. Supp. 1163 (E.D. Wis. 1991).
Vernonia School District v. Acton, 515 U.S. 646 (1995).
Video Game Dealers v. Schwarzenegger, 556 F.3d 950 (9th Cir. 2009).
Wallace v. Jaffree, 472 U.S. 38 (1985).
Walz v. Egg Harbor Township Board of Education, 342 F.3d 271 (3d Cir. 2003).
West Virginia Board of Education v. Barnette, 319 U.S. 624 (1943).
Widmar v. Vincent, 454 U.S. 263 (1981).
Wieman v. Updegraff, 344 U.S. 183 (1952).
Wilson v. Board of Education of the City of Chicago, 137 Ill. App. 187 (Ill. App. Ct. 1907).
Wisconsin v. Yoder, 406 U.S. 205 (1972).
Wooster v. Sunderland, 27 Cal. App. 51, 55 (Cal. App. Ct. 1915).
Wyner v. Douglas County School District, 728 F.3d 1062 (9th Cir. 2013).
Yeo v. Town of Lexington, 131 F.3d 241 (1st Cir. 1997).
Zucker v. Panitz, 299 F. Supp. 102 (S.D. N.Y. 1969).

Index

Abrams v. United States 105
age of majority 11–12
Alabama Student Party v. Student Government Association of the University of Alabama 68
Ambach v. Norwick 51, 104
"anti–Hazelwood" laws 73–75
Arnett, Jeffrey 90

Baker v. Downey City Board of Education 46–47
Baker, Edwin 100, 103. 129
Beard, Charles 90, 115
Bellotti v. Baird 13, 16
Bethel School District No. 403 v. Fraser 20, 49–51, 76, 111
B.H. v. Easton Area School District 61–62, 112
Blackwell v. Issaquena County Board of Education 41–45, 76
Board of Education of the Westside Community Schools v. Mergens 30
Board of Regents of the University of Wisconsin System v. Southworth 23, 69–70
Brandenburg v. Ohio 60
Brown v. Board of Education of Topeka 32, 104
Burbridge v. Sampson 65
Burnside v. Byars 41–45, 76

campus speech codes 70–71
Captive Voices 75
Chalifoux v. New Caney Independent School District 56, 157–158
Chaplinsky v. New Hampshire 109
children's rights movement 23
Chiras v. Miller 23
City of Madison Joint School District v. WERC 81
civics education 8
Cohen v. California 110

common-school movement 8, 22, 110
compelled speech 41, 69–70
compulsory education 17–19, 36, 83
Connick v. Myers 81
corporal punishment 25
creative writing 57
cyberbullying 5, 20

Davis v. Monroe County Board of Education 20
Dean v. Utica Community Schools 55, 135, 138
"Declaration of the Rights of the Child" 41
DeJohn v. Temple University 70–71, 84
Desilets v. Clearview Regional Board of Education 136
Dewey, John 108
Dixon v. Alabama State Board of Education 19
D.J.M. v. Hannibal Public School District #60 149
Doninger v. Niehoff 150
Draudt v. Wooster 135
drug testing 35
due process 36–37

Eisner v. Stamford Board of Education 47
emerging adulthood 90–91
Emerson, Thomas 100, 123, 156
Emmett v. Kent School District 151
Engle v. Vitale 28
Establishment Clause 26–31
Everson v. Board of Education 26
Ex Parte Crouse 17

Fine, Michelle 122
flags 48, 62–63
forum analysis 53, 55–56, 65–66, 85, 133–136

Index

Free Exercise Clause 26–31
free-speech zones 65

Garcetti v. Ceballos 82
Ginsberg v. New York 14, 99, 166
Gitlow v New York 40
Goss v. Lopez 36
Griswold v. Connecticut 6

Habermas, Jürgen 99–100
Hammond v. South Carolina State College 64
Harper v. Poway 57, 111
Hazelwood School District v. Kuhlmeier 52–55, 76, 132–136
Healy v. James 66–67, 84, 119–120
heckler's veto 45–46, 78
Holloman v. Harland 56
Hosty v. Carter 85–86
Hutchins Commission 129

"I [heart] boobies" 61–62, 112
Illinois ex rel. McCollum v. Board of Education of School District 71 27
imprimatur 54
in loco parentis 16, 19–21, 122
In re Gault 15
Ingraham v. Wright 36

James v. Board of Education 165
Jefferson, Thomas 7, 22, 103–104
Jones v. State of Arkansas 116, 123–124
J.S. v. Bethlehem 148–149
J.S. v. Blue Mountain School District 152–155

Karp v. Becken 48, 121
Khademi v. South Orange Community College District 65
Kincaid v. Gibson 133, 135
K.J. v. Sauk Prairie School District 61
Kowalski v. Berkeley County Schools 149–150

Lander v. Seaver 3, 38–39, 76
Lane, Robert Wheeler 102
Layshock v. Hermitage School District 152–153
Lee v. Weisman 29
Leeb v. DeLong 134

Mann, Horace 22
McCauley v. University of the Virgin Islands 83–84
Meiklejohn, Alexander 100–101, 105
Meyer v. Nebraska 18
Miami Herald v. Tornillo 139

Mill, John Stuart 12, 98–99, 114, 123
money as speech 68–70
Morse v. Frederick 4, 20, 58–60, 76
Mt. Healthy v. Doyle 81
Mozert v. Hawkins County Public Schools 27

Near v. Minnesota 127–128
Nebraska Press Association v. Stuart 128
New Jersey v. T.L.O. 19–20, 33–34
1985 Equal Access Act 30
Nixon v. Hardin 151
Nuxoll v. Indian Prairie 62

Office of the National Committee on the Employment of Youth 90
Oliver Wendell Holmes 11
On Liberty 12

parens patriae 16–18
Pew Internet Project 142
Pickering v. Board of Education 81
Pierce v. Society of Sisters 27
Planned Parenthood of Central Missouri v. Danforth 13, 16
Pledge of Allegiance 40–41, 56
Plessy v. Ferguson 32
prayer in school 28–29
Prejean, Carrie 160
Prince v. Massachusetts 17
privacy 33–35

qualified immunity 59, 85–86

Reno v. ACLU 146
Roe, Richard 119
Romano v. Harrington 134
Rosenberger v. Rector 30, 68–69
R.S. v. Minnewaska Area School District 150

Safford v. Redding 35
Schenck v. U.S. 40–41
Schlessinger, Laura 160
scholar 79–80
School District of Abington Township v. Schempp 28, 104
school safety 6, 20, 34, 57–58, 60, 123
search and seizure 33–35
Settle v. Dickson County School Board 121
Seyfried v. Walton 84, 94
SG v. Sayreville Board of Education 84, 111
Shamloo v. Mississippi State Board of Trustees 65
Spence v. Washington 157

204

Sherbert v. Verner 27
Stanton v. Brunswick School Department 49
State ex rel Dresser v. District Board of School District 1 39–40, 147
Stewart, Potter 129

t-shirts 62
Tatro v. University of Minnesota 71–73
Terminiello v. Chicago 45–46, 110
Thomas v. Board of Education, Granville Central School District 47, 144
Tinker et al. v. Des Moines Independent Community School District 4, 43–46, 76, 99
Title IX of the Educational Amendments of 1972 20–21, 32
26th Amendment 14, 19

U.S. Department of Education 21
United States v. Virginia 32
University of Missouri v. Horowitz 36

variable obscenity 14
vestibule adolescence 90

Wallace v. Jaffree 28
West Virginia v. Barnette 40–41
Widmar v. Vincent 29, 67–68
Wisconsin v. Yoder 18–19
Wooster v. Sunderland 40, 83
Wyner v. Douglas County School District 151

Yeo v. Town of Lexington 139

Zucker v. Panitz 46